Of Sneetches and Whos and the Good Dr. Seuss

Of Sneetches and Whos and the Good Dr. Seuss

Essays on the Writings and Life of Theodor Geisel

edited by THOMAS FENSCH

McFarland & Company, Inc., Publishers
Jefferson, North Carolina, and London

ALSO BY THOMAS FENSCH

Television News Anchors: An Anthology of Profiles of the Major Figures and Issues in United States Network Reporting (McFarland, 1993)

Oskar Schindler and His List: The Man, the Book, the Film, the Holocaust and Its Survivors (1995)

Conversations with James Thurber (1989)

Conversations with John Steinbeck (1988)

Steinbeck and Covici: The Story of a Friendship (1979)

Frontispiece: Theodor Seuss Geisel, circa 1980s (photo courtesy of Dr. Seuss Enterprises, L.P.)

British Library Cataloguing-in-Publication data are available

Library of Congress Cataloguing-in-Publication Data

Of Sneetches and Whos and the good Dr. Seuss / essays on the writings and life of Theodor Geisel / edited by Thomas Fensch.
　　p.　cm.
　　Includes bibliographical references (p.　) and index.
　　ISBN 0-7864-0388-8 (library binding : 50# alkaline paper) ∞
　　1. Geisel, Theodor Seuss, 1904–1991.　2. Children's stories, American—History and criticism.　3. Children's stories, American—Illustrations.　4. Authors, American—20th century—Biography.　5. Illustrators—United States—Biography.　6. Illustration of books—United States.　I. Fensch, Thomas.
PS3513.E2Z79　1997
813'.52—dc21
　[B]　　　　　　　　　　　　　　　　　　　　　　　　97-36069
　　　　　　　　　　　　　　　　　　　　　　　　　　　　　CIP

Manufactured in the United States of America

McFarland & Company, Inc., Publishers
　Box 611, Jefferson, North Carolina 28640

To the memory of my father,
Edwin A. Fensch, Ph.D., 1903–1995,
who gave me two priceless gifts:
the love of reading and the love of writing

Contents

Acknowledgments

Grateful acknowledgment is made to the following for permission to reprint copyrighted material:

Reprint permission for the Dr. Seuss poem "Signs of Civilization" granted by the Town Council of La Jolla, California. All other Dr. Seuss text and the photographs of Dr. Seuss are used by gracious consent of Dr. Seuss Enterprises, L.P. All rights reserved. *And to Think That I Saw It on Mulberry Street* ©1937, 1968, Dr. Seuss Enterprises, L.P.; *The 500 Hats of Bartholomew Cubbins* ©1938, 1965, Dr. Seuss Enterprises, L.P.; *The King's Stilts* ©1939, 1967, Dr. Seuss Enterprises, L.P.; *Horton Hatches the Egg* ©1940, 1968, Dr. Seuss Enterprises, L.P.; *McElligot's Pool* ©1947, 1975, Dr. Seuss Enterprises, L.P.; *Bartholomew and the Oobleck* ©1949, 1977, Dr. Seuss Enterprises, L.P.; *If I Ran the Zoo* ©1950, 1977, Dr. Seuss Enterprises, L.P.; *Scrambled Eggs Super!* ©1953, 1991, Dr. Seuss Enterprises, L.P.; *On Beyond Zebra!* ©1955, 1983, Dr. Seuss Enterprises, L.P.; *How the Grinch Stole Christmas!* ©1957, 1985, Dr. Seuss Enterprises, L.P.; *The Cat in the Hat* ©1957, 1985, Dr. Seuss Enterprises, L.P.; *The Cat in the Hat Comes Back* ©1958, 1986, Dr. Seuss Enterprises, L.P.; "Yertle the Turtle" from *Yertle the Turtle and Other Stories* ©1950, 1977, Dr. Seuss Enterprises, L.P.; *Happy Birthday to You!* ©1959, 1983, Dr. Seuss Enterprises, L.P.; *One Fish Two Fish Red Fish Blue Fish* ©1960, 1988, Dr. Seuss Enterprises, L.P.; *Dr. Seuss's Sleep Book* ©1962, 1990, Dr. Seuss Enterprises, L.P.; *Fox in Socks* ©1965, 1993, Dr. Seuss Enterprises, L.P.; *I Had Trouble Getting to Solla Sollew* ©1965, 1993, Dr. Seuss Enterprises, L.P.; "King Louis Katz" and "The Gunk that Got Thunk" from *I Can Lick 30 Tigers Today! and Other Stories* ©1969, 1997, Dr. Seuss Enterprises, L.P.; *The Lorax* ©1971, Dr. Seuss Enterprises, L.P.; *Marvin K. Mooney Will You Please Go Now!* ©1972, Dr. Seuss Enterprises, L.P.; *I Can Read with My Eyes Shut!* ©1978 Dr. Seuss Enterprises, L.P.; *The Butter Battle Book* ©1984, Dr. Seuss Enterprises, L.P.; *My Uncle Terwilliger on the Art of Eating Popovers* ©1989, Dr. Seuss Enterprises, L.P.; *Oh, the Places You'll Go!* ©1990, Dr. Seuss Enterprises, L.P.; *Daisy-Head Mayzie* ©1994, Dr. Seuss Enterprises, L.P.

"The Beginnings of Dr. Seuss" by Edward Connery Lathem reprinted with permission of *Dartmouth Alumni Magazine.*

"The Wacky World of Dr. Seuss" by Peter Bunzel, *Life* magazine, April 6, 1959. Reprinted by permission.

"Children's Friend" by E. J. Kahn, Jr., reprinted by permission, ©1960 *The New Yorker Magazine, Inc.* All rights reserved.

"25 Years of Working Wonder with Words" by Helen Renthal, copyright © The Chicago Tribune Company. All rights reserved. Used with permission.

"Then I Doodled a Tree" by Lewis Nichols, copyright ©1962 The New York Times Co. Reprinted by permission.

"Seuss for the Goose Is Seuss for the Gander" from *Down the Rabbit Hole: Adventures and Misadventures in the Realm of Children's Literature* by Selma G. Lanes (New York: Atheneum, 1971). Reprinted by permission of Selma G. Lanes.

"Dr. Seuss and the Naked Ladies" by Carolyn See. Reprinted by permission of Carolyn See.

"And, Dear Dr. Seuss, the Whole World's in Love with Yeuss" by George Kane. Reprinted by permission of *The Rocky Mountain News.*

"Dr. Seuss's Green-Eggs-and-Ham World" by Judith Frutig. Reprinted by permission of Judith Frutig.

"How the Grinch Stole Reading: The Serious Nonsense of Dr. Seuss" by Warren T. Greenleaf, copyright ©1982 National Association of Elementary School Principals. All rights reserved.

"The Good Dr. Seuss" from *Pipers at the Gates of Dawn: The Wisdom of Children's Literature* by Jonathan Cott (New York: Random House, 1983). Copyright ©1983 Jonathan Cott. Reprinted by permission of Jonathan Cott.

"'Somebody's got to win' in kids' books," copyright ©*1986 U.S. News & World Report* magazine. Reprinted by permission.

"The Private World of Dr. Seuss" by Hilliard Harper, copyright ©1986 *The Los Angeles Times.* Reprinted by permission.

"On Beyond Zebra with Dr. Seuss" by Rita Roth. Reprinted by permission of Rita Roth.

"Maurice Sendak and Dr. Seuss: A Conversation" by Glenn Edward Sadler, *The Horn Book Magazine*, September/October 1989. Reprinted by permission of The Horn Book, Inc., 11 Beacon St., Suite 1000, Boston, Mass., 02108.

"The Cabinet of Dr. Seuss" by Alison Lurie, copyright ©1990 by Alison Lurie. Originally appeared in *The New York Review of Books*, December 20, 1990. Reprinted by permission of Melanie Jackson Agency.

"The Mouse in the Corner, the Fly on the Wall: What Very Young Eyes See in Children's Books" by Karla Kuskin, copyright ©1993 The New York Times Co. Reprinted by permission.

"Dr. Seuss and Dr. Einstein: Children's Books and Scientific Imagination" by Chet Raymo, *The Horn Book Magazine*, September/October 1992. Reprinted by permission of the Horn Book, Inc., 11 Beacon Street, Suite 1000, Boston, Mass., 02108.

Introduction

"They snap. They crackle. And also pop. If the books of other more staid authors are the oatmeal of children's literature—solid, nourishing, and warm, but not much fun—those of Theodor Seuss Geisel are its Rice Krispies, blending nutrition with a happily explosive morning racket," Warren T. Greenleaf wrote, in the educators' magazine *Principal*, in May 1982.

And the year after that Dr. Seuss had become "a genre, a category, an institution," Jonathan Cott said, in his book *Pipers at the Gates of Dawn: The Wisdom of Children's Literature.*

Bennett Cerf, Geisel's publisher at Random House, called him "a genius, pure and simple," at a time when both William Faulkner and John O'Hara were being published by Random House. Rudolf Flesch said that Dr. Seuss would surely be read one hundred years from now, when Ernest Hemingway, William Faulkner, John Marquand and others may be forgotten.

Since Theodor (Ted) Geisel's death in September 1991, there have been five additional Seuss books published: *Daisy-Head Mayzie*, the only Seuss book featuring a little girl (1995); *The Secret Art of Dr. Seuss*, illustrations Geisel completed during his lifetime which didn't quite fit the Seuss books (1995); *My Many Colored Days*, with illustrations by Steve Johnson and Lou Fancher (1996); the collection *A Hatful of Seuss*, and *Seuss-isms*.

Longtime Geisel family friends Judith and Neil Morgan published a rich, evocative authorized biography, *Dr. Seuss and Mr. Geisel*, in 1995, but there has not yet been a comprehensive anthology devoted to Dr. Seuss's critical reception.

In "On Beyond Zebra with Dr. Seuss," Rita Roth writes that Seuss was "beloved by his audience, yet, until comparatively recently, he was held at arm's length by the children's literature establishment."

And Jonathan Cott writes, "Aside from *The Cat in the Hat* and its brilliant sequel *The Cat in the Hat Comes Back*, most of Dr. Seuss's Beginner and Bright and Early Books have often been overlooked, patronized and undervalued."

Held at arm's length. Overlooked, patronized and undervalued.

Thus it seems high time for a book that discusses, analyzes and studies the nation's best-known children's writer. For indeed, as Alison Lurie observes (quoted in Jonathan Cott), Dr. Seuss is now as well known as Mark Twain

1

and Lewis Carroll. Carrying that comparison further, certainly his life has been just as interesting.

What do we see if we examine the life of Theodor Geisel?

For one thing, we see that serendipity played a large part in his early success, as even Geisel acknowledged. Perhaps the first happy accident of fate was in the 1930s, when Geisel accidentally designed an advertising campaign. Looking for the name of an insecticide to use in a cartoon caption, he flipped a coin to decide on Flit, a popular brand of the day, rather than Fly-Tox, a competitor. The wife of a Flit advertising man later found the cartoon in a beauty parlor she normally didn't patronize—and the Flit account kept Geisel busy for 17 years.

It was surely serendipitous that during a return from Europe in 1936 on the oceanliner M.S. *Kungsholm*, Geisel found himself obsessed with the rhythmic throbbing of the oceanliner's engines. A less imaginative man might simply have been irritated by the noise. Geisel, however, repeated the beat until the words came:

...and to think that I saw it on Mulberry Street...

Ted Geisel kept playing with the meter until he completed his first book, using that line as the title.

Serendipity struck again one day on the sidewalk in New York City. At that point, *And to Think That I Saw It on Mulberry Street* had been rejected by somewhere between 20 and 30 book publishers (figures vary, even from Geisel himself). But on this day in New York, Geisel, with manuscript under his arm, chanced to meet an acquaintance from his Dartmouth College days, Marshall McClintock. McClintock, who had just been hired as a children's book editor, asked about Geisel's package, and an hour or so later, Geisel had a book contract.

It must have been serendipity that placed him, on a commuter train leaving New York City, behind a staid, hat-wearing businessman to whom he took an instant (though unexpressed) dislike. What would happen if I took that hat off his head? Geisel wondered. Would another grow in its place? Thus Dr. Seuss' second book, *The 500 Hats of Bartholomew Cubbins*, was born.

Not long afterward, serendipity, in the form of a breeze through an open window, blew some of Geisel's sketches about. A sketch of an elephant landed on a sketch of a tree. What would an elephant be doing in a tree? Geisel thought.

Hatching an egg!

So Dr. Seuss gave the world *Horton Hatches an Egg*.

Later, in Europe, Geisel overheard a G.I. complain about the weather: "Rain. Rain. Why doesn't something else fall from the sky?"

Why, indeed? Why couldn't, why shouldn't something else fall from the sky? Geisel thought.

Before long came another book: *Bartholomew and the Oobleck*.

Many years later, Geisel worked and worked over a book that just wouldn't jell. He fussed and he stewed, he worked and he worked, but nothing happened. Finally, his wife, Audrey, took him on a trip to Africa. There, Theodor Geisel saw elephants on a plain—and Dr. Seuss leaped to work. Writing furiously on whatever he could find, he completed the book. *The Lorax* was published in 1971.

Serendipity. Plus a big helping of imagination. His first wife, Helen Geisel, once said, "His mind never grew up." Asked about the strange Seussian animals and the equally strange Seussian places—Whoville, Solla Sollew and elsewhere—Seuss said, "Why, I've been to most of those places myself so the names are from memory."

And hard work. Geisel worked regular hours, day after day, year after year. He threw away far more material than he published.

Early in his career as a children's book author, he once asked, rather plaintively, if his agents thought he could make $5,000 a year on his books. Surely Geisel couldn't have anticipated that after World War Two, the baby boom would cause sales of children's books, and of the Dr. Seuss books in particular, to grow almost geometrically. Sales of all his books have now surpassed 150,000,000 copies. After his death, Audrey Geisel donated $20 million to the library of the University of California at San Diego, which was promptly renamed the Geisel Library. She also donated $1 million to the library in Geisel's hometown of Springfield, Massachusetts.

And to think it began with the sound of a ship!

At substantial risk of sounding like a dried-up academic, one could wager that the oceanliner with the rhythmic engine had throbbed out some variant of anapestic tetrameter. An *anapest* is a metric foot consisting of two short unstressed syllables followed by a stressed syllable. In *The Concise Oxford Dictionary of Literary Terms*, editor Chris Baldick writes that this form was originally a Greek marching beat. *Tetrameter* is four metric feet to a line.

A perfect example from *McElligot's Pool*:

> *'Cause you never can tell*
> *What goes on below!*
> This pool *might* be bigger
> Than you or I know!

And from *Horton Hatches the Egg*:

> And it should be, it *should* be, it SHOULD be like that!
> Because Horton was faithful! He sat and he sat!

The oceanliner engine gave Theodor Geisel a rhythm that pulls readers through the text. (Critics have suggested this is one reason children love the Seuss books.) Even more importantly, with the stress toward the end of the lines, the rhythm gallops. Children repeat it—they chant it, they sing the words.

Dr. Seuss's books always employ logical insanity. If there is a drawing of a two-headed anything, there are always two toothbrushes in the bathroom and two hats on two hooks. Children understand and accept that logic.

The drawings—Geisel said at least once that he couldn't really draw— also pull the reader through the book, and they perfectly match the text. Some authors do words; some books feature exquisite illustrations. The Dr. Seuss books offer story and illustrations perfectly matched to each other.

Are children sophisticated enough to accept mature subjects? Ted Geisel thought so. Dr. Seuss gave the world *Yertle the Turtle*, about the evils of dictatorship; *Horton Hears a Who!* about equality (a person's a person no matter how small); *The Sneetches*, about anti–Semitism; *The Lorax*, about despoiling the environment; *The Butter Battle Book*, about warfare; and *How the Grinch Stole Christmas*, about the commercialization of Christmas. All have become classics. Furthermore, as a body of work, their influence is enormous. Thanks to Dr. Seuss—and particularly to his first Beginner Book, *The Cat in the Hat*— American children's literature was liberated from all that was simplistic, stuffy and dull.

The Seuss canon is a part of American culture. *Green Eggs and Ham*, for example, is a national treasure. Jesse Jackson once recited it on *Saturday Night Live* as a black southern minister would in a church pulpit. Others have performed it as a rap song.

The throbbing ship engine that once spoke to Theodor Geisel now speaks to us all.

The Dr. Seuss animals—are they so fanciful? Nature gives us real Dr. Seuss animals, Chet Raymo writes. Consider the Thrips, who sometimes lay eggs, sometimes give birth to live young and sometimes do both. Or the Yapok, who takes its young to swim in a waterproof pouch. There is even a bird like Seuss's Grickily Gractus, who *does* lay its eggs in a cactus.

Nature imitates Seuss. And, Raymo writes, the wonderful Seuss creatures are the ideal way to teach children to appreciate science—not with the dry, unimaginative books most children are forced to read, and few appreciate.

Many a reader has gained encouragement from Seuss. In late January 1996, during a promotional tour for her book *It Takes a Village*, first lady Hillary Rodham Clinton noted that Seuss has spurred her on in difficult times. Reporter Doreen Caravajal wrote:

> On her book tour, she frequently cites her chapter about lessons for coping with adversity. It begins with a poem from Dr. Seuss:
>
> *You have brains in your head*
> *You have feet in your shoes*
> *You can steer yourself*
> *Any direction you choose.*
>
> (*Houston Chronicle*, January 20, 1996, p. 5A)

Dr. Seuss is even on the information superhighway. Several of his books are available online, including *Green Eggs and Ham*, *The Cat in the Hat*, and *How the Grinch Stole Christmas*. Addresses for Seuss sites include

http://www.afn.org/~afn15301/drseuss.html

http://www.seussville.com

http://www.usca.scarolina.edu/442-961/MistyJohnson.html

In the articles that follow, occasionally a Seuss title was misquoted or mistyped—for example, "Thudwick" for *Thidwick*, "Yerkle" for *Yertle*, or the very common error of *The Grinch Who Stole Christmas* for *How the Grinch Stole Christmas*. These have been corrected without comment. Otherwise the articles are reproduced faithfully and in full.

The articles in this collection represent newspapers, magazines, the academic world and sources in between. Since these articles were written at varying times for varying audiences, readers will find some aspects of the basic Geisel-Seuss story repeated. They will even discover that some tales grow and change over time. For example, the story of how Horton came to sit in that tree: It begins with a simple accident and eventually develops to include that breeze shuffling papers around. One can imagine the likely twinkle in Geisel's eye as he allowed his life story to sprout small embellishments, just as his creatures sprouted odd feathers and frills as they came to life on his drawing board.

Overall, then, the structure of the book conveys a significant benefit. It allows us to see Geisel from a variety of perspectives, as evinced in the work of many writers over some thirty-five years. And it provides valuable insight into the workings of the famous Seuss imagination.

Thus we come to know, appreciate, and celebrate the good Dr. Seuss.

—THOMAS FENSCH
Huntsville, Texas
Summer 1997

Chronology:
Key Dates in the Life
of Theodor Seuss Geisel

1904: March 2, Theodor Seuss Geisel born in Springfield, Massachusetts, the son of Theodor Robert and Henrietta Seuss Geisel.

1921–1925: Attends Dartmouth College, where he begins writing and drawing for the *Jack-O-Lantern*, the campus humor magazine. Graduates in June 1925.

1926–1927: Attends Oxford University in England, meets Helen Palmer and tours England and Europe.

1927: Sells a cartoon to *The Saturday Evening Post*. When it is published in July, it bears the name "Seuss."

November 29, marries Helen Palmer.

1928: Begins advertising campaign with the line "Quick Henry, the Flit," a phrase that becomes nationally popular.

1931: Illustrates *Boners*, published by the Viking Press.

1937: After numerous rejections, *And to Think That I Saw It on Mulberry Street* is published, by the Vanguard Press. It is the first Dr. Seuss book.

1938: *The 500 Hats of Bartholomew Cubbins* is published by the Vanguard Press.

1939: *The King's Stilts* is published, the first Seuss book with Random House. Thereafter all of Geisel's books in his lifetime, with one exception, would be Random House books.

The Seven Lady Godivas, an adult retelling of the Lady Godiva saga, is published. It is a failure.

1940: *Horton Hatches the Egg* is published.

1940–1942: Geisel works as an editorial cartoonist for the newspaper *PM*.

1943–1946: Serves in the United States Army Signal Corps, Information and Educational Division, under director Frank Capra; receives Legion of Merit for his work on informational films and receives first of three Academy Awards for his film *Hitler Lives* (originally written for the army under the title *Your Job in Germany*).

1947: *McElligot's Pool* is published and named a Caldecott Honor Book. Geisel wins second Academy Award, for *Design for Death* (written with Helen Geisel).

1948: *Thidwick the Big-Hearted Moose* is published. Geisel purchases hilltop home in La Jolla, California. He would live in La Jolla the rest of his life.

1949: *Bartholomew and the Oobleck* is published and named a Caldecott Honor Book.

1950: *If I Ran the Zoo* is published and named a Caldecott Honor Book.

1951: Geisel wins third Academy Award, for the cartoon film *Gerald McBoing-Boing*.

1952: Writes the script and songs and designs the sets for the film *The 5,000 Fingers of Dr. T.* It is not successful. Geisel abandons Hollywood.

1953: *Scrambled Eggs Super!* is published.

1954: *Horton Hears a Who!* is published.

1955: *On Beyond Zebra!* is published.

1956: *If I Ran the Circus* is published. Geisel receives honorary doctoral degree from Dartmouth, his alma mater.

1957: *How the Grinch Stole Christmas* is published and becomes one of his most popular books. *The Cat in the Hat* is published, the first of the Random House Beginner Books for young readers.

1958: *The Cat in the Hat Comes Back* and *Yertle the Turtle and Other Stories* are published. Geisel becomes president of Beginner Books, a division of Random House.

1959: *Happy Birthday to You!* is published.

1960: *Green Eggs and Ham* is published. In terms of sales, it would become his most popular book. *One Fish Two Fish Red Fish Blue Fish* is also published.

1961: *The Sneetches and Other Stories* is published. *Ten Apples Up on Top!* is published under a pseudonym, Theo. LeSieg (Geisel spelled backwards).

1962: *Dr. Seuss's Sleep Book* is published.

1963: *Dr. Seuss's ABC* and *Hop on Pop* are published.

1965: *Fox in Sox*, *I Had Trouble in Getting to Solla Sollew* and *I Wish I Had Duck Feet* (Theo. LeSieg, pseudonym) are all published.

1966: *Come Over to My House* (Theo LeSieg, pseudonym) is published.

1967: *Dr. Seuss's Lost World Revisited: A Forward-Looking Backward Glance,* a paperback, is published by Universal Publishing Co., New York. *The Cat in the Hat Song Book* is published.

October 23, Helen Palmer Geisel dies by her own hand, after lengthy physical and emotional illnesses.

1968: *The Eye Book* (Theo. LeSieg, pseudonym) is published, the first of the Bright and Early Books for readers *before* Beginner Books. *The Foot Book* is published. Geisel receives honorary doctoral degree from American International College.

August 5, Theodor Geisel marries Audrey Stone Diamond.

1969: *I Can Lick 30 Tigers Today! And Other Stories* and *My Book About Me —By Me, Myself. I Wrote It! I Drew It!* are published.

1970: *I Can Draw It Myself* and *Mr. Brown Can Moo! Can You?* are published.

1971: *I Can Write—By Me, Myself* (Theo. LeSieg, pseudonym) and *The Lorax* are published. *The Lorax,* which deals with the despoiling of the environment, becomes perhaps the most controversial Dr. Seuss book. Geisel receives a Peabody Award for his television specials "How the Grinch Stole Christmas" and "Horton Hears a Who."

1972: *In a People House* (Theo. LeSieg, pseudonym) and *Marvin K. Mooney Will You Please Go Now!* are published.

1973: *The Many Mice of Mr. Brice* (Theo. LeSieg, pseudonym), *Did I Ever Tell You How Lucky You Are?* and *The Shape of Me and Other Stuff* are published.

1974: *Great Day for Up!,* *There's a Wocket in My Pocket!* and *Wacky Wednesday* (Theo. LeSieg, pseudonym) are published.

1975: *Because a Little Bug Went Ka-Choo!* (Rosetta Stone, pseudonym), *Oh, the Thinks You Can Think!* and *Would You Rather Be a Bullfrog?* (Theo. LeSieg, pseudonym) are published.

1976: *Hooper Humperdink...? Not Him!* (Theo. LeSieg, pseudonym) and *The Cat's Quizzer* are published.

1977: *Please Try to Remember the First of Octember* (Theo. LeSieg, pseudonym) is published. Geisel receives honorary doctoral degree from Lake Forest College. He also receives Emmy Award for "Halloween Is Grinch Night."

1978: *I Can Read with My Eyes Shut!* is published.

1979: *Oh Say Can You Say?* is published.

1980: *Maybe You Should Fly a Jet! Maybe You Should Be a Vet!* (Theo. LeSieg, pseudonym) is published. Geisel receives honorary doctoral degree from

Whittier College; he also receives the Laura Ingalls Wilder Award from the American Library Association.

1981: *The Tooth Book* (Theo. LeSieg, pseudonym) is published.

1982: *Hunches in Bunches* is published. Geisel wins an Emmy for the television special "The Grinch Grinches the Cat in the Hat."

1983: Receives honorary doctoral degree from John F. Kennedy University.

1984: *The Butter Battle Book*, about warfare, is published. It becomes as controversial as *The Lorax*. Geisel wins a Pulitzer Prize for his contributions to children's literature.

1985: Receives honorary doctoral degree from Princeton University. The entire graduating class stands and recites *Green Eggs and Ham* in tribute.

1986: *You're Only Old Once!* is published. Geisel receives honorary doctoral degree from the University of Hartford.

1987: *I Am Not Going to Get Up Today!* is published. Geisel receives honorary doctoral degree from Brown University, his eighth honorary degree.

1990: *Oh, the Places You'll Go* is published.

1991: *Six by Seuss: A Treasury of Dr. Seuss Classics* is published. It includes *And to Think That I Saw It on Mulberry Street*; *The 500 Hats of Bartholomew Cubbins*; *Horton Hatches the Egg*; *Yertle the Turtle*; *How the Grinch Stole Christmas*; and *The Lorax*.

September 24, Theodor Seuss Geisel dies in La Jolla, California, at 87.

1995: *Daisy-Head Mayzie* is published. It is the only Dr. Seuss book featuring a little girl. *The Secret Art of Dr. Seuss* is also published. Audrey Geisel donates $20 million to the Main Library of the University of California at San Diego. The library is renamed the Geisel Library.

1996: *My Many Colored Days*, with illustrations by Steve Johnson and Lou Fancher, is published by Alfred A. Knopf. Audrey Geisel donates $1 million to the library in Theodor Geisel's hometown of Springfield, Massachusetts. Random House publishes *A Hatful of Seuss*, which includes *If I Ran the Zoo*; *The Sneetches and Other Stories*; *Horton Hears a Who!*; *Dr. Seuss's Sleep Book*; and *Bartholomew and the Oobleck*.

1997: *Seuss-isms: Wise and Witty Prescriptions for Living from the Good Doctor* is published.

This is one of the first major articles about Dr. Seuss. By 1959 he had published 17 books, including Horton Hatches the Egg *(1940),* McElligot's Pool *(1947),* Thidwick the Big-Hearted Moose *(1948),* Horton Hears a Who! *(1954), and two of his most famous,* How the Grinch Stole Christmas *(1957) and* The Cat in the Hat *(1957).*

The quotations from the three children in the last paragraph are three of the most quoted comments ever made about Dr. Seuss books.

1

The Wacky World of Dr. Seuss Delights the Child—and Adult— Readers of His Books

PETER BUNZEL

Life, **April 6, 1959**

"My animals look the way they do because I can't draw," explains Theodor Seuss Geisel, a man far better known as Dr. Seuss. But because his drawing and imagination are so outlandish, the weird menagerie of potbellied, strangely named creatures—some of which are shown here for the first time—has put Geisel in a class by himself as the creator of children's books and of a wacky world.

Geisel has been misdrawing animals since his childhood in Springfield, Mass., where his father, as park superintendent, supervised the zoo. A successful cartoonist, he hit national fame with his "Quick, Henry, the Flit!" ads in 1927. Ten years later he started a long line of children's books capped by last year's best-selling *The Cat in the Hat* (Random House). Restricted to a vocabulary of 225 words, it has launched him into a project called Beginner Books, designed to make first reading "a bit more entertaining" than present primers. "There's been too much 'Come here, Fido,' in kids' readers," says Geisel. "I sometimes wonder how any of us learned to read."

If you should ask Ted Geisel how he ever thought up an animal called a Bippo-no-Bungus from the wilds of Hippo-no-Hungus or a tizzle-topped Tufted Mazurka from the African island of Yerka, his answer would be disarmingly to the point: "Why, I've been to most of these places myself so the names are from memory. As for the animals, I have a special dictionary which gives most of them, and I just look up the spellings." Helen Geisel, Ted's chief editor, chief critic, business manager and wife, has another explanation. "His mind," she says of Ted, "has never grown up."

Mrs. Geisel goes on: "Ted doesn't sit down and write for children. He writes to amuse himself. Luckily what amuses him also amuses them." Her husband emphatically agrees. "Ninety percent of failures in children's books," says he, speaking with the authority of 16 successes, "come from writing to preconceptions of what kids like. When I'm writing a book I do it to please Helen and me. But when it finally comes out I take one look and think 'Oh, my God!'"

Most of Geisel's books point a moral, though he insists he never starts with one. "Kids," he says, "can see a moral coming a mile off and they gag at it. But there's an inherent moral in any story." *Horton Hatches the Egg*, whose theme is *I meant what I said and I said what I meant, an elephant's faithful, one hundred percent!*, teaches dedication. Despotism gets the works in *Yertle the Turtle*, while *McElligot's Pool* extols unity in nature.

For every book completed, Geisel throws out enough material to fill 35 others. Each book takes about 18 months to write because Geisel, a meticulous craftsman, runs into log jams that last for days. The problem may be a single line or even a word. Stuck in this situation, Geisel will pace the studio floor or throw himself on a bed where he thrashes convulsively, "Every once in a while it comes easily," says he. "Sometimes a lovely flow of words will carry me four whole lines." His troubles and intensity arise chiefly from his high regard for children who, he says, "have as much right to qualify as their elders," or, in the immortal words of Horton the Elephant, "a person's a person no matter how small."

All Dr. Seuss's books, as well as his Oscar-winning cartoon film *Gerald McBoing-Boing*, proceed from the simple premise that children will believe a ludicrous situation if pursued with relentless logic. "If I start with a two-headed animal I must never waver from that concept. There must be two hats in the closet, two toothbrushes in the bathroom and two sets of spectacles on the night table. Then my readers will accept the poor fellow without hesitation and so will I."

The Geisels have no children of their own. But he once dedicated a book to a girl named "Chrysanthemum-Pearl (aged 89 months, going on 90)." His wife explains: "Ted got tired hearing friends describe bright things their children said and did. At first he'd say, 'The child would have been a fool not to.' Then he invented Chrysanthemum-Pearl. She became so real that he repeated her bright sayings, though they were really quite stupid. But people fell for it. Some even sent her presents. There were times when even we believed it."

Geisel, now 55, has long since admitted to the hoax. To his pink stucco home, remodeled on an old watchtower overlooking the Pacific and Mexico, the postman brings him testimonials from a legion of various offspring, his real-life fans. "Dr. Seuss has an imagination with a long tail," said one child. ("That fellow will go places," says Geisel.) A nine-year-old once wrote, "It's the funniest book I ever read in nine years." But the accolade Geisel cherishes above all is a single word set down in a childish hand, "Whew!"

cal and sociological jargon. Geisel's own approach to the topic is down-to-earth. "If a book pleases me, it has a chance of pleasing children," he says. Many of the elders whom he also pleases are faithful to him because they feel that they can read, and reread, and re-reread a Dr. Seuss book to a child without imperilling their own mental balance or—by skipping paragraphs or whole pages—impairing their integrity. This is not to say that Geisel has no detractors. There are those who think his pictures and words are plain silly—a few of the leaders of this faction would just as soon seek to divert their children with the exterior of a cereal box—but most guardians of the young mind, it would appear, are willing to go along with the *Bulletin* of the Parents League of New York, which has enthusiastically endorsed Geisel's books. The League classifies them as "read-alouds." He himself fancies the description "logical insanity." The reading aloud of logical insanity, appropriately illustrated by its creator, has always been fun, but between Edward Lear's day and Dr. Seuss's the pickings, few people would deny, have been slim.

Geisel and his wife, who under her maiden name of Helen Palmer is herself the author of several successful but more or less conventional children's books—to name a few, *Tommy's Wonderful Rides*, *Johnny's Machines*, *Bobby and His Airplane*, and *Donald Duck Sees South America*—are childless. Some of their friends consider it a shame that a man who is so beloved by so many children has none of his own. Geisel does not agree. "You have 'em, I'll amuse 'em," he has said on more than one occasion, and he has also said, "You can't write books for children if too many of them are looking over your shoulder." With no children at all looking over his shoulder, Geisel painstakingly turns out books that, in the opinion of Rudolf Flesch, the *Why Johnny Can't Read* man, will be read a hundred years hence, when, also in Flesch's opinion, Hemingway, Faulkner, Marquand, and other current favorites may be gathering dust. Flesch rates Geisel "a genius pure and simple." Bennett Cerf, the president of Random House, has stated that Geisel is the only genius on his list, though Cerf would probably not have put it so baldly had Faulkner, whom he also publishes, been in his office at the time. For the last few years, Geisel has been the best-selling author of the Random House list, and possibly on any list anywhere. Once or twice a year, the *Times* put out a Sunday children's-book supplement and includes a roster of best-sellers; in last month's ratings three of the top four sellers were by Dr. Seuss. When Nevil Shute died, last January, his obituary in the *Times* proclaimed him the best-selling novelist of his day, adding that his yearly royalties amounted to a hundred and seventy-five thousand dollars. Geisel's book royalties came to nearly two hundred thousand dollars in 1959. To date, nearly three million copies of Dr. Seuss's books have been sold, and Random House now orders a first printing of a hundred thousand copies of any book that he writes. Even this figure proved inadequate for *Happy Birthday to You!*, which was issued in October, 1959; within a few weeks, stocks of the book were exhausted, and fifty thousand additional copies were run off. Geisel is staggered and a bit frightened by his opulence, for he has never learned to come to grips with money. Not quite trusting money, he hardly ever carries any, and he frequently grabs for restaurant checks only to discover that he can't pay them. He gave up trying to cope with checkbooks some thirty years ago, and turned them over to his wife. "I wish people would stop talking to me about money," he says. "All I want to do is to write books, and everybody's forever nagging at me to *keep* them."

Geisel's tastes are simple. "Ted has no extravagances," his wife says. "I can't think of anything he likes except cigarettes and rocks." His cigarette outlay runs comparatively high. A chain smoker, he now and then breaks off for a while and sucks on an unlighted corncob pipe filled with radish seeds. Whenever a compulsion to smoke sweeps over him—which is every few minutes—he waters seeds with an eyedropper. Once a crop of radish greens has sprouted from his pipe bowl—which he says takes about three days in a hospital environment—he goes back to cigarettes. Rocks are his outdoor hobby. At his home, astride a hilltop in La Jolla, California, he is an earnest rock gardener, and *Publishers' Weekly* is apt to be crowded off his parlor table by some lithic journal like *Guide for Beginning Fossil Hunters.* One of his most treasured possessions is a heavy stone slab with a dinosaur's foot-print in it, reputed to be something over a hundred and fifty million years old. Geisel himself is reputed to be something of a prankster, and, to his indignation, quite a few of his acquaintances refuse to believe that his hoary fossil is not homemade.

La Jolla is an upper-bracket community, and the relative austerity of the Geisels' way of life confounds their neighbors. Geisel and his wife have only one car, only one maid—part-time, at that—and only one swimming pool. After thirty-three years of married life, they are an uncommonly devoted couple, and they see no reason to have a second car, since they are rarely apart. Mrs. Geisel stopped writing books of her own fifteen years ago, so she could concentrate on helping her husband with his. This she does in part by keeping a vigilant critical eye on his output, in part by giving him the reassurance and praise for which he, like many another writer, has an insatiable need, and in part by shielding him from distractions. Along with his finances, she handles his correspondence. Geisel's—or, rather, Dr. Seuss's—mail is imposing. At the end of 1957, Random House announced that in the previous twelve months he had received nine thousand two hundred and sixty-seven pounds of it. No up-to-date statistics have been released, but whatever the avoirdupois of Geisel's current mail, it amounts to thousands of letters a week. Geisel's policy is to have his wife answer letters from teachers, librarians, sick or crippled children, and entire school classes. (Mrs. Geisel signs some of the replies "Mrs. Dr. Seuss.") The rest of his fan mail hardly ever gets to La Jolla. It is mercifully intercepted and screened by Random House, which sends the bulk of his correspondents a printed form letter that he has written and illustrated. The form letter in use until just recently explained that Dr. Seuss's mail service was unreliable, because he lived on a steep and inaccessible precipice and because his correspondence had to travel by Budget, an ungainly Seuss beast, driven by Nudget, a Seuss Budget-driver. Most children were satisfied with this reply, but now and then a persistent correspondent would grumble. "Did you get a letter from a girl named Olive or a boy named Bud?" an Oregon schoolchild wrote Dr. Seuss a year or so ago. "They are both in my classroom. Did you get their letter? I don't think you did the way your roads are but they will write to you again and then are you going to write to them again about the Budget and the Nudget? I want a letter from you again but not about the Budget and Nudget again." Geisel sought to curtail laments of this sort by fashioning a new illustrated form letter, which thanks the correspondent on behalf of Dr. Seuss himself and a friend—the Three-Muffed Apfel Moose.

It is only within the last couple of years that Geisel's fan mail and sales figures have soared into the literary stratosphere. As recently as 1954, he asked his agent, Phyllis Jackson, of the Music Corporation of America, whether she thought he could count on five thousand dollars annually from book royalties in the foreseeable future. She said he could, and now he knows he can. Not only does he write a new book or two every year but the sales of each book on his back list grow larger every year. All his old books are current best-sellers. An early one, *The King's Stilts*, which was published in 1939, sold 4,648 copies the first year. By 1941, its annual sales were down to 394. In 1958, the last year for which figures are obtainable, they were up to 11,037. *The King's Stilts* has been a more sluggish mover than any other Dr. Seuss book; its cumulative sales have climbed nearly to the 75,000 mark. Another early Dr. Seuss, *Horton Hatches the Egg*, which has had total sales of more than 200,000 and is still briskly hatching profits, sold 5,801 copies in 1940, the year it came out. It, too, fell off—to 1,645 the following year. In 1958, it sold 27,463 copies. What appears to have given all the Dr. Seuss books their recent boost was the publication, in 1957, of *The Cat in the Hat*, which seems likely to achieve a total sale of a million copies by the end of this year. Since the book is priced at a dollar ninety-five, this would bring its retail gross to nearly two million dollars—equivalent to the gross on six million copies of a thirty-five-cent paperback. Only two works of fiction, *God's Little Acre* and *Peyton Place*, have sold as well as that in paperback form. And *The Cat in the Hat* is aseptic.

The Cat in the Hat evolved from a 1954 article in *Life* by John Hersey, who complained of the sorry state of children's primers and suggested that someone like Dr. Seuss ought to give the kids a break by providing them with sprightlier fare. Among those who urged Geisel to accept this challenge was William Spaulding, then the textbook editor and now the president of Houghton Mifflin. Having long felt that the "See the red ball? The ball is red" school of literature left a good deal to be desired, Geisel did not need much prodding. He was somewhat taken aback to learn that a primer was supposed to have a severely limited vocabulary—a particularly inhibiting restriction for a writer whose metier is verse—but after a long struggle he came up with a book that had a plot, had humor, rhymed, and did it all on a vocabulary of only two hundred-odd words. Houghton Mifflin issued *The Cat in the Hat* as a textbook, and Random House as a trade book. Hersey called it a "gift to the art of reading" and a "harum-scarum masterpiece." Curiously, the Random House edition, sold through bookstores, has far outdistanced the Houghton Mifflin one, sold through school channels; the explanation may be that some old-line educators have tended to be suspicious of a primer produced by a man who signs himself "Dr." but has never written a doctoral dissertation, and that others have felt the teaching process is a solemn business, not to be interrupted by avoidable laughter.

Geisel, being fond of both cats and children, was glad that he had been able to use the one species to edify the other. In real life he sometimes finds the relationship between animals and human beings cruelly bewildering—not long ago he rescued a mouse that was floundering in his pool, only to see it scamper straight into a mousetrap he had set in his garage—but in his books he manages to reconcile his innate kindheartedness with some of the nasty practices implicit in the survival of the fittest. When a situation in *McElligot's Pool*, for instance, seemed to call for a picture of a worm on a hook, Geisel made it graphically clear that his worm was not skewered on his barb but instead had curled itself up there cozily. At the moment, the Geisels, who once kept twenty-five or thirty cats, have only one pet—an aging, wheezy Irish setter. Their home, though, is filled with Dr. Seuss animals—painted, carved into chair backs and chests of drawers, or sculptured by him out of any old objects that have come to hand, like shaving brushes—as well as with store-bought toy animals collected by his wife. As a wedding-anniversary present one year, she gave her husband a delicate life-size model of a cockroach. Geisel was touched, but professionally he shuns any animal that looks normal.

The animals that Geisel confects are anatomically absurd, as flexible and floppy-looking as rag dolls—or, indeed, as many children wish real pets were. "My animals look the way they do because I've never learned to draw," he explains. He does, in fact, draw very much like an untutored child; first he makes an outline of the creature he has in mind, and then he fills in the enclosed area with solid colors. In 1954, he appeared on a children's television program called *Excursion*, in the course of which he attempted to demonstrate how different the same animal could look to different artists by having six young abstract painters render their impressions of a horse. Geisel did not enter this sweepstakes himself, but he commented sympathetically on the utterly dissimilar, and universally unnaturalistic, results. In private, Geisel is less indulgent toward much contemporary art. To spoof a friend who had pretensions as a collector, he once told him at length about a nonexistent abstract painter called Escorobus. "I have some of his finest works at home," Geisel said, "and he's given me permission to act as his agent in selling them." Then he went home and dashed off a wallful of Escorobuses. The friend came around to see them, and was reaching for his checkbook when Geisel owned up to the hoax. "That experience made me suspect that a lot of modern art is malarkey," Geisel says. "If I can do it myself, it can't be any good."

Geisel's father, Theodor Robert Geisel, is superintendent of the Springfield, Massachusetts, public-park system, and since his dominion includes a zoo, it is sometimes thought that his son's predilection for animals—one of Dr. Seuss's best-sellers is *If I Ran the Zoo*—is traceable back to boyhood. But the elder Geisel—a vigorous, ramrod-straight, silver-haired man of eighty-three—did not start running his zoo until his son had grown up; before that, he ran a Springfield brewery that *his* father had founded. (The brewery's original name was Kuhlmbach & Geisel, which in Springfield taverns was traditionally amended to "Come back and guzzle.") The younger Theodor was born on March 2, 1904. His forebears on both sides were German—his mother, Henrietta Seuss, who died in 1928, was the daughter of a Springfield baker— and he was raised in a *Turnverein* and *Schützverein* atmosphere. His father was an international rifle champion, and his mother was a crack shot, too; he is not. During the First World War, the Geisels, although they were by then pretty well Americanized and vociferously loyal, felt uneasy. Germans, brewers, marksmen—who wouldn't? Geisel attributes much of his present diffidence to an incident that took place when the Springfield Boy Scouts, himself among them, were competitively peddling thrift stamps and Liberty Bonds. His grandfather Geisel was so doggedly open-handed a customer that young Ted compiled the second-best sales record in town. The day came when the leading salesboys were to be awarded medals, and Theodore Roosevelt arrived in Springfield to do the honors. "We all put on our Scout uniforms and marched to City Hall," Geisel recalls, "and after Roosevelt had given a fiery speech, we lined up onstage to be decorated. But somebody had made a mistake, and there were ten boys and only nine medals. I happened to be tenth in line. When I stepped forward, with my whole family sitting proudly in the audience, all ready to applaud, Roosevelt had nothing to pin on me. He just stood there, nonplussed. Then a Scoutmaster ran up and said there had been a misunderstanding, and shoved me off the stage. I've had a dread of platform appearances ever since."

After finishing public high school in Springfield, Geisel entered Dartmouth with the class of 1925, which the present Vice-President of the college has hailed—in no small measure because Dr. Seuss belongs to it—as Dartmouth's greatest class ever. (Some members of the class of '26 insist that they have a matching claim to fame, because their ranks include the composer of

"Rudolph, the Red-nosed Reindeer.") Geisel became editor of the college humor magazine, the *Jack-o-Lantern*, to which he contributed reams of cartoons, many of them involving bizarre animals. It was standard undergraduate fare: one cartoon, captioned "Financial Note: Goat Milk Is Higher Than Ever," showed a female mountain goat with her forefeet and her hind feet on two uneven peaks, which raised her udder above her head. Geisel's editorship of the magazine gave him the status of a big man on campus, and he has been a big man on campus, and he has been a big man there ever since. He has even judged a beauty-queen contest at the Dartmouth Winter Carnival. Whenever the Geisels come East nowadays, they try to fit in a visit to Dartmouth. The college library has a complete set of Dr. Seuss's works, and now and then, in an avuncular mood, it puts them on display. In the archives of the library are manuscripts by Sinclair Lewis, Booth Tarkington, and Robert Frost, and also the manuscript of Dr. Seuss's *The 500 Hats of Bartholomew Cubbins*. In 1955, Dartmouth legitimized Dr. Seuss's title by making Geisel an honorary Doctor of Humane Letters. His citation, composed by the president of the college, Dr. John S. Dickey, read, in part, "You single-handedly have stood as St. George between a generation of exhausted parents and the demon dragon of unexhausted children on a rainy day." Dartmouth's affection for Geisel '25 has been handsomely reciprocated by his for his alma mater. When he was asked to contribute to a building-fund drive a few years ago, he replied offhandedly that he was leaving Dartmouth a little something in his will. The little something proved to be the copyrights on most of his books. The income from a couple of others is earmarked, through a foundation the Geisels have established, for the San Diego Fine Arts Gallery, of which he is a trustee. But Dartmouth will inherit a large portion of his royalties, and its share of them, twenty or thirty years hence, may very well amount to a quarter of a million dollars a year—the equivalent in income of a six-million-dollar endowment. Dartmouth's promised legacy was endangered in the summer of 1958, when the Geisels paid an off-season visit to Hanover. Some faculty members who were there cooked up a surprise for Geisel. They had eighty children dress up as characters from his books and serenade him one morning, following which he was dragged onto the folded-down top of an ancient Packard phaeton and driven four times around the campus, while sticky-fingered urchins swarmed lovingly all over him. Geisel, though aware that his accolade had sprung from the best of intentions, was so shaken by it that he was tempted to call his lawyer and have his will redrawn. But he soon calmed down, and now he is a true-blue, or true-green, as ever. "Dartmouth will always be Number One for me," he has since said.

On receiving his bachelor's degree, Geisel thought he might like to go into teaching. He had somehow given his father the impression that he was in line for a fellowship in English literature at Oxford, and Geisel *père* had elatedly spread word of this around Springfield. Nothing of the sort came to pass, so Mr. Geisel offered to stake his son to a graduate course at Oxford anyway. Arriving at Lincoln College, young Geisel was miserable. The weather was dank, and, what was worse, he quickly decided that by comparison with his fellow-matriculants he was appallingly ignorant. Helen Palmer, a Wellesley graduate, had entered Oxford a year before him, and she, too, was in the dumps. An American Rhodes Scholar there, Joseph Sagmaster, who knew and pitied both of them, thought that misery deserved company, and introduced them in his rooms one afternoon over anchovy toast. Students at Oxford were not allowed motorcycles, but Geisel acquired one anyway. In the hope of avoiding detection, he passed himself off as a poultrymonger, a disguise he effected by always carrying two plucked ducks in a basket wired to his vehicle. Geisel proposed to Miss Palmer while they were both aboard this sputtering prop, and at the instant of her consent the machine went out of control and hurled them into a ditch. They were superficially bruised, but they were engaged. In the judgment of Sagmaster, who became an editorial writer in Cincinnati, and to whose family Dr. Seuss's "Yertle the Turtle" has been appreciatively dedicated, bringing the Geisels together was "the happiest inspiration I've ever had." The Geisels, who do a lot of traveling, still nostalgically go back to Oxford every so often. When Mrs. Geisel was a student there, she lived in a boarding house and bathed in a tub under a window that she could not, and her landlady would not, close. Thirty years later, the Geisels were in London, and he suggested impulsively one morning, "Let's go up to Oxford and see if that window is still open." They took the next train, found that it was, and took the next train back.

Geisel's friends at Oxford were aware that he much preferred drawing pictures to mastering the prescribed curriculum. Miss Palmer kept urging him to give up the academic life for the artistic, but he hesitated. He had already had one galling rebuff. The Oxford University Press had responded with dismaying chilliness to his proposal that he illustrate, and it publish, a new edition of *Paradise Lost*. (It was his plan—and this alone may well have prompted the rejection—to show the Archangel Uriel sliding down a sunbeam with a long-necked oil can in his hand, to slick his passage.) Geisel got even by leaving Oxford after one year and going to the University of Vienna, where he thought he might have a fling at studying nineteenth-century German drama. He couldn't find anyone there who taught it, so he backtracked to the Sorbonne, where he called on a Jonathan Swift specialist whose name had been given him by an Oxford don. The Swift man welcomed him warmly and outlined what he thought was a bang-up subject for a doctoral thesis. His notion was that Geisel should explore the only period of Swift's life, barring infancy, when he was not known to have written a single word—a stretch of several months in his teens. Though flattered at being thought capable of handling this scholarly opportunity, Geisel regarded it as depressingly negative in scope, and forthwith abandoned formal education for good. He took a cattle boat to Corsica, where he wrote a novel that has never been published, and then went to Italy. In November, 1927, he came home and married Miss Palmer, in New Jersey.

The Geisels had decided to get married on the strength of his having sold a couple of cartoons to *Judge*. He signed them "Dr. Seuss," feeling that he should save his patronym for more exalted artistic accomplishments and throwing in the title to give flair to the pseudonym. Over the next few years, he turned out a stream of cartoons and prose for *Judge* and for such other magazines as *College Humor, Liberty, Vanity Fair,* and the old *Life*. He made enough money to live in a Park Avenue apartment, where he produced, gratis, some of his most imaginative drawings for the customers of a neighborhood fish market that had a phone number differing from his by just one digit. On receiving a telephoned order for, say, two pounds of haddock, Geisel would obligingly draw a two-pound haddock, on an old shirt cardboard, and send it around to the customer.

For *Judge,* one week, Geisel did a cartoon showing a huge beast nuzzling a bed on which lay a knight in armor. The caption went, "Mediaeval tenant: 'Darn it all, another Dragon. And just after I'd sprayed the whole castle with Flit!'" A toss of a coin had impelled Geisel to make it Flit instead of Fly-Tox, another insecticide of the day, and it was a lucky toss, for the wife of a Flit advertising man picked up a copy of that *Judge* in a beauty parlor, and the next thing Geisel knew, he was under contract to do Flit Ads. The famous "Quick, Henry! The Flit!" was the outcome. Actually, Geisel's line for the first ad was "Quick, Mama! The Flit!," and it accompanied a drawing of a cave boy clutched in a dinosaur's jaws. Geisel did cartoons for Flit for seventeen years, varying his basic caption only occasionally, for the purpose of having, say, a bug-beset whale cry to a passenger in *its* jaws, "Quick, Jonah! The Flit!"

The firm that made Flit was a subsidiary of the Standard Oil Company of New Jersey (the only cartoon-ad idea that did not originate with Geisel or his wife was submitted by the first Mrs. John D. Rockefeller, Jr., and while he can't remember what it was, he recalls that it was droll), and every now and then he would be farmed out to another subsidiary, like the Essomarine fuel outfit. In this connection, he presided over a celebrated publicity stunt of the thirties—the Seuss Navy. The idea was spawned at the 1936 Motor Boat Show, and enrollment in the Navy was at first limited to owners of boats with inboard motors. Later, gossip columnists got in, some of them landlubbers. Every member was an admiral except Dr. Seuss, who was Admiral-in-Chief, and by 1940, when his Navy no longer seemed quite so funny, and petered out, it boated a couple of thousand admirals. Its burgee was a Geisel-designed herring, mostly bones, and its official seal was a flippered seal. Annually, at Motor Boat Show time, Essomarine picked up the tab for a Seuss Navy banquet, attended by nearly a thousand admirals, whom Geisel would sonorously lead in an oath of allegiance to Mother Neptune—a mermaidlike creature he had rigged up out of a dressmaker's dummy and a fishtail. "The Seuss Navy was a rather corny outfit," Geisel says now.

Geisel has toiled on many advertising campaigns over the years. For another Standard Oil offshoot, he created a series of bloodcurdling, or engine-curdling, monsters who roamed the nation's billboards—the Moto-Raspus, the Zerodoccus, the Moto-Munchus, the Karbo-Nockus, and the Oilio-Gobelus. Geisel did his last billboard job in 1956. In that year, the La Jolla Town Council—of which he was, and still is, an active and conscientious member—issued a pamphlet, written and illustrated by Dr. Seuss, that merrily lambasted all billboards. It was an account of the rivalry of two Neanderthal business establishments—Guss's Guss-ma-Tuss and Zaxx's Zaxx-ma-Taxx—and it concluded with these lines:

> And, thus between them, with impunity
> They loused up the entire community.
> Sign after sign after sign, until
> Their property values slumped to nil.
> And even the dinosaurs moved away
> From that messed-up spot in the U.S.A.
> Which is why our businessmen never shall
> Allow such to happen in La Jolla, Cal.

On reading this, Geisel's current billboard sponsor abruptly terminated his contract.

Geisel frequently says that his life has been a series of accidents, and it was pretty much accidental that he began writing books in the first place. Back in 1931, during his *Judge* and Esso days, the Viking Press asked him to illustrate, for a modest flat fee, a collection of schoolboys' howlers that was to be brought out under the title *Boners*. The book and a sequel, *More Boners*, did very well, and Geisel looked on with envy as the author's royalties piled up. "I suddenly realized there was no sense in just illustrating books," he says. The following year, he wrote an ABC book, which consisted mainly of pictures of wacky animals of the kind that populate most of his books—a long-necked whizzleworp, for example, and a green-striped chomondelet. Nobody was interested in publishing the book, but Dartmouth consolingly exhibited the manuscript. "The idea is obviously an excellent one," an undergraduate critic commented in a campus publication, "but if juvenile impressions are as important as the child psychologists say they are, it is interesting to consider the strange new neuroses which such pictures could bring about."

Geisel shied away from trying another children's book for four years. Then, in 1936, while returning from a European trip, he became mesmerized, as he tells the tale, by the rhythm of the ship's engines. "Da da *da* da de *dum* dum de *da* de de *da*," it sent. To be sure, he could have come up with the identical rhythm merely be reciting " 'Twas the night before Christmas, when all through the house," but one cannot anticipate inspiration. The words that seemed to him to fit his magic meter most neatly were "And to think that I saw it on Mulberry Street," and within a few months he had written and illustrated a book with that title. A score of publishers rejected it. Then, one morning, while walking, manuscript in hand, along Madison Avenue, a byway to which his advertising stints often summoned him, he bumped in to a Dartmouth contemporary, Marshall McClintock, who the day before had given the class of '26 an upward nudge by becoming juvenile editor of the Vanguard Press, and who was aprowl for something to edit. Never did supply and demand more fortuitously collide. *Mulberry Street* has to do with a boy named Marco who, on the way home from school, sees an ordinary horse and wagon and progressively enlarges his recollection of them until his fancy has soared to rarefied descriptive heights. The book has gone through fifteen editions, totaling a hundred and twenty thousand copies; it has been read or dramatized on radio more than a hundred times; and it has been used in a fiction-writing course at N.Y.U. to illustrate what the instructor in charge called "the principle of intensification," Demms Taylor based what he called "a set of variations for orchestra" on it, and in 1943 the New York Philharmonic played the piece at Carnegie Hall.

Since *Mulberry Street*, Geisel has about every triumph conceivable for a writer of children's books except one—he is largely without honor outside of his own country. It may have been easy for Deems Taylor to convert *Mulberry Street* into music, but there have been obvious difficulties in translating the bulk of Dr. Seuss's work—most of which not only rhymes but deals with creatures called Nizzards, Ziffs, Zuffs, and Ham-ikka-Schnim-ikka-Schnam-ikka-Schnopps—into foreign languages. In Polish, for instance, a cat in a hat becomes a *kot w kapeluszu*, and a drum-tummied snumm a *brzuchaty snumm*—there evidently being no Polish word for "snumm." In *The 500 Hats of Bartholomew Cubbins*, Geisel, who likes hats and once collected them, had some magicians chanting, "Winkibus, Tinkibus, Fotichee, Klay! Hat on this demon's head, fly far away!" The Japanese translation of this book omitted the passage entirely. In Germany, a translator came up with "*Winkibus, Pinkibus, Lupf um die Eck. Hut von dem Hexc-rich, Fliege weit weg!*" The chant hasn't yet been tried in Poland. A few Dr. Seuss books have been published in England, but they haven't done especially well there. One reason may be the British have no word for "snumm," either.

Geisel is a high-principled man, and most of his books have a moral—usually served up, like children's medicine, in mild and palatable doses. In his books, might never makes right, the meek inherit the earth, and pride frequently goeth before a fall—usually a pratfall. When his *Horton Hears a Who!*

came out, in 1954, the *Times* called it "probably the most moral tale since the first 'Elsie Dinsmore,'" and the Des Moines *Register* characterized it as "a rhymed lesson in protection of minorities and their rights." The hero, Horton, is an elephant who takes it upon himself, in the face of considerable scoffing, to champion the cause of a colony of Whos, microscopic creatures who inhabit a grain of dust. "A person's a person, no matter how small," Horton declares. In 1940, Geisel was working on an earlier Horton book, *Horton Hatches the Egg* (in this one Horton dutifully sits on an abandoned egg in a bird's nest until, as a reward for his patience, he hatches a winged infant with the head of an elephant), when Paris fell to the Nazis. With Europe in turmoil and this country, to Geisel's way of thinking, misguidedly complacent, he could not stick to the writing of children's books, and instead began drawing cartoons that hit out at American isolationists. He was unable to find any newspaper publisher who felt that his political views needed airing until he ran into Virginia Vanderlip Schoales, an old friend, who was working on *PM*. Mrs. Schoales introduced him to Ralph Ingersoll, the editor of the paper, and Geisel at once became *PM's* editorial cartoonist.

While *PM's* stated philosophy—that it was against people who pushed other people around—tied in very aptly with Horton's view that a person's a person regardless of size, some of Geisel's friends, aware that he was then living on Park Avenue and that his major patron was Standard Oil, thought Ingersoll's up-the-rebels journal an odd haven for him to have sailed into. (Actually, he was a no more incongruous figure there than Ingersoll himself, whose blood is very blue, or than Mrs. Schoales, the daughter of a bank president and the wife of a Morgan Stanley partner.) Geisel's contributions to *PM*, like nearly everything else in that now defunct paper, were dead serious. He portrayed Pierre Laval as a louse on Hitler's finger, and, for once drawing a reasonably recognizable animal, the archetypal Nazi as a particularly close-to-the-ground dachshund. This provoked so many protests from hundred-per-cent-American dachshund fanciers that he resolved never again to compete, artistically, with photographers and taxidermists. He depicted the America First Committee and the Nazi Party as Siamese twins linked by a straggly beard. This provoked some threats of a boycott against Standard Oil by a few irate isolationist customers, who thought the company's right-hand advertising man was straying too far left.

Geisel did three cartoons a week for *PM* and occasional drawings for the Treasury Department, the War Production Board, and Nelson Rockefeller's Committee on Inter-American Affairs, but after the United States got into the war, he felt so out of the main current of events that at the end of 1942 he decided to join the armed forces. He was presently stationed in California, as an Army captain attached to Frank Capra's celebrated wartime documentary-film-making unit, for which he wrote and directed scripts calculated to elevate G.I. morals and morale. In the fall of 1944, Geisel was shipped to Europe for a spell, in connection with his film work, and at General Omar Bradley's headquarters in Luxembourg, he ran into Ingersoll, by then a lieutenant colonel. Ingersoll said he supposed that Geisel, like most Stateside tourists, would like to have a peek at some actual fighting while he was in the area—without, of course, getting too dangerously exposed. Unfolding a top-secret map, he studied it carefully and circled "Bastogne." Then he summoned a jeep and urged Geisel to ride on up there and take in the sights. Geisel was trapped for three days in the Battle of the Bulge, eventually being rescued by the British. "Nobody came along and put a sign saying, 'This is the Battle of the Bulge,'" he explained later. "How was I supposed to know? I thought the fact that we didn't seem to be able to find any friendly troops in any direction was just one of the normal occurrences of combat.'"

After Allied soldiers crossed the Rhine, Geisel had the task of lugging around an indoctrination film he'd worked on for future American occupation troops, with instructions to show it to generals in the field and obtain their imprimatur. The picture was a strong sermon against fraternization, and one point is kept hammering home was that in no circumstances should an American military man shake the hand of a German. (The ending of the finished product was somewhat tamer than the one Geisel had proposed, in which he had a War Department narrator saying, "Just be a good soldier. Leave all the bungling to the State Department.") One Army headquarters at which he paused with his can of anti-handshake film was in a captured German city, and he was invited to accompany some staff officers to a municipal reception. Geisel, by then a major, was under orders not to let the film out of his sight, and he dutifully carried it to the party, where he shortly found himself at the tail end of a line of officers being greeted, with ceremonious handshakes, by their German hosts. As he moved forward, he ruefully shifted his burden from his right hand to his left so that he could follow the leader.

Shortly before the first atomic bomb was exploded, Geisel returned to California, where he was ordered to come up with another film for postwar occupation troops—one that would keep them on the alert by reminding them that inattention could lead to a third world war. "Make that third war a real doozy, Geisel," he was told. Seeking inspiration, he leafed through the magazine section of a recent Sunday *Times,* where his eye was caught by an article suggesting that there was enough latent energy in a tumbler of water, if man could ever figure out a way of harnessing it, to blow up half the earth. Without further ado, or further research, Geisel knocked out the draft of a script suggesting the possibility of unimaginably devastating explosions, and passed it along to his superiors. Two days later, the Pentagon was on the phone, urgently asking where he'd got his facts.

"From the *Times?*" he replied.

"Burn your source of information, Geisel," came the command.

"Burn the *Times*?" he asked.

"Yes, and report by phone as soon as you've carried out your orders," he was told.

"I had long since thrown away the copy of the paper in question," Geisel recalls, "but I wanted to be a good soldier, so I rushed my most reliable sergeant to an out-of-town news dealer, and he bought me a copy of the latest *Times*. We put it in a metal bucket and all marched out into a courtyard and stood in formation and gave the Boy Scout salute while a trusted lieutenant lit a match to it. Then I called Washington and said, 'Mission accomplished, sir. We have burned the *Times*.' 'Well done, Geisel,' I was told and then they went on with the war."

Mustered out, as a lieutenant colonel, early in 1946, Geisel proceeded to divide his time for several years between children's books and motion pictures. With his wife, he wrote a documentary film about Japan, *Design for Death*, which won an Oscar in 1947, but which soured its authors on Hollywood values. The object of the picture was to show that the Japanese were at heart not much different from any other human beings ("A person's a person, no matter how small"), and that they had allowed themselves to be dominated by a gang of ruthless leaders. One sequence, of which both Geisels were particularly fond, as illustrative of the serenity of Japanese culture, was devoted to sixteenth-century Japan. No actors were involved—just fog and water, with a muted tone poem as the musical background. While looking at some rushes one evening, the Geisels were horrified to discover that one of the producers had livened up his tranquil stretch with shots of American tanks barreling through a crowd of shrieking Japanese. The producer refused to delete the tanks, on the ground that, anachronism or no anachronism, they gave the dreary old century some vitality. Just before the picture was released, the Geisels sneaked into a cutting room and, abetted by a film editor, snipped out the lively footage. The producer had the last word, though. Weeks later, when the Geisels passed a theater where the film was playing, they found it advertised with posters that showed terrified white women in ripped chemises being carted off in cages by transparently ill-mentioned Japanese soldiers.

On his own, Geisel invented the movie-cartoon character Gerald McBoing-Boing, whose adventures also won an Oscar, and he not only conceived but wrote the scenario and designed the sets and costumes for a full-length screen musical with live actors, called *The 5,000 Fingers of Dr. T.* This was a fantasy about a whipcracking music teacher, Dr. Terwilliker, who made five hundred boys practice their scales simultaneously day in and out at the keyboard of an enormous piano. Geisel wrote the words of twenty songs for the picture, too. Most of them were never used. One that was, "Ten Happy Fingers," was supposed to be a satire on conventional piano exercises. The lyricist was bemused when a sheet-music publisher later brought it out as a conventional piano exercise. A hundred more or less piano-playing boys were hired for the movie, and Geisel has vivid memories of this group in action. "The kids were paid in cash," he says, "and one day, during a violent rainstorm that flooded the studio, they descended on the commissary en masse. They all rapidly got sick on candy. It was like a nightmarish Noah's Ark. Water was pouring in on the set, and the boys were moaning, and their mothers and their music teachers were all hopping up and down, and their ordinary teachers were running around trying to organize arithmetic classes, because the law said they should, and we had to call off work for three days and take the director to a hospital. It was the damnedest, nerve-rackingest, screamingest experience of my life." Upon learning that a movie theater in San Diego was holding the West Coast premiere of the picture and, as a special honor to him, was featuring his name on its marquee, Geisel became so edgy that he grabbed his wife and fled to Japan, explaining over his shoulder that he had some blocked yen in royalties that he wanted to spend. (The royalties, unsurprisingly, amounted to twenty-seven dollars and fifty cents.) He hasn't seen the finished movie yet, he says, and he has never again worked for motion pictures.

The Geisels had become addicted to California, though, if not to the movies. In 1948, they settled in La Jolla, a town of twenty thousand that was put on the map by the late E. W. Scripps. Among various La Jolla landmarks that the publisher endowed is the Scripps Institution of Oceanography, on whose staff is a Ph.D. named Hans Seuss. He sometimes receives requests from first-grade teachers that have been addressed simply "Dr. Seuss, La Jolla," and Geisel, in turn, receives requests from bathyorographically oriented professors. La Jolla is both a summer resort and a year-round haven for the retired, most of whom know their literary neighbor and are proud of him. La Jolla has four bookstores, and nearly every day one or another of them sends Geisel a batch of his books to be autographed for its customers. Many persons who spend vacations at La Jolla, moreover, order their Dr. Seuss books from La Jolla stores all the year round, to get them inscribed. During a couple of weeks last December, Geisel autographed a hundred and fifty Christmas-gift books a day.

The highest spot in La Jolla is Mount Soledad, and it is on its summit that the Geisels live, in a pink stucco house they built around an observation tower, from which they can look out across the Pacific or down into Mexico. The tower was erected many years ago by a real-estate man, who used it to point out low-lying sites to prospects. When the Geisels bought the place, a lot of La Jollans were surprised; they had always believed that the tower, a favorite aerie for young couples, was municipally owned. When the Geisels moved in, they found the walls and beams of its topmost room covered with heart-framed initials and other romantic graffiti, many of them scribbled in lipstick, and Geisel insists that he removed five thousand empty beer cans from one of the closets. During the first few months after the Geisels took possession, sailors from the San Diego naval base and their girls would roll up to the house and head happily for the tower stairs. Even today, an occasional married couple who became engaged at the summit stop by to ask if they may make an anniversary visit to their former trysting place.

The Geisels are also beleaguered by visitors who want to enjoy a view of Dr. Seuss. "It sometimes seems to me that half the teachers and librarians in America come to La Jolla for their holidays," Geisel said wearily one evening last summer. He likes to work at night and sleep late, but for a while he was aroused at seven o'clock every Sunday morning by an idolatrous neighboring pack of Cub Scouts, who would hike across a ravine or two and ring his doorbell. "I would stagger downstairs and let them in," Geisel says, "and the chief, or whatever he was, would announce cheerfully, 'Well, here we are!' Then they'd all march inside and sit down. I would be too groggy to say anything, and they would be too winded. One morning, we all sat and stared at each other for five minutes without exchanging a word, and finally one eight-year-old piped up, 'We saw a snake on the way over.' Then we all sat for another five minutes, until Helen rescued me by handing out cookies and easing them out. Eventually, I got them to quit through a friend who knew a cousin of a Scoutmaster."

Notwithstanding such impressive demonstrations of popularity, Geisel still finds it hard to believe in his own renown. A few months ago, he tried unavailingly, through somebody else's cousin, to wangle an introduction to an eminent dowager he had admired from afar; he ultimately met her after she had stood in line for an hour at a bookstore autographing session, holding a copy of a book of his that she wanted inscribed for a grandchild. In 1956, some of the illustrations for his books were exhibited at the San Diego Fine Arts Gallery. Just before the opening night, Geisel expressed grave doubts about whether anyone would show up. When he himself did, he was instantly pounced on by a mob of three or four hundred children and parents, who pinned him against a wall and kept him at bay for more than an hour.

As a trustee of the gallery, Geisel is busy these days helping map plans for a children's wing to be added to it, which the museum hopes to call the Dr. Seuss Wing. Five years ago, he wrote and acted in an *Omnibus* television show devoted to an imaginary Seuss Museum. It differed from the general run of museums in that children going through it were not forbidden to touch the displays; on the contrary, the exhibits were all marked "Do Touch." Geisel, who dedicated *Happy Birthday to You!* to "my good friends, the Children of San Diego County," hopes that the new museum, toward which he has contributed substantially, will carry out this idea, at least to a degree. "I want a museum that will have a real, operable printing press alongside a shelf of books, and blocks of wood and chisels alongside woodcuts, so that children can watch and work at the same time," he says. "I want every kid in San Diego to be able to blow a glass bottle while looking at some Venetian glass, and to make a tapestry in front of a Gobelin."

Geisel used to do most of his writing and drawing in any corner of his house that happened to be reasonably uncluttered. A few years ago, Ray Freiman, the production manager at Random House, told him he really ought to provide himself with, and certainly could afford, a permanent and comfortable studio. Geisel obediently built a spacious atelier on the Pacific side of his tower. The room has cork walls, on which he can tack the illustrations for a work in progress. His desk, which is littered with cans and jars of brushes and pens, seems to indicate that he regards himself as artist first and writer second, for it is a drafting table, with a sloping work surface; he keeps his typewriter on top of it, and types at a tilt. Ideas come hard to Geisel, and their implementation is a drawn-out, painful process. Once, he says, he chanced to sketch an elephant on an old pad of tracing paper. Afterward, he saw that he had-superimposed the animal on a previously doodled tree in such a manner as to make the elephant seem perched in it. "I stopped, dumfounded," he says. "I said to myself, 'That's a hell of a situation. An elephant in a tree! What's he doing there?' I brooded over it for three or four weeks, and finally I said to myself, 'Of course! He's hatching an egg!'" This is his conscious recollection of the genesis of *Horton Hatches the Egg*, but his subconscious might demur, since he had done a cartoon for *Judge*, years before, showing a whale in a tree.

Being harshly self-critical, Geisel at one point or another in the evolution of each of his books has hurled his accumulated words and pictures onto the floor or into a fireplace, whence they are customarily retrieved by his wife and restored to his hands when he is in a less fractious mood. Perfectionism is his creed. He insists on retyping a page of copy if one word has been crossed out, and he has spent up to three days worrying about the appositeness of a single adjective. It is his habit, once he has finished a book, to deliver it in person to Random House, and as the time for setting off cross country draws near, he becomes increasingly morose. The night before he heads East, he usually goes without sleep. He spreads the pages of his book out on the floor of his living room and crawls back and forth in anguish among them, hovering over the composite parts with the awkward concern of his brood elephant. Sometimes, for last-minute advice or plain bucking up, he summons his next-door neighbor, a seventy-five-year-old businessman named Bert L. Hupp—one of the few people around, aside from Mrs. Geisel, in whose judgment of Dr. Seuss's output Geisel has any faith. Hupp, who is the board chairman of the Sunshine Biscuit Company and was formerly a director of the Santa Fe Railroad, drops to his knees, too, and encourages Geisel with the kind of pep talk that a football coach might deliver in a locker room.

When Random House hears that Geisel is on the way with another pot of gold, excitement runs high, and when he arrives, all hands convene in the office of Louise Bonino, the juvenile editor, for a reading and showing of the latest Dr. Seuss. Even the switchboard operators have been known to leave their post, to the consternation of television producers, lecture agents, Nobel Prize winners, and other outsiders vainly seeking the ear of Bennett Cerf. Geisel, always a high-strung man, is at his tensest during these performances. At the close of one of them, he retreated in dejection to the Madison Hotel, where he usually stays while in New York, and spent a week rewriting three pages, because he felt that nobody at Random House had laughed hard enough at them. Many authors who have turned in a manuscript and learned that it has been accepted are happy to leave the technicalities of its transformation into a book up to their publishers. Not Geisel. Invading the production department, he will dump three or four moldy bits of crayon, or some scraps torn from matchbooks, onto Ray Freiman's desk and say that they are precisely the shades of color he wants used in this or that illustration. That it is often extremely difficult to match up printing ink with crayon does not bother him. Random House has learned to ride with his punches. "From a genius you tolerate a little bit more," one editor there has observed. Just to keep Geisel pacified, his publisher spends twenty-five per cent more on the paper in his books than on that in any other author's, and two or three times as much as the norm on preparing his color plates for the press. Nevertheless, Geisel still complains loudly if, in the thirteenth or fourteenth printing of one of his works, he perceives one color to be a tiny bit off register. After more than a hundred thousand copies of *The Cat in the Hat Comes Back* had been sold, he decided that a single black line on the original jacket was too black, and a new jacket was made up. In this vigorous policing of his output he is encouraged by his neighbor Hupp, who keeps telling him, as they jointly prune a camellia or spray a lemon tree in La Jolla, "Be tough. Keep your standards up. It's your product, and don't you let anybody talk you into letting it slip."

During the last couple of years, the Geisels have visited New York with increasing frequency. In an office on the top floor of the Random House building, at 457 Madison Avenue, are the headquarters of Beginner Books, a publishing venture that they launched two years ago, emboldened by the sales of *The Cat in the Hat*, to bring out volumes for the very young. Geisel is president of the outfit; the day-in-and-day-out chief executive officer is Cerf's wife, Phyllis; and the two of them, along with Mrs. Geisel, make up the editorial board. (Among the animals on display in La Jolla is a portrait of Dr. Seuss's cat in the hat, done in needlepoint for Mrs. Geisel by Mrs. Cerf; an accompanying gold plaque bears the inscription "This cat started a publishing house and 'no other cat can make this claim.'") When Beginner Books began, there was no standard, authoritative word list for first-graders, so Mrs. Cerf compiled her own, culling it from time respected but verbally varied primers. Authors who are about to tackle a Beginner Book are given her list, but they are not immutably bound by it. If someone is writing a book about the moon, say, he is allowed to use the word "moon," although it is not a first-grade staple. There are some severely enforced rules of composition, however. The text of a Beginner Book may describe nothing that is not pictured, and each page must have no more than one illustration. Another strict rule, laid down by the president, is that no book shall be "cute"—an adjective that he applies to much contemporary literature for children. Geisel calls cute books "bunny-bunny books," or "the fuzzy, mysterious literature of the young," and he once delivered a lecture at a summer writing course entitled "Mrs. Mulvaney and the Billion-Dollar Bunny"—a satirical account of the origin and subsequent swift acclaim of a mythical children's book called "Bunny, Bunny, Bunny, Bunny, Bunny, Bunny, Bunny." He planned to illustrate his talk with a blackboard mural depicting the history of children's books. Since he is a shy lecturer and a slow limner, he went to the classroom well ahead of time and sketched on the blackboard the outlines of his illustrations—in faint strokes that could be seen only from close up, and that he planned to retrace in an apparently freehand performance. When he reentered the room, however, a few minutes before he was scheduled to go on, the outlines were gone, and a janitor was walking out, carrying a sponge and mop bucket. "Some wise guy has been messing up your blackboard, Doctor," Geisel recalls the man's saying, "but fortunately there are people like me in the world to take care of people like him." Despite the haphazard art work, the lecture must have left a lasting impression on at least one of his listeners, for a few months later a real book with a title much like Geisel's "Bunny, Bunny, etc.," was published, and became an immediate success.

Last August, Beginner Books became a full-fledged division of Random House, but with the same officers and editorial board. According to the present arrangement, Random House proper will continue to publish Geisel's regular works, and Beginner Books will do his low-vocabulary ones. So far, eighteen Beginner Books have been published, four of them written by Dr. Seuss. As an editor, Geisel is no less of a driving perfectionist than he is when it comes to his own work. He cannot abide a book that he thinks could stand improvement, and some Beginner Books at his demand, have been revised as many as eight times. Among his authors is a La Jolla neighbor named Fred Phleger, who is a professor of oceanography at the Scripps Institution and a world-famed expert on a kind of plankton called foraminifera. Phleger spent six years on a book. *Ecology and Distribution of Recent Foraminifera*, which was published last summer by the Johns Hopkins University Press and which in ten years, if all goes well, should rack up a sale of perhaps three thousand copies. After hesitantly accepting Geisel's invitation to try his hand at a children's book about whales, the Professor was pleasantly dazed to hear that the result, *The Whales Go By,* had attained a sale of nearly a hundred thousand copies in a little over a year. Still another specialist now published by Geisel is Cerf himself, who is represented by a Beginner Book called *Bennett Cerf's Book of Laughs.* (Cerf ordinarily turns out joke books at an assembly-line clip, but in this instance Geisel's finicky insistence on alterations slowed him down almost to the pace of an author.) Nobody can say whether the spectacular success of Beginner Books is the result of the exacting demands that Geisel makes on his authors and illustrators or of the fact that there has long been a need for easy-to-read volumes—a need that other publishing houses, noting Geisel's surging progress, have been hurriedly doing their bit to fill by putting out low-word-count books of their own. In any event, Beginner Books has shown itself to be a booming business. Its capital in 1958 consisted of a hundred shares of stock, worth thirty dollars a piece. The Geisels owned twenty-two shares. Under the terms of last August's agreement with Random House, each share was traded in for two hundred and fifty shares of stock in the parent company, and two hundred and fifty Random House shares are now worth eight thousand dollars.

Over the years, many companies have besought Geisel to let them manufacture Dr. Seuss products of one kind or another. He has permitted R.C.A. Victor to record some of his books, but in the main he has steered clear of by-products that he cannot personally create. Two years ago, though, he was persuaded by Revell, Inc., a toy company in Venice, California, to authorize, and help design, a series of Dr. Seuss toys and games. It has proved to be a challenging collaboration. Revell, which is run by Mr. and Mrs. Lew Glaser, a resourceful and articulate young couple, was geared to turning out small-scale models of ships, planes, and cars. To translate Dr. Seuss's animals into three dimensions was a different matter entirely. "None of my animals have joints and none of them balance," Geisel explained to the Glasers. "And when it comes to that, none of them are animals. They're all people, sort of." Whatever they were, not even he could clearly visualize them with flesh on their bones. Revell sent two sculptors to La Jolla, and for months, with Geisel working alongside them, they modeled Dr. Seuss creatures, shaping and rehaping hundreds of jointless legs and unbalanced heads before he was satisfied. By then, the Glasers had learned enough of Geisel's meticulous ways and second thoughts to stipulate that he give his assent in writing to each successive step of production as soon as agreement was reached on it. Mrs. Glaser, who calls herself Revell's Vice-President in Charge of Geisel, keeps a notebook containing reminders like "Test shots of eye decorations to T.G. for approval." The first Dr. Seuss toys went on the market in September, 1959, and before the year was out they had achieved retail sales of a million and a half dollars.

During the past year, two Dr. Seuss Beginner Books have come out— *One Fish, Two Fish, Red Fish, Blue Fish* and *Green Eggs and Ham. One Fish* is actually a *pre*-beginner book, or, as the educators say, a reading-readiness book. "It's a book based on an educational theory I have, but one I unfortunately can't define," Geisel says. In essence, it is an attempt to initiate very young children into the mysteries of reading by seeing to it that almost every word in the text is neatly juxtaposed with an illustration of the object it describes. Children's memories being the marvelous things they are, a child who has once had the book read to him can go back to it and pick out the familiar words for himself, guided by the pictures. Not all educators are persuaded that this is necessarily a good idea. *One Fish* elicited from a Columbia professor the opinion that a bright four-year-old could learn from the book to read in a week—a conclusion that somewhat disturbed the professor, since many of his colleagues believe that four is a trifle young for a child to get mixed up in the reading business. Geisel's answer to such alarmists is that he may someday facilitate prenatal reading, by investing a two-hundred-and-fifty word pill that expectant mothers can swallow.

Geisel has produced only one book—*The Seven Lady Godivas*—that was aimed at an unequivocally grown-up audience. It was an unequivocal flop. An enhancement of the old legend, it dealt with seven Lady Godivas, all sisters, and seven brothers named Peeping (one, of course, was Tom), who courted them. It was published by Random House in 1939, and Geisel clearly had some misgivings about it beforehand; nailed to the Godiva family tree, which he drew for the end papers, was a small bucket of sap labeled "Bennett Cerf." One trouble was that all the Godivas were shown in the nude, a situation with which Geisel feels he did not cope adequately. "I tried to draw the sexiest-looking women I could," he explains, "and they came out just ridiculous." Although a review in the *Dartmouth Alumni Magazine* called the book "a particularly triumphant job," only twenty-five hundred copies of a first printing of ten thousand were sold. "I think maybe it all went to prove that I don't know anything about adults," Geisel says.

By the mid–1960s, Dr. Seuss books had charmed several generations of children—and parents. Here, in a short essay, are all the reasons why.

3

25 Years of Working Wonder with Words

HELEN RENTHAL

The Chicago Tribune, **November 11, 1962**

From Mulberry Street to the habitat of the Sneetches, from the earth's highest river to the haunts of the Cat in the Hat, lies the mad, revolutionary world of Dr. Seuss. It came into being 25 years ago, and no theory about children's books has been safe there ever since.

In 1937 a Dr. Seuss, who seemed as improbable as his characters, wrote and illustrated a children's book that a score of publishers turned down before it appeared under the title, *And to Think That I Saw It on Mulberry Street.* Now, 25 years and 21 books later, just about everyone but the Flunnel, "the softish nice fellow who hides in a tunnel," knows what was evident long ago to any child who came upon that surprising book: Dr. Seuss was a worker of wonders who could send his imagination on prodigious flights and fill him with delight.

Somehow, the human race produces what it needs, space ships or wonder drugs or a Dr. Seuss. It is common knowledge now that Dr. Seuss is the alias assumed by a shy, gentle man named Theodor Seuss Geisel, upon whom, in 1957, Darthmouth College conferred the honorary degree of Doctor of Humane Letters.

Nothing could have been more appropriate. What Dr. Seuss brought to children's literature were qualities that are rare in any literature and that children especially need, cherish, and too rarely find: a genuine comic spirit and a sense of the power and joy of language.

37

This quarter century, this Age of Dr. Seuss, has seen a new kind of mythology appear. The blue-haired Iota with a Mona Lisa smile, the microscopic but progressive-minded Who, the elephant in a tree and the parachuting fish and blissful Thing 1 and Thing 2:—all of the outlandish creatures conjured up by Dr. Seuss inhabit a comic world that has its own mad logic. No more bizarre than a winged horse or a fire-breathing dragon, they are only funnier. Viewed as a whole, the work of Dr. Seuss looms among contemporary children's books like one of his own whale-like species, unlike anything else in shape, size, or function.

After 25 years and 21 books, it seems reasonably clear that Dr. Seuss has been making one long, joyous assault on the prosaic world of orderly disorder, of people who hear only the obvious, see only the superficial, believe only the commonplace. What Marco sees on Mulberry street, what Horton suffers to keep his word to the undeserving Mayzie, what Bartholomew Cubbins discovers about the vanity of rulers, and Gerald McGrew boldly sets out to search for—all express a kind of freedom from conventional ways of thinking and acting.

It is this spirit that makes the world of Dr. Seuss uproariously comic and explains why children love him. Children regard themselves as superior to adults, storytellers who honestly agree. "Grownups," he has ruefully remarked, "have lost their sense of humor."

All ages, all tastes, even the child indifferent to all books, are swept up in the Dr. Seuss merriment. Those who have outgrown picture books cling to him in unashamed joy. A Dr. Seuss book never comes to rest in a library but is passed on among children as a special favor they do for each other. They delight in his rollicking rhythms, his unexpected rhymes, in sounds they can feel and taste on their tongues, in hearing his whip crack over the galloping syllables. His drawings are bold and vivid and full of outrageous surprises. Words and drawings are inseparable, each illuminating the other. And at the heart of his fantasy there is always reality curled like the worm in an apple.

For the world of Dr. Seuss is beset by lazy Mayzie birds and beady-eyed hunters, by die-hard Duke Wilfreds and all those without Horton's sense of honor or Marco's vision. Marco, whose imagination soars and transforms Mulberry street, must eventually come to terms with reality at home. What the Sneetches awake to are the economic facts of life.

Nevertheless, such fresh and exuberant books as *McElligot's Pool, Horton Hatches the Egg,* and *If I Ran the Zoo* are not only wildly funny but irrepressibly hopeful. In steadily growing numbers parents have found that Dr. Seuss books will bear reading repeatedly without going stale, and that they and the children may discover in them the experience of uninhibited laughter together.

It no longer is fashionable to speak of the moral of a book. The tales of Dr. Seuss not only are full of shrewd insights but have brought back the old-fashioned fairy tale moral that unequivocally takes sides between right and wrong. Can it be that in this relativistic world a child needs a Dr. Seuss? What makes his moralizing something rare is the way children take sides with him, elated at each triumph, seized by every setback. When that amazing winged elephant emerges from the egg Horton has hatched, Dr. Seuss speaks for the heart of every child who has been following his logical insanity:

> For Horton was faithful, he sat and he sat
> And it should be, it *should* be, it SHOULD be like that!*

Clearly, Dr. Seuss has an unfailing instinct for what should be, in the depths of the sea or on a speck of dust. In *The 500 Hats of Bartholomew Cubbins,* power and custom and cruelty are undone by the simple, innocent Bartholomew and his magic hat. In *Horton Hears a Who!,* the heroic elephant acts on the principle: "A person's a person, no matter how small."

Possibly in an unguarded moment, Dr. Seuss told something about his secret for creating deliriously funny creatures. "I don't draw animals," said Dr. Seuss, "I draw people." On their faces may be seen expressions of arrogance and smugness and foolishness. Whatever else a Sneetch, an Obsk or a Yuzz-a-ma-Tuzz may be, Dr. Seuss is dealing with human follies and frailties as well as possibilities.

If these was doubt about Dr. Seuss' genius, *The Cat in the Hat* went a long way toward dispelling it. John Hersey had publicly suggested that if something could be done about the dull, deplorable books inflicted on 1st-graders, Dr. Seuss was the man to do it. Needless to say, he took up the challenge—only to be shaken by his discovery of how limited the vocabulary of such books must be. He was handed a list of exciting words he could work with—am, is, but, if, in, into, no, yes, milk, about 200 in all. What he produced was a beginning reader that had plot, character, life, laughter; in one stroke he revolutionized 1st grade readers.

While working on *The Cat in the Hat,* Dr. Seuss tried early versions on his nephew Norval, but by the time it was finished Norval couldn't be bothered—he was out of 1st grade and learning calculus. Calculus? The mind trembles—in our age of scientific revolution, the need to speed up the learning of mathematics is urgent, and if anyone can bring life, excitement, laughter to calculus.... But perhaps Dr. Seuss is working on it.

---

* *These lines are transposed. Properly, the stanza reads: "And it should be, it should be, it SHOULD be like that! Because Horton was faithful! He sat and he sat!"—T.F.*

The New York Times *celebrated the twenty-fifth anniversary of the Dr. Seuss books with this essay by Lewis Nichols. The very hardest question Geisel had to answer—and the question he dreaded most—was "How do you write your books?" The answer is, at least in part, serendipity—as when he discovered an elephant in a tree.*

4

"Then I Doodled a Tree"

LEWIS NICHOLS

The New York Times Book Review, **November 11, 1962**

It was just twenty-five years ago this fall that bookstore browsers, looking for something to read to Johnny, could have picked up a thin book with a blush jacket. The first pages seemed to be in a sort of galloping poetry, with small illustrations. In subsequent pages, the poetry still galloped but there was less of it, and the illustrations grew larger. If the browser bought it and held on, he now has a collector's item for the grandchildren, the first edition of *And to Think That I Saw It on Mulberry Street,* first book by the author, one Dr. Seuss.

Statistics are pretty lifeless companions for such as Yertle, the turtle, and Thidwick, the moose, but those about the Seuss library of people and animals are astounding. A quarter-century later, twenty-one books later, *Mulberry Street* still is in print, still sells some 15,000 copies a year. Total sales of Dr. Seuss' first book have been 200,000 copies. This is an agreeable figure in itself, but the joker here is that for recent Seuss books, the first printing is 100,000 copies, and that is often exhausted before actual publication. Sales of all twenty-two Seuss books are in the neighborhood of 7,250,000 copies, give or take.

Just how many readers there are in the Seuss circle lies completely outside conjecture, even by Dr. Seuss, himself. Parents read the books to children, children read them to other children and—wryly pleasing to the pedagogue that still lurks within him—Dr. Seuss is studied in school. When the most recent one came out last summer, *Dr. Seuss's Sleep Book,* adults found themselves so swayed by the drowsy rhythm they were perfectly willing to go

41

to bed at the same hour as the children. What effect this one might have on the world if read during a violent meeting of the United Nations also lies outside conjecture. But it's the sort of thing you think of after an hour or so with Dr. Seuss.

He is a tall man with graying hair, who on hotel registers about the world identifies himself as Theodore S. Geisel of La Jolla, California. That "S" is for Seuss, his mother's family name. When he walks into a restaurant or other place where he is known, however, he immediately is called "Doctor"—tacit recognition of a personality split. There are other indications, self-acknowledged. Part of Dr. Seuss is the humorist, part is the humorist-moralist, part is the pedagogue. This last is shown by his enthusiastic presidency of the Beginner Books division of Random House, for which he has written such items as *The Cat in the Hat* and *The Cat in the Hat Comes Back.*

"I'd say that the most useful of the books is *The Cat in the Hat.*" he replied the other day when asked about his favorites. "That had a different purpose, to help reading, and it goes back to my old ambition to be an educator. The happiest book, I would think, is *Horton Hatches the Egg.* And I remember I did the last three pages just as Paris was falling, and all around us was isolationist talk.

"The favorite animals—this is a little hard. The most popular with the kids are the weird ones. My own choices—the cat, probably, and Horton, and a very odd one, the pair of pants in the story 'What Was I Scared Of?' in *The Sneetches and Other Stories.* I think there's more life in the pair of green pants with no one inside them than a good many of the others."

Since this is, after all, the anniversary year for *Mulberry Street,* and *Mulberry Street* is in middle-aged consciousness like *Penrod* and *Seventeen,* what about that one? The man is a traitor to his class. "I think I was a little aloof, too outside there," he said. "It was written from the point of view of my mind, not the mind of a child." For the records, there was no particular Mulberry Street in view, although there was one of that name in Springfield, Mass., where Mr. Geisel was born, and the subconscious may have taken him back.

There is no wish to annotate Dr. Seuss here, as they do *Alice in Wonderland,* but it might be noted that various academic big brothers are watching him. There have been a couple of doctoral dissertations written about him, and a number of masters' theses. This pleases Dr. Seuss, quite naturally, but it also somewhat amuses him. When Seuss was still Geisel, he went from Dartmouth (class of '25) to Oxford and the Sorbonne—aim, scholarship and teaching. What pushed him away from same was the suggestion he might make a real name for himself as a scholar if he made a study of a few years in the life of Swift—the years when Swift wrote nothing. Geisel promptly came home, began sending drawings around, became famous for the "Quick, Henry, the Flit" ads, finally took his walk along Mulberry Street.

Which comes first, the drawings or the story? Dr. Seuss is weary of answering that one.

"I get a plot, start off with words. But words are deceptive things, and I get stuck with them, and when fully stuck try drawings. 'Horton' came one day when I drew a picture of an elephant, a sort of doodle. Then I doodled a tree, and in an accidental shuffle, the transparent paper showed an elephant in a tree. Then all I had to do was figure out why an elephant would be sitting in a tree. There are millions of figures—drawings, kids, clothes—which haunt me because I can't seem to do anything about them, dozens of ideas which never have jelled. Sometimes I can take chunks and drop them in somewhere, but the rest just float around waiting."

Doodles for a time were pretty much doodles, but now they are being saved, again by the academic world with which Dr. Seuss seems unable to avoid contact. The manuscript of *Mulberry Street* is at Dartmouth, the rest—along with such peripheral material as doodles—have been given to the University of California at Los Angeles. There's a course there for the study of a work of art from the doodle through the script and the plates to the book, and so Dr. Seuss, if *in absentia*, finally is teaching. Teaching there as well as in the Beginner Books.

One further note, this directed to those writers of dissertations and theses on the subject of Dr. Seuss. On the table in his hotel room the other day were these objects: One copy of *Live and Let Live [sic]*, by Ian Fleming; one folder of delicacies offered by Room Service; six partly used folders of matches; two bars of chocolate; one large pear. Dr. Seuss could make something of this. Can the scholars?

Fan mail? Dr. Seuss naturally gets it, and since it comes from the young, it is good mail. Often school classes make projects on Seuss, one arriving at 45 feet in length. Had to unroll it in the back yard to read it.

*Selma G. Lanes was one of the first children's literature experts
to take Dr. Seuss seriously as a topic for analysis and criticism.
This article, from her 1971 book* Down the Rabbit Hole, *pre-dates almost all other serious Seuss criticism.*

5

Seuss for the Goose Is
Seuss for the Gander

SELMA G. LANES

from *Down the Rabbit Hole: Adventures and
Misadventures in the Realm of Children's Literature*, 1971

*And on a day that I remember it came to me that
"reading" was not "The Cat Lay on the Mat," but
a means to everything that would make me happy.*
RUDYARD KIPLING, Something of Myself

Dr. Seuss, born Theodor Seuss Geisel, has won a formidable book-buy-ing public by providing anxiety-filled diversion for listeners and readers at precisely the "Cat Lay on the Mat" stage of development. As it often is in life, this anxiety is disguised and controlled by laughter. While his books are a far cry from what Kipling meant by "everything that would make me happy," Seuss has managed, almost single-handedly, to provide a safety valve for the overscheduled, overburdened and overstimulated child of modern civiliza-tion. In recognizing that children's craving for excitement, in their books as in their lives, is often merely the means for releasing pent-up anxiety, Seuss cannily manages to magnify and multiply the sense of suspense in his sto-ries, not so much by the ingenuity of his plots as by a clever and relentless piling on of gratuitous anxiety until the child is fairly ready to cry "uncle" and settle for any resolution, however mundane, that will end his at once mar-velous, exquisite and finally unbearable tension. The process is not unlike the blowing up of a balloon: bigger, bigger, bigger and finally, when the burst-ing point is reached, Seuss simply releases his grip and all tension, like trapped air, is freed. If, as the British psychoanalyst Charles Ryecroft defined it, an orgastic experience consists of "a subjective sense of excitation followed by a feeling of discharge," then Dr. Seuss in his books—like Wilhelm Reich with his orgone box—can be said to provide his young disciples with a literary release not so far removed from orgasm.

Like many another illustrator and author, Seuss comes to children's books from the world of advertising. It was he who gave America in the '30s the battle cry "Quick, Henry, the Flit!" and breakneck speed has been his narrative hallmark ever since. His first book for children, in 1937, *And to Think That I Saw It on Mulberry Street,* was a prototype, low-key version of all Seuss plots and characters to follow. The hero, Marco, is—like his creator—a varnisher of truth. Despite his father's stern warning to

> Stop telling such outlandish tales
> Stop turning minnows into whales

(precisely the talents that have won the book's author a firm place beside Edward Lear and Lewis Carroll as one of the inspired creators of nonsense in the English language), he cannot. Left to his own devices on a walk down Mulberry Street, Marco finds it impossible to suppress his gift for brightening up reality. From a garden-variety horse and wagon he sees on his walk, Marco compulsively builds bigger and better variations until he ends up with "a Rajah, with rubies, perched high on a throne" atop an elephant who, with two giraffe assistants, is pulling an enormous brass band, with a trailer behind—the entire entourage escorted by motorcycle policemen past the mayor's reviewing stand while a small airplane drops confetti down on the frenetic scene—all of it, of course, on Mulberry Street. Seuss's doggerel moves at a steady gallop and the artist's pen slides effortlessly from one outlandish embellishment to the next. The reader is at a mild fever pitch by the time the final invention is heaped on Marco's rapidly expanding universe. It is a blessed relief when the hero, home at last, is confronted by his fact-loving father's query: "Did *nothing* excite you or make your heart beat?" and he replies:

> "Nothing," I said, growing red as a beet,
> "But a plain horse and wagon on Mulberry Street."

Why does Marco grow "red as a beet?" Because adults, alas, are incapable of understanding what gives children deep pleasure, and it is always embarrassing to be forced to lie, even to keep the peace. The anxiety in Seuss's books always arises from the flouting of authority, parental or societal. It is central to the Seuss formula that the action of all his books with children as protagonists takes place either (1) in the absence of grownups, or (2) in the imagination. *The Cat in the Hat* performs his forbidden games when "Our mother was out of the house for the day" and *The Cat in the Hat Comes Back* only "when our mother went down to the town for the day." Young Morris McGurk daydreams *If I Ran the Circus* out behind Sneelock's Store without Sneelock ever realizing how pivotal a role he plays in young Morris' imaginings. In *Scrambled Eggs Super!* of 1953, Peter T. Hooper confesses,

> Why, only last Tuesday, when mother was out
> I really cooked something worth talking about.

Seuss's books are obsessed with having "lots of good fun." What Seuss means by fun, however, is the sort of thing which, if it took place in real life, would place an anxiety burden on most children impossible for them to bear. Genuine fun to small children—like squeezing all the toothpaste out of inviting new tubes or taking apart Aunt Zelda's gift alarm clock—is always accompanied by anxiety because retribution is sure to follow. Only on rare occasions in life, therefore, will a sensible child yield to such temptation. But when the Cat in the Hat says, "We can have lots of good fun that is funny" (by which he really means fun that is forbidden), the child can sit back and experience genuine pleasure, knowing that the anxiety building up in him is vicarious and that no punishment will follow Seuss's forbidden pleasures.

Every detail in a Seuss illustration is calculated to add its bit to increasing the child's vicarious anxiety. Nervous projections and curlicues wriggle about everywhere. No drawing detail seems to be at rest. The hero of *Scrambled Eggs Super!* works in a kitchen where the coffee pot is ominously bubbling over as well as perched at a precarious angle on the stove. Milk glasses, filled, stand teetering on counter brinks; batter is splattered everywhere; baking ingredients are spilled. (And no cake in any Seuss book is ever intact. Large—and doubtless forbidden—slices are always removed.) It is just the sort of world no child's mother would put up with for one instant. The greatest pleasure in Seuss is derived from the sense of having a season pass to utter chaos with no personal responsibility for any of it. Seuss has a perfect understanding of grownups' love of order and the rule of their laws—and of the enormous anxiety burden this places on small children everywhere.

After the Cat in the Hat wreaks his havoc, the children's pet fish, a superego surrogate, warns:

> But your mother will come.
> She will find this big mess!
> And this mess is so big
> And so deep and so tall,
> We can not pick it up.
> There is no way at all!

Wolves and monsters be damned! This is the content of every child's worst nightmare. Seuss, of course, can and will clean up the mess with some magical last-minute plot invention, but it is the marvelous, wonderful heaping on of anxiety, almost more than the final release, that is Seuss's real success with children.

The denouement formula remains the same in *The Cat in the Hat* of 1957 as it was twenty years earlier in *And to Think That I Saw It on Mulberry Street*. Parents, burdened by household chores, the reupholsterer's unpaid bill and the compulsion to build character in their children, are incapable of taking a lighthearted view of spills, breakage and imaginative highjinks:

> Then our mother came in
> And she said to us two,
> "Did you have any fun?
> Tell me. What did you do?"

So, like Marco, the children tell her nothing at all—though they put the matter to a democratic readers' vote:

> Well ... What would YOU do
> If your mother asked you?

There is another sort of Seuss book, no less subversive of authority, but in this case more of societal authority than the strictly parental. Stories like *Thidwick, the Big-Hearted Moose* and *Horton Hatches the Egg* take as their point of departure maxims which no child can attain the age of four without having run up against (usually because he has violated them). Seuss holds a noble sentiment up for admiration, then proceeds to turn it inside out. "A host above all must be nice to his guests," says the well-mannered Thidwick, and barely misses becoming a decoration for the Harvard Club wall in the adage's defense. "I meant what I said and I said what I meant," intones the upright Horton, "an elephant's faithful one hundred per cent," and everyone but he cashes in on this dogged virtue.

Sometimes Seuss is simply subversive of authoritarian rule in general, whatever form it takes, as in *Yertle the Turtle* of 1950 or *King Louis Katz* in 1969. What child will ever doubt that absolute power corrupts absolutely after reading of King Yertle's appalling *hubris* and ignominious downfall (the direct result of "a lowly burp" from the lowliest of his subjects, a turtle named Mack). *King Louis Katz* is a mellower and at once more revolutionary fable. By an act of open and willful rebellion, almost Marcusian in its purity, Zooie Katzenbein, the last cat in the line, shatters feline tradition in King Louis' realm. He simply yelled,

> "I QUIT!
> I cannot, shall not, will not

Lug this stupid thing around!"
He slammed the tail of Prooie Katz!
He slammed it on the ground.

And in one of Seuss's most satisfying conclusions—as up to date as student confrontations on the nation's campuses—he tells his young audience:

And since that day in Katzen-stein,
All cats have been more grown-up.
They're all more demo-catic
Because each cat holds his own up.

For all his exaggerated zaniness (and subversive alliance with the child's free spirit against all forms of authoritarianism), the ultimate moral Seuss presents is always same and mature, one to which adults as well as children can subscribe. Though Yertle is undone, who can say it is not for the greater good?

And today the great Yertle, that Marvelous he
Is King of the Mud. That is all he can see.
And the turtles, of course, all the turtles are free
As turtles and, maybe, all creatures should be.

Though his sympathies are with the child, his sense of proportion is distinctly adult. This dual view finds representation in both pictures and text of several of his books. The early *The 500 Hats of Bartholomew Cubbins* starts out with King Derwin viewing his realm from the castle's ramparts and feeling "mighty important." On the following double-page spread, however, his small subject Bartholomew Cubbins sees exactly the same view in reverse—from a poor peasant's cottage down in the fields and feels "mighty small." The lowly turtle Mack, in *Yertle the Turtle,* complains:

I know up on top you are seeing great sights,
But down at the bottom we, too, should have rights.

It is an adult voice, lobbying for the lowly, often forgotten child.

It is entirely possible that history will judge Seuss as the Patrick Henry of today's nursery set. Even where authority is benevolent and benign, as in *The King's Stilts,* one gets the feeling that it rests on wobbly foundations which ought not to be tampered with. The wicked Lord Droon has only to hide the King's stilts to bring the kingdom to near-ruin.

Another of Seuss's charms for children is his unfailingly direct language. In his doggerel, he has raised the vernacular nearly to an art form. Hear Mayzie, a lazy bird, complaining of her lot:

I'm tired and I'm bored
And I've kinks in my leg

> From sitting, just sitting here day after day.
> It's *work!* How I hate it!
> I'd *much* rather play.

Or another vindictive bird about to flaunt her feathers:

> "And NOW," giggled Gertrude, "the next thing to do
> Is to fly right straight home and show Lolla-Lee-Lou
> And when Lolla sees *these,* why her face will get red
> And she'll let out a scream and she'll fall right down dead!"

It is a language children instinctively understand and appreciate for its honesty. It is the way people talk to one another: "the stuff people bake," "I sort of got thinking it's sort of a shame," etc. He is not afraid of contractions or inelegant phraseology. It is living language he uses to rich effect. Yet Seuss can turn a phrase with the best of authors. Consider his Grinch, a character unflinchingly mean because "his heart was two sizes too small."

Though there is a sameness of rhyme, occasionally even of ideas, in Seuss now that the number of his books is pushing into the thirties, his audience has not dwindled because the good Doctor's inventiveness of language and zany hyperbole never flags. There are few places where a child can get a better sense of the richness of language, the infinite possibilities it offers a lively imagination. Consider some of the new places Seuss has christened: Lake Wina-Bango; the towns of North Nubb, East Ounce, West Bungelfield, Yupster and Jounce; the Zweiback Motel and Foona Laguna. Or the letters he has added to the alphabet in *On Beyond Zebra* for children tired of the old twenty-six: Yuzz, Wum, Glikk, Snee and Spazz (indispensable for spelling "Spazzim/A Beast who belongs to the Nazzim of Bazzim"). He has given children and their book-reading parents birds as varied as the tizzle-topped grouse, the flannel-wing jay and the mop-noodled finch; and animals as startling as the seersucker, the straggle-foot mullagatawny and the Hammikka-Schnim-ikka-Schnam-ikka-Schnopp. There are also new taste sensations:

> And the yolks of these eggs, I am told, taste like fleece
> While the whites taste like very old bicycle grease.

It's hard to resist watching for what will spring next from the mind of a man who would feed an "obsk" a vegetarian diet of "corn on the cobsk."

In a day when children's books are almost unrelievedly beautiful and elevating, his are intentionally rough-drawn, tough-talking and almost downright ugly. They have no need to insinuate their way into our affections. A thing of beauty may be a joy forever, but Seuss is always a joy for whatever moments we choose to devote to him. At a time when the great majority of picture books are a spare 32 pages—occasionally a lengthy 48—his go on and on for 64 wild pages. Seuss's guaranteed audience, of mass-market proportions, keeps production costs down and the price of his books reasonable. We not only get our money's worth, but are left with a reservoir of sane thoughts and an appetite for his next outlandish invention. Long live Theodor Seuss Geisel, physician to the psyche of the beleaguered modern child!

*In his article "Children's Friend," E. J. Kahn, Jr., mentioned
the only unsuccessful book Dr. Seuss ever published,
The Seven Lady Godivas. Here's why it didn't work.*

6

Dr. Seuss and the Naked Ladies:
Blowing the Lid Off the Private Life
of America's Most Beloved Author

CAROLYN SEE

Esquire, June 1974

In March of 1969, a scant month after Philip Roth had published *Port-noy's Complaint*, Theodor Seuss Geisel, the celebrated "Dr. Seuss," creator of grinches and hippogrifs, foxes in socks and cats in hats, wrote a five-page out-line for a dirty book. He sent it to Robert Bernstein, successor to Bennett Cerf, and Seuss's own editor at Random House. Bernstein blanched, it is to be supposed, made emergency phone calls and called emergency meetings, all to discuss this more than dangerous aberration to which one of their lead-ing, and certainly most wholesome, writers had succumbed. Dr. Seuss stayed home, meanwhile, didn't answer the phone, and laughed himself sick.

"I finally called Bernstein, after about a week, and let him off the hook. He'd caught on by that time anyway."

Dr. Seuss lives in La Jolla, one of the most elegant and affluent beach resorts in Southern California, in an old observation post at the very high-est point in the community. He has transformed it into a dwelling both Ital-ianate and cozy. A miniature fountain tinkles in his richly furnished living room; a dozen or so "Seuss-Hepplewhite" chairs—each one with a unique Seuss character carved into a medallion at its back—cluster in the dim and formal dining room. A swimming pool, blue as the banks of voraciously blooming petunias which surround it, awaits the pleasure of the master of the house.

Dr. Seuss is having lunch—a perfect soufflé, bleached Belgian asparagus with a soupcon of capers. He uses a gold fork. When from time to time his attention wanders, he looks out his window, which commands a view of the entire Pacific.

Sex, Seuss relates, has played a key part in his life, his work, his failures and success; although his youth was comparatively austere. "After graduating from Dartmouth in 1925, I had gone on to pursue my studies at Oxford. The astonishing irrelevance of graduate work in English, the committing to memory, for instance, of all the vowel changes in Old English—from ā to ē, from ē to ī, and so on—had daunted but not defeated me. I was determined to be a Ph.D. in English literature. While continuing my studies at the Sorbonne, I had tea one day with my academic adviser, Emile Legouis, the world's foremost expert on Jonathan Swift. He suggested I devote the next two years of my life to discovering whether Swift had written anything at the age of seventeen. I threw in my doctoral towel and took the next freighter to Corsica."

During the following year Seuss wrote his first novel. "I was heavily influenced at that time by Carl Van Vechten, who often lapsed into Italian during the course of his books. Accordingly, I lapsed into Italian in *my* book, for pages at a time. I don't even speak Italian. I picked up the manuscript a few years ago—it was very long, and mercifully never published—and couldn't understand a word of it."

Like most of the literary expatriates of his generation, Seuss returned inevitably to his homeland toward the end of the Twenties. Still a very young man, he began to make his way in the world of American advertising, where he invented the immortal phrase, "Quick, Henry, the Flit!" He also wrote his first two children's books, *And to Think That I Saw It on Mulberry Street* in 1937 and *The 500 Hats of Bartholomew Cubbins* in 1938.

It was then that sex first revealed its hydra head to Dr. Seuss, leading him down a primrose path to the "most expensive failure" of his career. Seuss was inspired to right an ancient wrong, to set the world straight about what really happened to the Lady Godiva, and thus, in 1939, wrote his third (and first adult) book, *The Seven Lady Godivas*, which took the position that there were seven Ladies Godiva; Clementina, Dorcas, Arabella, Mitzi, Lulu, Gussie, and Hedwig, and that, contrary to common legend, there was not one Peeping Tom, "an illicit snooper of questionable intentions," but that Peeping was the old family name of a respected English family. Seuss told his story about seven sisters so saddened by the untimely death of their father in an equestrian accident that they swore to abstain from marriage until they had each discovered a "horse truth." (To take only one example from this slim, ambitious volume, the first sister, "Teeny," a girl of noble proportions, stares down the throat of a steed her uncle Ethelbert had sent the Godiva family the Christmas before. Ethelbert bites Teeny's nose off to the quick, but teaches her, in the biting, that most valuable horse truth, "Never look a gift horse in the mouth.")

"The book failed," Dr. Seuss recalls, pensive, "because for one reason, I can't get their knees right." There is something left undone in the chest area of the Ladies Godiva too, but in 1939, and to a child, the ladies were racy fare indeed. Librarians across the country, conditioned to think of Dr. Seuss as a children's writer, put *The Seven Lady Godivas* next to *The 500 Hats of Bartholomew Cubbins*. Across the nation there was a rash of veritable tiny riots as thousands of genuine peeping toms scrambled to check out the book.

Grown-ups, on the other hand, were far from crazy about it. In 1939 America was feeling too blue to be cheered up by pictures of silly ladies with no nipples and funny knees. The book had an ignominious end; it was remaindered in the then famous chain of Shulte's Cigar Stores across New York City. Dr. Seuss turned his brooding genius to the burgeoning war effort.

Few people know the part that Major Seuss played in that worldwide drama. Quartered for the most part in "Fort Fox," the informal appellation which its occupants gave to a commandeered Hollywood movie studio, Seuss produced important documentaries on Germany and Japan. He was then placed "in charge of malaria," and finally, "promoted to syphilis." Again, sex—and its consequences—dealt Seuss a crushing blow.

"They wanted me to make an anti-V.D. film ... one that the men wouldn't laugh at. It was, I believe, an impossible task. Instead of using actors, actresses and so-called real situations, we tried to get our message across by means of abstract animated figures. The film made no sense whatever. As far as I know it was never shown."

In 1945, the war almost over, Major Seuss made a last contribution to the war effort by "...inventing the atomic bomb. It was during the period after V.E. Day and before the Japanese surrender. The problem was to keep soldiers interested in the entire project. My assignment, together with a team of other artists and writers, was to make a film which would motivate American boys to stay in the Army. The previous Sunday, leafing listlessly through The New York *Times*, I had come across an article which mentioned a 'source of energy so strong that the amount contained in a glass of water might wipe out Minneapolis!' My colleagues and I sat down and wrote a scenario around this then hypothetical but certainly interesting statement." Seuss sent the script to the Pentagon, for what he thought would be routine approval. Instead, he was contacted by some of the highest and most hysterical brass in the nation. They swore Seuss to secrecy and directed him "to destroy his source of information" instanter. Seuss got together a platoon of enlisted men, stuffed the offending *Times* in a wastebasket and ceremoniously lit it, his men meanwhile holding their guns in their left hands so that they might give the Boy Scout salute with their right.

Exhausted by the stresses of wartime life, the newly civilian Dr. Seuss decided to move to La Jolla, California, a peaceful resort on one of the most beautiful of our Western shores, where he bought that deserted observation tower on the highest point of land in the community. He planned to devote the rest of his career and his life to writing children's books; in those days, let us remember, a peculiarly modest enterprise. There was fun in writing children's books, of course, and prestige enough—if they were literate. But it was impossible to make a living writing children's books, simply because there weren't enough children.

Sex, again, changed the good doctor's life—sex and the G.I. Bill. Thanks to that generous legislation, every returning war veteran could get married and have all the kids he wanted. Moreover, each new father could afford to go to college, thus developing a respect for books which he might then pass on to the next generation. This happy combination of social history and the mass indulgence in fleshy desire made Dr. Seuss rich. He began to build on to his modest observation post, room by stately room, until it became the kindly palace it is today. His industrious pen turned out *Thidwick the Big-Hearted Moose, Bartholomew and the Oobleck, Horton Hears a Who!, On Beyond Zebra!, Yertle the Turtle*, and many, many, many more.

As the television contracts rolled in, and invitations from Presidents, and book awards and film awards and fascinating people calling on the phone, Dr. Seuss forgot about such things as his melancholy first novel which continually lapsed into Italian, or the days when he invented the A-bomb concurrent with the dedicated men at Oak Ridge. He even forgot about sex until that recent, unchecked whim which prompted him to write the five-page outline.

Dr. Seuss says now that he can't remember the plot of that five-page outline and wouldn't tell me if he could.

"It was awful," he says, "outrageous. The worst thing you can imagine."

Well, if he can't remember the plot, what about the characters?

But Dr. Seuss shakes his head. And those who remember Thidwick, or Horton, or what happens beyond Zebra might well concur with his wish to draw a curtain of chastity across those five pages. There are some scenes, some tableaux vivants, as it were, that the human mind cannot encompass. The worst vice has its limits.

"I told Bernstein to destroy that outline," Seuss says, peering through the picture windows of his stately drawing room off across the sequined coruscations of the Pacific to where the thin rim of Mainland China is just visible. "I told him that the outline must never get out of his hands."

One only hopes that Bernstein had enough éclat to destroy the outline in something approaching the manner that Seuss destroyed his A-bomb documents. One hopes as well—shall we say it?—that Bernstein had the *savoir-faire*, the *sens commun*, to keep a carbon copy.

*This article reveals much about Geisel's inventive mind—
how he discovered a loophole in his contract with Standard
Oil that allowed him to work six months of every year on
his own projects, and how the "sad lack" of animals in his
hometown zoo inspired him to create fantastic new species.
As a writer of allegories, says Kane, Seuss has "possibly only three
equals: Hans Christian Andersen, Aesop and Jonathan Swift."*

7

And, Dear Dr. Seuss, the Whole World's in Love with Yeuss

GEORGE KANE

The Rocky Mountain News, **February 15, 1976**

Once Upon a Time in the mythical kingdom of Standard Oil of New Jersey there lived a writer/artist named Theodor Geisel.

He struggled and struggled and one day his dreams, ensconced in the ethereal but necessary world of corporate advertising (which is what he wrote for a Living), came closer to reality.

His telephone rang. It was an inside line, direct from "upstairs." The voice of The Director said: "Ted. It is up to you to design our corporate Christmas card. It must have an appropriate message."

Being Dec. 1, Ted hurried but still took the time to do His Best. Because the reality of Real Writing loomed. Do Good and Good will be done upon you.

When writer/artist Theodor Geisel delivered his Christmas cards, The Director said: "You're late." But, after all, it WAS the first time. The Director said: "Design the next one in January. And with it submit 12 Christmas messages." Within one week in January, the writer/artist designed The Best of Christmas cards and wrote 12 Wonderful captions.

On Dec. 1, The Director and His Swad still had not chosen from the captions THE most suitable. Just before Christmas, they decided upon "Very Merry Christmas and a Happy New Year." The cards were late.

"This is the high directorial level," said a perennially smiling Theodor Seuss Geisel, the 71-year-old father of sneetches and nerkles and grinches and all manner of wonderful animals. The "Seuss" is actually pronounced "Soyce," the name being his mother's family name, but Geisel says he gave up long ago correcting that in conversation and goes along with the Dr. "Soos" by which millions of readers worldwide know him.

Dr. Seuss is a legend—even around the kingdom of Standard Oil of New Jersey. For it was Standard which produced Flit, a bug-killer, and Geisel who produced for Standard the slogan "Quick! Henry! The Flit!" which carried the ad campaign for 17 years.

Geisel was with the oil giant only a dozen years, many of those during the '30s Depression, and did his job so successfully that he found great amounts of time on his hands—he figures about six months out of each 12.

The company had a clear and simple rule which affected Geisel, who wanted to write: No outside work. What to do with six months' free time? First, find a loophole in the company policy. He did. The rule did not prohibit writing for children. Second, he began writing for children.

And so, since 1937, Dr. Seuss has written 37 books, all but one of them for "children." That one, titled *The Seven Lady Godivas* and published by Random House circa 1940, died a woeful death. Geisel, in Denver doing one of the things which he finds almost un-understandable—autographing his own books for buyers—wanted to be a novelist.

"I was headed toward a career of professional boredom (teaching) after Dartmouth and Oxford," he said, "and I began to write the great American novel. Who hasn't?

"I found the book not too long ago," he said with the ever-constant glint in his eye of bonhomie and gentleness. "I boiled the Great American Novel down to a short story. It didn't sell. So it became a two-line joke and I sold it."

Dr. Seuss/Geisel (he holds a doctorate of humane letters from Dartmouth) is unpretentious to the point that he seems totally underwhelmed by, if not oblivious to, his own talents. For he is a spinner of tales which occupy two levels—a writer of allegories who has had possibly only three equals: Hans Christian Andersen, Aesop and Jonathan Swift.

His first two books—*And to Think That I Saw It on Mulberry Street* and *The 500 Hats of Bartholomew Cubbins*—he published himself through a vanity press.* But then came Random House and a relationship which has since endured.

---

* *Theodor Geisel never published with a vanity press. The writer confuses the publisher of his first two books, The Vanguard Press, with a vanity publisher. In part to gain legal access to Geisel's books, Random House later bought Vanguard Press.—T.F.*

For Random House, he has produced the books which have made him famous world-wide (with the exception of his only adult book), and he has been called upon to ghost-write occasionally for that publishing house when another children's author failed to meet deadlines.

"In fact," he said seriously, "an author failed us this year, so I wrote the book in one day. It was *Because the Small Bug Went Ka-chooooo*. The author's name we selected for the book was Rosetta Stone." The merry little twinkle came back.

With his own books, he spends far more time. Which is evident to anyone who has read Dr. Seuss' *Horton Hears a Who!*, *How the Grinch Stole Christmas*, *The Cat in the Hat Songbook* and most particularly *I Had Trouble Getting to Solla Sollew*.

It takes him a year, as an average, to write a book—seemingly a very long time for a man to put simple rhyming words together. But the impact of those words is unmistakable.

At his autograph session in Denver, adults in their mid–40s kept him at his cramped station 2½ hours overtime. He loved it. Denver, he said, is like Cleveland—"a book town."

"Some towns aren't. In Boston once, only two people showed up at the autograph table," he said. "They were both children and one was a little boy looking for the bathroom."

As pertinent as his words are his cartoons. Geisel illustrated commercials for Esso Marine Products and did animated television commercials for Ford Motor Co., then won three Academy Awards—two for the best documentary features (1946 and 1947) and one for best animated cartoon—*Gerald McBoing-Boing*" (1951).

His animated specials on CBS-TV have been without parallel. *Grinch* and *Horton* both gained Geisel the Peabody Award and *The Lorax* won him the Critics Award at the International Animated Cartoon Festival, held in Europe, and a Silver Medal at the International film and TV Festival in New York.

Geisel works (he says he sits) at his desk in his California resort-town home for eight hours a day, seven days a week. "If I didn't, I would become a bum," he said. "I have that schedule whether I write anything or not."

He writes. And the lessons he teaches—whether he wanted to be a teacher or not—are pertinent, rather like Fromm in simple form (witness "Solla Sollew").

"Only occasionally," he said, "do I find myself wanting to write a novel. About one in the morning once in a while. So I paint and that energy goes there."

The most successful writer of children's books in the world (Dr. Seuss has sold 50 million copies and has been translated into a dozen languages), Geisel has no formula for writing other than his own.

A publisher once handed him a "word list," a sheet containing those words which youngsters are said to be able to "understand" immediately, from which Geisel was to work.

Geisel considered the list rubbish. "I found only two words that rhymed in the entire list: cat and hat." Ergo: "The Cat in the Hat."

"A kid," he said, "is a very sophisticated market." But Geisel still avoids obvious moralizing. "I spent three months on the last page of 'The Grinch.' "It kept turning into a religious tract." And he confided with a grin, "The Grinch looks a little like Bennett Cerf."

Born in Springfield, Mass., Geisel was the son of a brewer who was later put out of business by that invitation to lawlessness known as Prohibition. Young Geisel's father became director of the Springfield zoo, but there was a sad lack in the variety of animals.

Geisel began inventing his own, started writing about them and attempting to sell his illustrated yarns, "throwing in the illustrations for free."

He sold to *Judge, Life, Vanity Fair,* and *The Saturday Evening Post* and didn't make much of a living at it, so did advertising posters and originated ad campaigns for various companies.

"Some of them used the barter system," he recalled. "I was once paid in Little Gem Nail Clippers. A hundred gross of them which they thought I could sell for a profit. I finally gave up trying to sell them."

But once he was paid for an ad campaign in cases of Hankey-Bannister Scotch. "If they'd go back to that system," he said, "it would cut down considerably on income tax work."

Theodor Seuss Geisel, the gentle genius who has brought delight to three generations of children, ironically had no children of his own. His first wife, the late Helen Palmer Geisel who co-authored one of his award-winning films, died without giving him his own audience of offspring.

Although he was a reluctant interview subject, Ted Geisel reminisced about his early days with a fellow Dartmouth College alumnus, Edward Connery Lathem. In 1955, Theodor Geisel received an honorary doctorate from Dartmouth College (the first of several honorary degrees he would receive during his lifetime), thus making the "Dr." Seuss legitimate.

8

The Beginnings of Dr. Seuss: A Conversation with Theodor S. Geisel

EDWARD CONNERY LATHEM, ED.

Dartmouth Alumni Magazine, **April 1976**

"Dr. Seuss" is of course a pseudonym, one known to millions upon millions of adults and children alike, in the United States and throughout the world.

It derives from the middle name of author-artist Theodor Seuss Geisel '25, and any telling of the story of "Dr. Seuss" must involve a tracing, also, of the career of Geisel himself.

Both born and raised in Springfield, Massachusetts, he attended Springfield's Central High School, where among his special extracurricular concerns was the student newspaper, the Central Recorder, *for which he did articles, verse, humorous squibs, and occasional cartoons, as well as serving as one of the paper's editors.*

At the conclusion of his high school years he, along with a large number of others from Central High, entered Dartmouth, apparently because of the influence of Edwin A. Smith, a 1917 graduate of the College:

The reason so many kids went to Dartmouth at that particular time from the Springfield high school was probably Red Smith, a young English teacher who, rather than being just an English teacher, was one of the gang—a real stimulating guy who probably was responsible for my starting to write.

I think many kids were excited by this fellow. (His family ran a candy factory in White River Junction, Vermont, I remember that.) And I think when time came to go to college we all said, "Let's go where Red Smith went."

Accordingly, in the autumn of 1921, Geisel headed for Hanover, some hundred and thirty miles up the Connecticut River from Springfield.

And what was to prove, as viewed now in retrospect, especially a stimulus to him at Dartmouth?

Well, my big inspiration for writing there was Ben Pressey [W. Benfield Pressey of the Department of English]. He was important to me in college as Smith was in high school.

He seemed to like the stuff I wrote. He was very informal, and he had little seminars at his house (plus a very beautiful wife who served us cocoa). In between sips of cocoa, we students read our trash aloud.

He's the only person I took any creative writing courses from ever, anywhere, and he was very kind and encouraging.

I remember being in a big argument at one of Ben's seminars. I maintained that subject matter wasn't as important as method. (I don't believe that at all now.)

To prove my point, I did a book review of the Boston and Maine Railroad timetable. As I remember, nobody in the class thought it was funny—except Ben and me.

From the outset at Dartmouth, Freshman Geisel gravitated toward associations with the humor magazine, Jack O'Lantern:

That was an extension of my activities in high school—and a lot less dangerous than doing somersaults off the ski jump.

I think I had something in *Jack O'Lantern* within a couple of months after I got to college.

Jack O'Lantern *proved increasingly an object of Geisel's attentions throughout his four years in Hanover, and at the end of his junior year he became editor-in-chief:*

Another guy who was a great encouragement was Norman Maclean. He was the editor preceding me. He found that I was a workhorse, so we used to write practically the whole thing ourselves every month.

Norman, at the same time, was writing a novel. And the further he got involved with his novel, the less time he had for his *Jack O'Lantern*. So, pretty soon I was essentially writing the whole thing myself.

One night Norman finished the novel and went out to celebrate. While he was out celebrating, his boarding house burned down and his novel burned up. Unlike Thomas Carlyle, I don't think he ever rewrote it.*

The general practice of Jack O'Lantern *was that its literary content appeared*

---

* *Norman Maclean went on to teach at the University of Chicago and eventually to publish a novel,* A River Runs Through It, *that became an American classic—T.F.*

unsigned, a circumstance which renders it impossible to compile today a compre-
hensive listing of Geisel's writings for its pages. The author himself has only vague
recollections of what he in fact wrote for the publication, although he does remem-
ber that certain contributions were written jointly with Maclean, including ones
which came about in a singular fashion:

Norman and I had a rather peculiar method of creating literary gems.
Hunched behind his typewriter, he would bang out a line of words.

Sometimes he'd tell me what he'd written, sometimes not. But, then,
he'd always say, "The next line's yours." And, always, I'd supply it.

This may have made for rough reading. But it was great sport writing.

The art work included in Jack O'Lantern *was, unlike its "lit," usually signed,*
and the magazine's issues of 1921–1925 are liberally sprinkled with cartoons bear-
ing explicit evidence of having come from Ted Geisel's pen.

The 1920s were seemingly "the era of the pun," and many of the individual
cartoons are found to have involved puns or currently popular expressions.

Going back, now, over the pages of Jacko *for his undergraduate years, Geisel*
is rather stern in his judgment of the cartoons that were included, and particularly
of those he himself drew.

In summing up his assessment he says:

You have to look at these things in the perspective of 50 years ago. These
things may have been considered funny then, I hope—but today I sort of
wonder.

The best I can say about the *Jacko* of this era is that they were doing just
as badly on the Harvard *Lampoon,* the Yale *Record,* and the Columbia *Jester.*

During his student days Geisel also went into print from time to time in
another campus publication, The Dartmouth, *"America's Oldest College News-*
paper":

Whit Campbell was editor of *The Daily Dartmouth* at the time. I filled-
in occasionally and did a few journalistic squibs with him.

Almost every night I'd be working in the *Jack O'Lantern* office, and while
waiting for Whit's morning paper across the hall to go to press, we used to
play a bit of poker.

Once in a while, if one of Whit's news stories turned sour, we'd put our
royal-straight flushes face down on the table, rewrite the story together, and
then pick up our royal-straight flushes again—and sometimes raise each other
as much as a quarter.

This did little to affect the history of journalism in America. But it did
cement the strongest personal friendship I made at Dartmouth.

There were two especially noteworthy aspects of the extensive work Geisel did
for Dartmouth's humor magazine.

The first of these emerged during his junior year, and he identifies it as having been in his undergraduate period "the only clue to my future life." It involved a technique of presentation, the approach to a form for combining humorous writing and zany drawings:

This was the year I discovered the excitement of "marrying" words to pictures.

I began to get it through my skull that words and pictures were Yin and Yan. I began thinking that words and pictures, married, might possibly produce a progeny more interesting than either parent.

It took me almost a quarter of a century to find the proper way to get my words and pictures married. At Dartmouth I couldn't even get them engaged.

The other particularly significant feature of Geisel's Jack O'Lantern *career relates to the spring of 1925, when apparently he first used the signature "Seuss." The circumstances that surrounded his employment of the later-famous pseudonym he outlines as follows:*

The night before Easter of my senior year there were ten of us gathered in my room at the Randall Club. We had a pint of gin for ten people, so that proves nobody was *really* drinking.

But Pa Randall, who hated merriment, called Chief Rood, the chief of police, and he himself in person raided us.

We all had to go before the dean, Craven Laycock, and we were all put on probation for defying the laws of Prohibition, and especially on Easter Evening.

The disciplinary action imposed by Dean Laycock meant that the editor-in-chief of Jack O'Lantern *was relieved forthwith of his official responsibilities for running the magazine. There existed, however, the practical necessity of helping to bring out its succeeding numbers during the remainder of the academic year.*

Articles and jokes presented no problem, since they normally appeared anonymously; thus, anything the deposed editor might do in that area could be completely invisible as to its source.

Cartoons, on the other hand, usually being signed contributions, did present a dilemma; and it was a dilemma Theodor Seuss Geisel resolved by publishing some of his cartoons entirely without signature and by attributing others of them to fictitious sources.

The final four Jacko *issues in the spring of 1925 contained, accordingly, a number of Geisel cartoons anonymously inserted or carrying utterly fanciful cognomens (such as "L. Burbank," "Thos. Mott Osborne '27," and "D. G. Rossetti '25"), and two cartoons, in the number of April twenty-second, had affixed to them his own middle name (in one case "Seuss" alone and in the other "T. Seuss"):*

To what extent this corny subterfuge fooled the dean, I never found out.

But that's how "Seuss" first came to be used as my signature. The "Dr." was added later on.

In June of 1925, Ted Geisel finished his undergraduate course at Dartmouth and prepared to embark upon a further academic adventure. It was one he had ardently desired to pursue, but it proved, in the end, to have a slightly different route of approach than he had anticipated.

I remember my father writing me and asking, "What are you going to do after you graduate?"

I wrote back, "Don't you worry about me, I'm going to win a thing called the Campbell Fellowship in English Literature and I'm going to Oxford."

He read the letter rather hurriedly. The editor of the *Springfield Union* lived across the street from us (that was Maurice Sherman; he was also a Dartmouth man), and my father ran across the street and said, "Hey, what do you know? Ted won a fellowship called the Campbell Fellowship and he's going to Oxford."

So, Maurice Sherman, being a staunch Dartmouth man, ran my picture in the paper (I think it was on the front page): GEISEL WINS FELLOWSHIP TO GO TO OXFORD. And everybody called up my father and congratulated him.

Well, it so happened that that year they found *nobody* in the College worthy of giving the Campbell Fellowship to. So, my father, to save face with Maurice Sherman and others, had to dig up the money to send me to Oxford, anyway.

In the autumn of 1925 Geisel entered Oxford as a member of Lincoln College:

My tutor was A.J. Carlyle, the nephew of the great, frightening Thomas Carlyle. I was surprised to see him alive. He was surprised to see me in any form.

He was the oldest man I've ever seen riding a bicycle. I was the only man he'd ever seen who never ever should have come to Oxford.

This brilliant scholar had taken "Firsts" in every school in Oxford, excepting medicine, without studying. Every year, up to his eighties, he went up for a different "First," just for the hell of it.

Patiently, he had me write essays and listened to me read them, in the usual manner of the Oxford tutorial system. But he realized I was getting stultified in English schools.

I was bogged down with old High German and Gothic and stuff of that sort, in which I have no interest whatsoever—and I don't think anybody really should.

Well, he was a great historian, and he quickly discovered that I didn't know *any* history. Somehow or other I got through high school and Dartmouth without taking one history course.

He very correctly told me I was ignorant, and he was the man who suggested that I do what I finally did: just travel around Europe with a bundle of high school history books and visit the places I was reading about—go to the museums and look at pictures and read as I went. That's what I finally did.

As an example of one factor contributing to the stultifying atmosphere he encountered at Oxford, he still has vivid memories of a don at the university who had produced a variorum edition of Shakespeare and who was chiefly interested in punctuational differences in Shakespearean texts:

That was the man who really drove me out of Oxford. I'll never forget his two-hour lecture on the punctuation of *King Lear*.

He had dug up all of the old folios, as far back as he could go. Some had more semicolons than commas. Some had more commas than periods. Some had no punctuation at all.

For the first hour and a half he talked about the first two pages in *King Lear*, lamenting the fact that modern people would never comprehend the true essence of Shakespeare, because it's punctuated badly these days.

It got unbelievable. I got up, went back to my room, and started packing.

A notebook used by Geisel during his time at Oxford has survived among his papers:

I think this demonstrates that I wasn't very interested in the subtle niceties and complexities of English literature. As you go through the notebook, there's a growing incidence of flying cows and strange beasts. And, finally, at the last page of the notebook there are no notes on English literature at all. There are just strange beasts.

This period, despite its academic frustrations, was not, however, without its diversions and recreations—one such having been, actually, an outgrowth of Miltonic studies:

While I was at Oxford I illustrated a great hunk of *Paradise Lost*.

With the imagery of *Paradise Lost*, Milton's sense of humor failed him in a couple of places. I remember one line, "Thither came the angel Uriel, sliding down a sunbeam."

I illustrated that: Uriel had a long, locomotive oil can and was greasing the sunbeam as he descended, to lessen the friction on his coccyx. And I worked a lot on Adam and Eve.

Blackwell, the great bookseller and publisher, was right around the corner from Lincoln, and I remember I had the crust to go in there and ask them to commission me to do the whole thing.

Somebody took it into a back room and then came back with it very promptly and said, "This isn't quite the Blackwell type of humor."

So, I was thrown out. But I got my revenge years later. I went to Oxford about 20 years later. I went past Blackwell's and found the whole window full of my books. It had apparently *become* "the Blackwell type of humor."

Clearly, the most important circumstance associated with Ted Geisel's interval at the University of Oxford was his meeting there a young lady from New Jersey named Helen Palmer.

A graduate of Wellesley College, Miss Palmer had in the autumn of 1924 entered upon studies at Oxford to complete her preparations for becoming a schoolteacher back home in America.

She was a gal who was sitting next to me when I was doing this notebook, and she was the one who said, "You're not very interested in the lectures." (She "picked me up" by looking over and saying, "I think that's a very good flying cow.")

It was she who finally convinced me that flying cows were a better future than tracing long and short E through Anglo Saxon.

She was the one who convinced me that I wasn't for pedagogy at all.

On the other hand, *she* did complete the English schools that year; took her degree in English Lit. This enabled her to get a job teaching English in the States. This enabled us to get married.

Upon quitting Oxford, Geisel did engage briefly in one final scholastic interlude, this time in Paris:

At Oxford I went to a lecture (I was very interested in Jonathan Swift) by the great Emile Legouis. Although he was a Frenchman, he was the greatest Swift authority in the world at that time.

He talked to me at the end of the lecture and began selling me on going to study with him at the Sorbonne. And, after I left Oxford, I did so.

I registered at the Sorbonne, and I went over to his house to find out exactly what he wanted me to do.

He said, "I have a most interesting assignment which should only take you about two years to complete." He said that nobody had ever discovered anything that Jonathan Swift wrote from the age of 16 and a half to 17.

He said I should devote two years to finding out whether he *had* written anything. If he had, I could analyze what he wrote as my D.Phil. thesis. Unfortunately, if he hadn't written anything, I wouldn't get my doctorate.

I remember leaving his charming home and walking straight to the American Express Company and booking myself a passage on a cattle boat to Corsica.

There I proceeded to paint donkeys for a month. Then, I proceeded with Carlyle's idea and began living all around the Continent, reading history books, going to museums, and drawing pictures.

I remember a long period in which I drew nothing but gargoyles. They were easier than Mona Lisas.

And what of those months of junketing?—
While floating around Europe trying to figure out what I wanted to do with my life, I decided at one point that I would be the Great American Novelist. And so I sat down and wrote the Great American Novel.

It turned out to be not so great, so I boiled it down into the Great American Short Story. It wasn't very great in that form either.

Two years later I boiled it down once more and sold it as a two-line joke to *Judge*.

Home once again in Springfield, Geisel lived with his parents and began submitting cartoons to national magazines:
I was trying to become self-sufficient—and my father was hoping I'd become self-sufficient and get out of the house, because I was working at his desk.

Finally, a submission to The Saturday Evening Post *was accepted. It was a cartoon depicting two tourists on a camel, and it appeared in the magazine's issue for July 16, 1927.*
The drawing was signed simply "Seuss" by its draftsman-humorist, resurrecting the pseudonym he had used in the Dartmouth Jack O'Lantern *two years earlier:*
The main reason that I picked "Seuss" professionally is that I still thought I was one day going to write the Great American Novel. I was saving my real name for that—and it looks like I still am.

Actually, the Post *in publishing his cartoon accorded "Seuss" no pseudonymity whatsoever, for it supplied the identification "Drawn by Theodor Seuss Geisel" in a by-line of type, right along the edge of the drawing itself.*
When the *Post* paid me 25 bucks for that picture, I informed my parents that my future success was assured; I would quickly make my fame and fortune in *The Saturday Evening Post*.

It didn't quite work out that way. It took 37 years before they bought a second Seuss: an article in 1964 called "If at First You Don't Succeed—Quit!"

But success during the summer of 1927 in placing something with The Saturday Evening Post *was a cause for great elation—and, moreover, for a decision on the cartoonist's part to leave Springfield:*
Bubbling over with self-assurance, I told my parents they no longer had to feed or clothe me.

I had a thousand dollars saved up from the *Jack O'Lantern* (in those days college magazines made a profit), and with this I jumped onto the New York, New Haven, and Hartford Railroad; and I invaded the Big City, where I knew that all the editors would be waiting to buy my wares.

In New York, Geisel moved in with an artist friend from his Dartmouth undergraduate days, John C. Rose, who had a one-room studio in Greenwich Village, upstairs over Don Dickerman's night club called the Pirates Den:
The last thing we used to do at night was to stand on chairs and, with canes we'd bought for that purpose, play polo with the rats, and try to drive them out so they wouldn't nibble us while we slept. God! what a place.

And I wasn't selling any wares. I tried to do sophisticated things for *Vanity Fair;* I tried unsophisticated things for the *Daily Mirror.*

I wasn't getting anywhere at all, until John suddenly said one day, "There's a guy called Beef Vernon, of my class at Dartmouth, who has just landed a job as a salesman to sell advertising for *Judge.*

"His job won't last long, because nobody buys any advertising in *Judge.* But maybe, before Beef gets fired, we can con him into introducing you to Norman Anthony, the editor."

The result of the Geisel-Anthony meeting was the offer of a job as a staff writer-artist for the humor magazine, at a salary of 75 dollars per week—enough encouragement to cause Ted Geisel and Helen Palmer (who had been teaching during the year since the completion of her Oxford studies) to marry. The wedding took place at Westfield, New Jersey, on November 29, 1927:
We got married on the strength of that. Then the magazine went semi-bust the next week, and my salary went down to 50 dollars.

And the *next* week they instituted another fiscal policy (I was getting a little bit worried by this time) in which they dispensed with money entirely and paid contributors with due bills. Due bills…?

Judge had practically no advertising. And the advertisers it attracted seldom paid for the ads with money; they paid the magazine with due bills. And that's what we, the artists and writers, ended up with in lieu of salary.

For instance: a hundred dollars, the only way for me to get the hundred dollars was to go down to the Hotel Traymore in Atlantic City and move into a hundred-dollar suite.

So, Helen and I spent many weeks of our first marriage year in sumptuous suites in Atlantic City—where we didn't want to be at all.

Under the due-bill system I got paid once, believe it or not, in a hundred cartons of Barbasol shaving cream. Another time I got paid in 13 gross of Little Gem nail clippers.

Looking back on it, it wasn't really so bad, because I didn't have to balance any checkbooks—or file any income tax.

How can you file an income tax when you're being paid in cases of White Rock soda?

And where did the newlywed Geisels set up housekeeping in New York?
Oh, we went to a place across from a stable in Hell's Kitchen on 18th Street.

Horses frequently died in the stable, and they'd drag them out and leave them in the street, where they'd be picked up by sanitation two or three days later.

That's where I learned to carry a "loaded" cane. It was about a three-block walk to the subway. It you weren't carrying a weapon of some sort you'd be sure to get mugged.

So, Helen and I worked harder than ever to get out of this place, and we finally managed to move north to 79th Street and West End Avenue. There there were many fewer dead horses.

"Seuss" work in Judge *consisted not only of cartoons:*
I was writing some crazy stories, as well. It was a combination, about fifty-fifty, the articles always tied in with drawings.

Among these combination pieces, extending the type of thing he had begun doing as an undergraduate at Dartmouth, Geisel produced for Judge *a succession of regular contributions signed in a way that brought his pseudonym into the final form of its evolution:*
I started to do a feature called "Boids and Beasties." It was a mock-zoological thing, and I put the "Dr." on the "Seuss" to make me sound more professorial.

At first the self-bestowed "Dr." was accompanied by "Theophrastus" or "Theo." in by-lines and as a signature for drawings, but with the passage of time "Dr. Seuss" was settled on as the standard form of his identification.
"Dr. Seuss" soon found his way into other magazines of the day, besides Judge, *including* Liberty, College Humor, *and* Life. *He even teamed up, at one point, with humorist Corey Ford in a collaboration for* Vanity Fair *that was, in the end, to be abandoned out of pure frustration:*
I illustrated some stories for Corey Ford in *Vanity Fair,* but I gave that up because it got a little ludicrous. The art director of *Vanity Fair* was more concerned with style than content.

The last thing I did with Corey was a spoof on political cartooning in the 1890s—a Boss Tweed type thing.

The art director laid the thing out before I did the drawings, and he insisted that my average picture was to be nine inches wide and three-quarters of an inch high. This caused Boss Tweed and me to roll over in our graves.

Corey and I remained good friends, but we didn't work together after that.

An occurrence early in Geisel's period of association with Judge *was to have a particular impact on his subsequent career:*
I'd been working for *Judge* about four months when I drew this accidental cartoon which changed my whole life. It was an insecticide gag.

It was a picture of a knight who had gone to bed. He had stacked his armor beside the bed. There was this covered canopy over the bed, and a tremendous dragon was sort of nuzzling him.

He looked up and said, "Darn it all, another Dragon. And just after I'd sprayed the whole castle with..."

With *what?* I wondered.

There were two well-known insecticides. One was Flit and one was Fly Tox. So, I tossed a coin. It came up heads, for Flit.

So, the caption read, "...another Dragon. And just after I'd sprayed the whole castle with Flit."

Here's where luck comes in.

Very few people ever bought *Judge*. It was continually in bankruptcy— and everybody else was bankrupt, too.

But one day the wife of Lincoln L. Cleaves, who was the account executive on Flit at the McCann-Erikson advertising agency, failed to get an appointment at her favorite hairdresser and went to a second-rate hairdresser's, where they had second-rate magazines around.

She opened *Judge* while waiting to get her hair dressed, and she found this picture. She ripped it out of the magazine, put it in her reticule, took it home, bearded her husband with it, and said, "Lincoln, you've got to hire this young man; it's the best Flit ad I've ever seen."

He said, "Go away." He said, "You're my wife, and you're to have nothing to do with my business."

So, she pestered him for about two weeks, and finally he said, "All right, I'll have him in, and I'll buy one picture."

He had me in. I drew one picture, which I captioned "Quick, Henry, the Flit!"—and it was published.

Then, they hired me to do two more—and 17 years later I was still doing them.

The only good thing Adolph Hitler did in starting World War II was that he enabled me to join the Army and finally stop drawing "Quick, Henry, the Flit!"

I'd drawn them by the millions—newspaper ads, magazine ads, booklets, window displays, 24-sheet posters, even "Quick, Henry, the Flit!" animated cartoons. Flit was pouring out of my ears and beginning to itch me.

The Standard Oil Company of New Jersey, the manufacturers of Flit, had another product with which Geisel was to become concerned, in an ad campaign that led to something of a naval career for "Dr. Seuss":

They had a product called Esso Marine, a lubricating oil for boats, and they didn't have a lot of money to spend on advertising.

They decided to see what we could do with public relations. So, Harry Bruno, a great PR man, Ted Cook and Verne Carrier of Esso, and I cooked up the Seuss Navy.

Starting small at one of the New York motorboat shows, we printed up a few diplomas, and we took about 15 prominent people into membership—Vincent Astor and sailors like that, who had tremendous yachts—so we could photograph them at the boat show receiving their certificates.

We waited to see what happened. Well, Astor and Guy Lombardo and a few other celebrities hung these things in their yachts. And very soon everyone who had a putt-putt wanted to join the Seuss Navy.

The next year we started giving annual banquets at the Biltmore. It was cheaper to give a party for a few thousand people, furnishing all booze, than it was to advertise in full-page ads.

And it was successful because we never mentioned the product at all. Reporters would cover the party, and *they* would write our commercials for us. So, we would end up with national coverage about "The Seuss Navy met ...," and then they would have to explain it by talking about Esso Marine.

At the time it was declared, in 1941, we had the biggest navy in the world. We commissioned the whole Standard Oil fleet, and we also had, for example, the *Queen Mary* and most of the ships of the U.S. lines.

Then, an interesting thing happened. I left to join the Army. And somebody said, "Thank God, Geisel's gone, he was wasting a great opportunity. He wasn't *selling* the product. We have Seuss Navy hats, and we have Seuss Navy glasses and Seuss Navy flags." He said, "These things should carry advertising on them."

They put advertising on them, and the Navy promptly died. The fun had gone out of it, and the Seuss Navy sank.

Concurrently with his advertising and promotional activity relating to Flit and Esso Marine, "Dr. Seuss" continued to contribute to the humor magazines; but he was not entirely free:

My contract with the Standard Oil Company was an exclusive one and forbade me from doing an awful lot of stuff.

Flit being seasonal, its ad campaign was only run during the summer months. I'd get my year's work done in about three months, and I had all this spare time and nothing to do.

They let me work for magazines, because I'd already established that. But it crimped future expansion into other things.

Restless to explore new avenues of activity, Geisel ultimately hit upon the notion of preparing a volume for children:
I would like to say I went into children's-book work because of my great understanding of children. I went in because it wasn't excluded by my Standard Oil contract.

Another evident cause for his focusing on the possibility of doing books at some point was a commission he received to provide "Dr. Seuss" illustrations for an anthology of amusing gaffes unconsciously and innocently perpetrated by school children, a work that styled itself as "compiled from classrooms and examination papers" by Alexander Abingdon:
The book was originally published in England, where it was called *Schoolboy Howlers*. Some smart person at Viking Press in New York (I think it was Marshall Best) brought out a reprint of the English edition, under the title *Boners*.

Whereupon hundreds of teachers in the U.S.A. began sending in boners from *their* examination papers. And the Boner Business boomed.

Boners and its sequel, More Boners, *were both published in 1931:*
That was a big Depression year. And although by Depression standards I was adequately paid a flat fee for illustrating these bestsellers, I was money-worried. The two books were booming and I was not.

This is the point when I first began to realize that if I hoped to succeed in the book world, I'd have to write, as well as draw.

The actual coming into being of a book of his own, the first of what was to be so substantial and celebrated a series of volumes written and illustrated by "Dr. Seuss," derived from a curious stimulus and through decidedly unusual means:
I was on a long, stormy crossing of the Atlantic, and it was too rough to go out on deck. Everybody in the ship just sat in the bar for a week, listening to the engines turn over: da-da-ta-ta, da-da-ta-ta, da-da-ta-ta....

To keep from going nuts, I began reciting silly words to the rhythm of the engines. Out of nowhere I found myself saying, "And that is a story that no one can beat; and to think that I saw it on Mulberry Street."

When I finally got off the ship, this refrain kept going through my head. I couldn't shake it. To therapeutize myself I added more words in the same rhythm.

Six months later I found I had a book on my hands, called *And to Think That I Saw It on Mulberry Street*. So, what to do with it?

I submitted it to 27 publishers. It was turned down by all 27. The main reason they all gave was there was nothing similar on the market, so of course it wouldn't sell.

After the 27th publisher had turned it down, I was taking the book home to my apartment, to burn it in the incinerator, and I bumped into Mike McClintock (Marshall McClintock, Dartmouth 1926) coming down Madison Avenue.

He said, "What's that under your arm?"

I said, "That's a book no one will publish. I'm lugging it home to burn."

Then I asked Mike, "What are *you* doing?"

He said, "This morning I was appointed juvenile editor of Vanguard Press, and we happen to be standing in front of my office; would you like to come inside?"

So, we went inside, and he looked at the book and he took me to the president of Vanguard Press. Twenty minutes later we were signing contracts.

That's one of the reasons I believe in luck. If I'd been going down the other side of Madison Avenue, I would be in the dry-cleaning business today!

And what reception did the public accord And to Think That I Saw It on Mulberry Street *when the book was released in 1937?*

In those days children's books didn't sell very well, and it became a bestseller at 10,000 copies, believe it or not. (Today, at "Beginner Books," if we're bringing out a *doubtful* book we print 20,000 copies.)

But, we were in the Depression era, and *Mulberry Street* cost a dollar, which was then a lot of money.

I remember what a big day it was in my life when Mike McClintock called up and announced, "I just sold a thousand copies of your book to Marshall Field. Congratulations! You *are* an author."

In addition to favorable sales, the comment of one particular reviewer was especially significant in encouraging the fledgling author of children's books toward further effort in this new-to-him field:

Clifton Fadiman, I think, was partially responsible for my going on in children's books. He wrote a review for *The New Yorker*, a one-sentence review.

He said, "They say it's for children, but better get a copy for yourself and marvel at the good Dr. Seuss's impossible pictures and the moral tale of the little boy who exaggerated not wisely but too well."

I remember that impressed me very much: if the great Kip Fadiman likes it I'll have to do another.

Another he did do (The 500 Hats of Bartholomew Cubbins, *in 1938) and then another and another and another—to the point that there have been to date nearly 50 volumes of his authorship, in addition to widely acclaimed motion pictures and animated specials for television. Besides this Theodor Seuss Geisel presides over and gives editorial direction to a major publishing enterprise, "Beginner Books," a division of Random House.*

In 1955 Ted Geisel returned to Dartmouth in order that his alma mater might, fondly and proudly, bestow upon him an honorary degree. President John Sloan Dickey's citation on that occasion proclaimed, in part:

"Your affinity for flying elephants and man-eating mosquitoes makes us rejoice you were not around to be Director of Admissions on Mr. Noah's ark. But our rejoicing in your career is far more positive: as author and artist you single-handedly have stood as St. George between a generation of exhausted parents and the demon dragon of unexhuasted children on a rainy day.... As always with the best of humor, behind the fun there has been intelligence, kindness, and a feel for humankind."

In this article, Seuss explains that he writes as much for adults
as for children, saying that his books are "satires on satires.
I have the parents in mind." Perhaps this is one of the reasons people
remember the Seuss books so vividly when they are grown:
They don't outgrow the lessons learned from Seuss.

9

Dr. Seuss's Green-Eggs-and-Ham World

Judith Frutig

The Christian Science Monitor, **May 12, 1978**

La Jolla, California—Just about the time sleepy children climb into bed, sober-minded adults from here to New Zealand can be heard nightly reading such logical absurdities as: "I like to box ... so every day I box a gox. In yellow socks I box my gox. I box in yellow gox box socks."

Anatomically outrageous, bursting with adventure and humor, rhymed with repetitive wit, and laced with imagination and a gentle moral, there are Nerkles, Sneetches, and Nutches ("who live in small caves known as nitches for hutches").

There are stories about Horton the Elephant who sits in a tree nursing a bird's egg; about the Grinch who tries to steal Christmas with a little help from his dog, Max; and about learning to love green eggs and ham for breakfast. Then, of course, there is the Cat in the Hat, the Circus McGurkus, McElligot's Pool, Yertle the Turtle, Thidwick the Big-Hearted Moose, the Fox in Socks.

These are the cuddly—sometimes creepy—creatures of Dr. Seuss, whose 40-odd books have sold 85 million copies around the world.

Forty years of imaginative verse—set off by his own quixotic illustrations—have firmly implanted Theodor Seuss Geisel (who says he has been saving his real name for 74 years now in the hope of attaching it to the great American novel) in the reluctant role of grandfather to the saucer-eyed set.

Along the way, it has established him as king of the kids, made him a multimillionaire, bestowed on him an honorary degree as doctor of humane letters (from Dartmouth, his alma mater), and built his airy glass-enclosed house atop the highest hill in this flower-festooned southern California resort community.

It also has left him to sit through countless well-intentioned breakfasts of green eggs and ham. "Deplorable stuff," he says. "The worst time was on a yacht in six-foot seas."

If that is not enough, Dr. Seuss is branching out. In addition to television, records, and Seuss toys, there is a new book out in September, and the Children's Theater in Minneapolis is preparing to put on the first stage production of *The 500 Hats of Bartholomew Cubbins*.

At the undisputed top of his profession, Mr. Geisel remains a charmingly unassuming man, tense in an interview, often apologetic, frequently asking his questioner whether he is providing the proper material.

A visit with the Geisels starts with a tour of their house. It is an elegant Spanish-style home which began as an observation tower and slowly grew from a weekend retreat to nine tastefully appointed rooms, including a somber and mirrored formal dining room.

Lining the walls are what Mr. Geisel calls "serious examples of Seuss art," oil paintings featuring fey felines with Seussian titles. There is a "Plethora of Cats," "Venetian Cat Singing O Solo Meow," "Alley Cat for a Very Long Alley," "Green Cat in the Lueaborg, Finland, Subway," and "I Dreamed I Was a Doorman at the Hotel Coronado."*

"Some people," observed Mr. Geisel, "say I should throw out the paintings and keep the titles."

It was a cat drawing that first launched Mr. Geisel's lucrative career. That was in the mid–1950s when the "why-Johnny-can't-read" crisis swept American public schools. Mr. Geisel stepped into the literary breach and agreed to write a primer-style book intended to replace the plodding Dick and Jane series.

He was given a list of 400 words with instructions to winnow them down to a working list of 220. The assumption: that children can absorb only so many words at a given age.

"I decided that the first two words on the list that rhymed would be the title," he said. And so the world received "The Cat in the Hat," a character that has grossed close to $5 million, along with Horton, the Grinch, and the rest of Mr. Geisel's colorful stable of characters.

Mr. Geisel's English lessons are based on fun—and tight writing. "You can fool an adult into thinking he's reading profundities by sprinkling your prose with purple passages," he said. "But with a kid you can't get away with that.

---

* *These paintings were published in the 1995 book* The Secret Art of Dr. Seuss.—*T.F.*

"Two sentences in a children's book is the equivalent of two chapters in an adult book."

Dr. Seuss has written some adult books, too. *The Seven Lady Godivas* sold 50 copies out of a printing of 10,000.

Then there was his first attempt at his great American novel, never published, which he now says he wrote when he was "23 and under the influence of everyone."

"I can't tell you what it was about," he says, "because I read it recently and I didn't understand it. There's a chapter in there with people talking in Italian. I'm not sure how they got there."

His children's books come to life along the expansive and cork-lined walls of his study overlooking the cool, blue Pacific Ocean, where Mr. Geisel is even now preparing his newest assault against dull children's literature.

In story-board form, he traces his drawings, first in black and white, then with colored pencils, fashioning the words and pictures into one idea, then fastening them with tacks as they progress. His desk is cluttered with colored pencils; he is an artist first, a writer second.

The new book is another adventure of the cocky Cat in the Hat. The title: *I Can Read with My Eyes Shut.* Scheduled for publication in September, the book is being finished with scrupulous detail for the printer, with each color carefully labeled and numbered on every inch of page.

When he writes, Mr. Geisel does not have children in mind. "I write for myself," he says, "and for the pleasure of saying, 'Audrey [his wife], don't you think this is funny?' For beginner books all I do is to strike out the complex sentence structure, throw out the unnecessary long words, and simplify."

But on the bigger books—he calls them novels—he usually tries them first on children. "There are several levels," he says of the story line; "most are satires on satires. I also have the parents in mind."

The secret of his success, he says, is overwriting. "For a 60-page book, I'll probably write 500 pages," he says—and toss out 90 percent or more of his drawings. "I think that's why it works. I winnow out."

Mr. Geisel is a publisher in his own right, as editor in chief of Beginner Books, a division of Random House in New York, and the original publisher of *The Cat in the Hat.*

His first wife, Helen, preceded him as publisher. When she passed on in 1967, he stepped into her position.

With a deep and growing interest in the reading habits of children—his books are available on four continents—a major Geisel concern is learning how to interest youngsters in reading.

"I personally don't think that television is the great evil demon it's made out to be," he says. "The average kids know more geography, more politics than their parents did at their age. The trouble is they can't spell.

"Teaching a child to read is a family setup," he says. "It's the business of having books around the house, not forcing them. Parents should have 20 books stacked on tables or set around the living room. The average kid will pick one up, find something interesting. And pretty soon he's reading."

Mr. Geisel grew up in Springfield, Massachusetts, with the same sharp reading skills he's trying to instill in the newest generation. But when it came to early expression of art talent, his teacher gently suggested he drop the class.

His first published children's book was *And to Think That I Saw It on Mulberry Street*. It drew 28 rejection slips before a major publisher decided to give it a chance. Since then it has sold out more than 25 editions.

Mr. Geisel began his writing career as an advertising copywriter, producing sparse copy for the Flit Company by penning cartoons subtitled: "Quick, Henry! The Flit."

To this day his schedule is virtually the same as it always has been. Breakfast with his wife, Audrey, who assists him with color schemes and as his chief critic.

He spends six hours a day at his desk. "I make it a rule to sit at my desk six hours a day whether anything's happening or not," he says. "It's disconcerting to look out here," he adds, sweeping his arm in the direction of the ocean, "and see the surfers."

When nothing is happening, he draws "hundreds of characters." But along the way something clicks. "Part of a character will evolve and part of another character will evolve and then I'll put them into conversation," he says. "One of them says something and the other says something back. I never know what's going to happen next but when you get them acting and reacting, you're on to a story."

That's what happened to *Horton Hatches the Egg*. I was sitting in my studio one day," he recalls, "working on transparent tracing paper, and the window blew open. The wind simply picked up a picture of an elephant I'd drawn and deposited it on top of another sheet of paper that had a tree.

"All I had to do was figure out what the elephant was doing on that tree. I've left my window open since then," he added, "but nothing's happened."

His favorite story is *The Lorax*. His story with the fewest words: *Green Eggs and Ham*.

The Lorax book was intended to be propaganda," he said. "I was angry about the ecology problems." The trouble was the story did not come together.

That was when Mrs. Geisel intervened. "Let's go to Africa," she recalls saying. He agreed.

Sitting by the pool at their hotel in Kenya, Mr. Geisel watched a herd of elephants amble over the hill. "And something just clicked," he said.

Mrs. Geisel picks up the story: "He wrote on the backs of everything ... on laundry lists," she said. "It came in a rush.

"Going over the Serengetti Plain one afternoon, he looked up and said, 'Look at that tree.' He said, 'They've stolen my trees.'"

Green Eggs and Ham was created in a quite different way. Since its first publication in 1960, it has become one of the best-selling Seuss books of all time.

"It began as a boast," said Mr. Geisel. "A friend said, "I'll bet you can't write a book in just 100 words. "I said I'll bet I can do it in 50." He did.

In 1960, E. J. Kahn noted that Dr. Seuss books did not sell well outside the United States because of the translation difficulties they presented. By 1979, however, when Cynthia Gorney wrote this article for The Washington Post, *Seuss books were translated or republished in 45 countries, including, she writes, "Brazil, Japan, the entire British commonwealth and the Netherlands, where 'There's a Wocket in My Pocket' translates to 'Ik heb een Gak in Myn Zak!'" capturing both the meaning and mood of Seuss.*

10

Dr. Seuss at 75: Grinch, Cat in Hat, Wocket and Generations of Kids in His Pocket

CYNTHIA GORNEY

The Washington Post, **May 21, 1979**

LA JOLLA, Calif.—One afternoon in 1957, as he bent over the big drawing board in his California studio, Theodor Seuss Geisel found himself drawing a turtle.

He was not sure why.

He drew another turtle and saw that it was underneath the first turtle, holding him up.

He drew another, and another, until he had an enormous pileup of turtles, each standing on the back of the turtle below it and hanging its turtle head, looking pained.

Geisel looked at his turtle pile. He asked himself, not unreasonably, What does this mean? Who is the turtle on top?

Then he understood that the turtle on top was Adolf Hitler.

"I couldn't draw Hitler as a turtle," Geisel says, now hunched over the same drawing board, making pencil scribbles of the original Yertle the Turtle drawings as he remembers them. "So I drew him as King What-ever-his-name-was, King" (scribble) "of the Pond." (Scribble.) "He wanted to be king as far as he could see. So he kept piling them up. He conquered Central Europe and France, and there it was." (Scribble.)

"Then I had this great pileup, and I said, 'How do you get rid of this impostor?'"

"Believe it or not, I said, 'The voice of the people.' I said, 'Well, I'll just simply have the guy on the bottom burp.'"

Geisel looks up from his drawing board and smiles—just a little, because a man is taking his picture and he has never gotten used to people who want to take his picture.

Dr. Seuss, American Institution, wild orchestrator of plausible nonsense, booster of things that matter (like fair play, kindness, Drum-Tummied Snumms, Hooded Klopfers, and infinite winding spools of birthday hot dogs), detractor of things that don't (like bullying, snobbery, condescension, gravity and walls), is 75 years old this year.

As usual, he is somewhat embarrassed by all the fuss.

"It's getting awful," Geisel says, "because I meet old, old people, who can scarcely walk, and they say, 'I was brought up on your books.' It's an awful shock."

There is probably not a single children's book author in America who has matched the impact, popularity and international fame of the spare, bearded California prodigy who signs his books Dr. Seuss.

Since 1936, when Ted Geisel the advertising illustrator first wrote *And to Think That I Saw It on Mulberry Street,* his books have sold 80 million copies in this country alone.

"Mulberry Street" was an effort, he explained later, to expel from his brain the maddening rhythm of a ship engine he had heard during the whole of a transatlantic voyage (da da Da da da Da da da Da da da da).

The late Bennett Cerf—at a time when his Random House writers included William Faulkner and John O'Hara—is on record as having called Geisel the only genius of the lot.

The drawings, manuscripts, and half-formed doodles of Dr. Seuss (who did not officially become a doctor until 1956, when Dartmouth College made him an honorary Dr. of Humane Letters), are kept in locked stacks of the Special Collections Division of the UCLA library. He won two Academy Awards for his World War II era documentary film and one for the cartoon *Gerald McBoing-Boing,* which he created. His books are published in about 45 countries outside the United States, including Brazil, Japan, the entire British commonwealth and the Netherlands, where "There's a Wocket in my Pocket" translates to "Ik heb een Gak in Myn Zak!"

On his last visit to Australia, his plane was met by reporters, television cameras, person-sized Cats in Hats, small children with "I love you, Dr. Seuss" badges, and a newspaper headline that read "Dr. Seuss Is Here." An official in the Afghan embassy sent him a collection of brilliant blue sculpted animals with mysterious shapes and corkscrew necks, all made according to traditional design in a tiny Afghanistan town whose name Geisel could never pronounce, but which he says has been unofficially renamed Seussville. "Somebody discovered they were stealing my stuff 3,000 years ago," Geisel says, gazing down admiringly at a small sort of yak. "They're pretty good Seuss, though."

Geisel has lived for 30 years in La Jolla, which is a coastal town just north of San Diego that has developed a flowery, almost Caribbean sparkle as the wealthy build homes up the side of the mountain. At the very top of one of the mountains, with the diminishing acres of wild land to the east and to the west the wide blue curve of the Pacific, Geisel and his wife Audrey share an old stucco observatory tower and the elegant, helter-skelter maze of rooms they have built around it. "It just grew," Audrey Geisel said, "Seuss-like."

They have a swimming pool, a small Yorkshire terrier whose front end is indistinguishable from the back at first glance ("I've been accused of having drawn him," Geisel says), and a gray Cadillac Seville with GRINCH license plates—which took them several years to obtain, because when they first applied they learned that an ardent Seuss-lover with four children had already put GRINCH on the license plates and both sides of his RV. He finally moved to Iowa City and released GRINCH back to the Geisels, with a note of apology for having hogged it so long.

San Diego children know Dr. Seuss lives in a white castle on the hill, and on occasion they will pack up peanut butter and jelly sandwiches and set out for the summit, seeking an audience. Mrs. Geisel has come to expect this. "Breathing on the intercom," she calls it. Geisel has no children of his own (Mrs. Geisel, whom he married 12 years ago after the death of his first wife, has two from a previous marriage), and although he is almost always polite to his callers, the sheer numbers of intercom breathers sometimes overwhelm him.

He cannot answer all his letters, either, because they come every month by the hundreds to his home and the Random House offices in New York— love letters, valentines, air letters from India and New Zealand, photographs of cakes decorated with Hippoheimers or Loraxes, various homemade varieties of Oobleck, the nasty green slime that rains on Bartholomew Cubbins; and in one dismaying delivery, Geisel says, a carefully wrapped package of green eggs and ham.

"These days I spend my birthday in Las Vegas," Geisel says, with unconvincing grumpiness. "Nobody will look for a children's book author in Las Vegas."

He is a private, engaging, intensely driven man, with a lean and sharp-nosed look that gives him an air of severity at first. His house is scattered with his own paintings and busts of creatures unlike anything anybody ever saw before, and as he leads visitors through the halls he makes congenial introductions, as though presenting boarders: "This is a green cat in the Uleaborg, Finland ... this is a cat who was born on the wrong side of town ... this is my religious period. This is Archbishop Katz ... this is called, 'Good god, do I look as old as all that?'"

He will not wear conventional neck ties—only bow ties. He reads paperback books—history, biography, detective novels—so voraciously that his wife makes regular bookstore runs (often to a certain store that saves new books for him in a special Geisel cubbyhole) and then stashes the paperbacks away so she can hand him new ones in the evening, one at a time. He reads for distraction. He needs it. When he is at work, the names, the verse, the story line, the colors, the shapes and sizes of his extraordinary characters all press upon him. He tapes the working drawings to the wall and stares at them, rearranging, reading aloud to himself, feeling the rhythm of the words.

In his new book, a volume of tongue twisters coming out in the fall, Geisel has drawn a green parrot. He has studied all the colors on the Random House art department printing chart—his usual procedure—looking for the printer's ink shade that most closely matches his working drawings in colored pencil. There are 60 different shades of green on the chart, and Geisel cannot find the right one. This one is too yellow, that one too red. He does not explain to the art department why each green is wrong—just not parrotty enough, or something.

They know better than to ask. They will have the printer make up the precise shade of green.

"His color sense," says Grace Clarke, executive art director of the Random House junior books division, "is the most sophisticated I've ever run into." Geisel had to completely relearn color during the last two years, after undergoing an operation for removal of a cataract. The right eye saw brilliant color, following the operation: "the other eye, which still has a small cataract, sees everything like Whistler's Mother." The second cataract is to be removed next year, after which, says Geisel, deadpanned, "They claim I'll be as good as Picasso."

Geisel does not read childrens' literature, unless he is editing it, which is part of his job as the founder and head of the special early readers Random House Division called Beginner Books. Then he is fierce in his judgment, dismissing instantly the noxious breed of childrens' books that coo and mince and pat little heads.

"Bunny-bunny books," he calls them. "Sugar plums, treacle, whimsy." He once turned down a manuscript from Truman Capote. (Diplomatically, neither Geisel nor the Random House people remember what it was about.) "I try to treat the child as an equal," Geisel has said, "and go on the assumption that a child can understand anything that is read to him if the writer takes care to state it clearly and simply enough."

There is a vast difference, of course, between respectful simplicity and invention, and Geisel is as mystified about that as anybody—about what makes one man dull a ship engine's throb with aspirim, or neat whiskey, while another hears the beginnings of an imaginary backstreet elephant-and-giraffe parade. Geisel never set out to be a children's book writer. He was born in

Springfield, Mass., the son of a German immigrant* who had been, at various times, a brewer, a park superintendent, and a world champion rifle shot. Ted Geisel grew up in Springfield, graduated from Dartmouth, and spent a year at Oxford, during which time he is reported to have proposed (unsuccessfully) a new edition of *Paradise Lost,* which would include such illustrations as the Archangel Uriel sliding down a sunbeam with an oil can to lubricate his trip.

He lived in New York, selling drawings, stories and political cartoons to magazines of the day—*Judge, Vanity Fair, The Saturday Evening Post*—and for 15 years he worked in advertising for Standard Oil of New Jersey.

He drew insecticide ads. "Quick, Henry! The Flit!" That was Geisel's creation.

He illustrated two volumes of jokes, tried unsuccessfully to sell an alphabet book, and then in 1936 laid out the wonderfully paced mad fantasy of the boy named Marco in *And to Think That I Saw It on Mulberry Street.* Before a publishing friend of Geisel's took the book in at Vanguard Press, 20 publishers turned it down.

He had an easier time with the next one. "I was sitting in a railroad train, going up somewhere in Connecticut," Geisel says. "And there was a fellow sitting ahead of me, who I didn't like. I didn't know who he was. He had a real ridiculous Wall Street broker's hat on, very stuffy, on this commuting train. And I just began playing around with the idea of what his reaction would be if I took his hat off and threw it out the window."

Geisel smiles a small, slightly evil smile.

"And I said, 'He'd probably just grow another one and ignore me.'"

Which gave us *The 500 Hats of Bartholomew Cubbins.* Boy, confronted in castle by snooty royalty, cannot doff his hat because new hats keep appearing to replace it.

"In those days 90 percent of the stuff that was written was literary fairy tales," Geisel says. "I began to think of appurtenances around the castle, and one of them would be a bowman, and then it occurred to me there would also be an executioner. And I said, 'We gotta get a little bastard of a crowned prince in here.' And I would draw and semi-write that sequence up. Then I would put in on the wall and see how they fit. I'm not a consecutive writer."

Once in a while there is an echo of something like anguish in Geisel's accounts of the workings of his own imagination—some constant, furious homage to the 1902 rifle target, its bullseye perforated by his father's exacting shots, that Geisel keeps mounted on the wall.

"To remind me of perfection," he says.

He will sometimes work late into the night, or break off into an entirely

---

* *The statement that Geisel was "the son of a German immigrant" is incorrect. Geisel's parents were of German extraction, but both were born in America.—T.F.*

different project, when some flaw in a book begins to gnaw at him. He spent a full year struggling over the smallish gopher-like creature called the Lorax. "Once he was mechanized. That didn't work. He was big at one point. I did the obvious thing of making him green, shrinking him, growing him."

And then? "I looked at him and he looked like a Lorax."

But he was equally stumped by the story itself, a dismal tale about the Once-ler, who hacks down all the Truffula Trees to mass-produce Thneeds, thereby driving away the Swomee-Swans, starving out the Brown Bar-ba-loots, and—as the wheezing, outraged Lorax cries—"glumping the pond where the Humming-fish hummed." It was the angriest story Geisel had ever written, and he could not figure out how to make sense of it, how to keep it from turning into a lecture—a preachment," as Geisel says. Geisel has a horror of preachments. Audrey Geisel, who quite rightly believes that the best way to come unstuck is to stand on your head and try looking at things that way, suggested they go to Africa for a while, which they did.

"I hadn't thought of the Lorax for three weeks," Geisel says. "And a herd of elephants came across the hill—about a half mile away—one of those lucky things, that never happened since. And I picked up a laundry pad and wrote the whole book that afternoon on a laundry pad." The final version of *The Lorax* still begins in its ominous, haunting way:

> At the far end of town
> Where the Grickle-grass grows
> And the wind smells slow-and-sour when it blows
> And no birds ever sing excepting old crows...

But it ends with some hope. One Truffula-Tree seed makes it through. And that, for Geisel, redeems the preachment. Happy endings, he has said, are vital: "A child identifies with the hero, and it is a personal tragedy to him when things don't come out all right."

Geisel, in an early fit of misguided inspiration, once wrote a book for adults. "My greatest failure," he says, pulling a rare copy off the bookshelf. "This is a book that nobody bought."

Its thesis is that there were in fact seven Lady Godivas (Gussie, Hedwig, Lulu, Teenie, Mitzi, Arabella, and Dorcas J.), each of them engaged to one of the seven Peeping Brothers. In order to avenge the unfortunate death of their father, who was tossed by an arrogant horse enroute to the Battle of Hastings, the Ladies Godiva set out to discover Horse Truths (don't look a gift horse in the mouth, and so on) while displaying limited but alluring portions of their anatomies.

"I don't think I drew proper naked ladies," Geisel says sadly. "I think their ankles came out wrong, and things like that." The book was published in 1937, priced steeply during the depression at $2 a copy, and less than a quarter of the 10,000 sold. They now go for $100 to $200. Geisel has a private fantasy about making the Godivas into an animated film, but he is not certain about how to present nudity—the ankles, and things like that.

But the bulk of Geisel's audience will always be children. "Writing for adults doesn't really interest me anymore," he said. "I think I've found the form in writing for kids, with which I can say everything I have to say a little more distinctly than if I had to put it in adult prose."

He pulls from a file some typewritten pages from his new book. "You want to try reading one?" Geisel asks.

His visitor, reading slowly, makes a stab at it:

> One year we had a Christmas brunch
> With Merry Christmas Mush to munch.
> But I don't think you'd care for such
> We didn't like to munch mush much.

There is a rather bad moment of tongue-twisting at the end, and Geisel looks delighted. "These things are written way over the ability of first grade kids, and I think it's going to work," he said. "They're stinkers, (the tongue-twisters, not the children.)"

"I think one reason kids are not reading up to their potential is a lack of being urged—you can't urge them with a big stick, but you can urge them with competition."

Well now, demands his visitor, Geisel has to read one.

"Not wearing the right glasses," Geisel says quickly. "I can't."

This is a school administrator writing—a noteworthy point because, inexplicably, few school administrators seem willing to confess to a passion for children's literature of any kind. Taking this strange fact into consideration, this article speaks volumes for the remarkable qualities of Dr. Seuss.

11

How the Grinch Stole Reading: The Serious Nonsense of Dr. Seuss

WARREN T. GREENLEAF
Principal, **May 1982**

They snap. They crackle, And also pop. If the books of other, more staid authors are the oatmeal of children's literature—solid, nourishing, and warm, but not much fun—those of Theodor Seuss Geisel are its Rice Krispies, blending nutrition with a happily explosive morning racket.

There has been a lot of such pleasant noise since 1937, when the first Dr. Seuss—*And to Think That I Saw It on Mulberry Street*—appeared. Geisel has written forty-one books for children; eighty million of them have been sold in forty-five countries. They have been translated into languages as disparate as Japanese, Polish, and Dutch. In addition to making Geisel a millionaire, they have brought him international fame and affection: when he visited Australia some years ago, he was greeted at the airport by hundreds of children and parents and by a headline in the local paper reading, DR. SEUSS HERE. A village in Afghanistan has been informally named Seussville. Rudolf Flesch called him "a genius pure and simple," and Bennett Cerf, the late president of Random House, once said Geisel was the *only* genius on his list—at a time when Cerf was also publishing William Faulkner and John O'Hara. His fan mail is of such proportions that, abandoning any attempt to count it, Random House weighed it instead; one year it totaled 9,267 pounds.

But the books of Dr. Seuss are not simply popular. They are written in dead earnest, with a serious though sketchy theory of reading behind them, and they have been recognized as important contributions to children's literature by people who do not equate best sellers with worthwhile reading. Three of Geisel's books have won the Caldecott Honor award, television specials based on them have won a Peabody and an Emmy, and in 1980, the American Library Association gave Geisel its Laura Ingalls Wilder Award.

How come? What makes these books so special? Why—in view of the hundreds of authors competing for the attention of children—has Theodor Geisel won a place in their hearts that other generations have reserved for Hans Christian Andersen, the Brothers Grimm, and Lewis Carroll?

Part of the answer was suggested by Elaine Banks, NAESP President, when she gave Geisel the association's first Special Award for Distinguished Service to Children at the Atlanta convention. "Few authors have created so much delight for young children as Mr. Geisel," she said. "Since a critical part of helping children achieve literacy is to prove to them that reading can be a source of deep pleasure, we think he deserves credit for having launched millions of youngsters on a lifetime of exploration through books."

The crucial word is *delight*, and one of the distinctive characteristics of the Dr. Seuss books is that they provide delight not only to children, but to adults. As any parent learns, reading to children—pleasant as it may be, and important though it undoubtedly is—can also become a tedious chore. Youngsters tend to become attached to one book at a time, and want to have it read and reread to them constantly; endless renditions of *Johnny Takes a Jet Plane* or *Ruth Visits the Dentist* tempt any parent to turn two pages at once in an effort (often detected by the irate young listener) to hurry a boring tale to its insipid conclusion.

But the Seuss books are written in such an engaging, bump-biddy-bump meter—one writer characterized it as "anapestic tetrameter"—that reading the rhymes aloud is a pleasure. The fact that the rhymes are often outrageous and the Seuss creatures—the Grinch, the Lorax, the Gootch, the Thweril—equally so, helps.

And finally, most of the Seuss books have a plot—usually a daffy one, to be sure, but a real plot with the classical requirement of a beginning, middle, and end.

Take, for example, *The Cat in the Hat Comes Back.* Two children are told to shovel a deep snow from their walk while their mother is downtown. As soon as they begin, the Cat in the Hat appears, bounds through the front door, leaps into the tub and—sitting beneath an umbrella while water pours from both the faucet and the shower—proceeds to eat a piece of cake. This creates a problem, for, when the children rout the Cat and drain the water, there is a bright pink ring around the tub. Not to worry, the Cat assures them:

> "Have no fear of that ring,"
> Laughed the Cat in the Hat.
> "Why, I can take cat rings
> Off tubs. Just like that!"

> Do you know how he did it?
> WITH MOTHER'S WHITE DRESS!
> Now the tub was all clean,
> But her dress was a mess!

In due order, the serenely confident but increasingly inept Cat transfers the pink spot from Mother's dress to the wall to Dad's $10 shoes (this was 1958) to the rug to the bedspread. At this point, viewing the carnage he has wrought, the Cat takes off his Hat.

> "It is good I have some one
> To help me," he said.
> "Right here in my hat
> On the top of my head!
>
> It is good that I have him
> Here with me today.
> He helps me a lot.
> This is Little Cat A."

And, of course, under Little Cat A's hat is Little Cat B, and so forth through an entire roster of diminishing cats until we are presented with Little Cat Z, so tiny he is invisible. While the other Cats have succeeded only in transferring the pink stain from the house to the snow outside, Little Cat Z has under *his* hat the ultimate detergent: something called Voom.

> Now, don't ask me what Voom is.
> I never will know.
> But, boy! Let me tell you
> It DOES clean up snow!

With the house and the snow spotless once more—Geisel always insists on a happy ending—the Cat departs with brothers A through Z all tucked back in his Hat, but volunteering to return with them if the children ever have spots again. The book's last page is a rhymed recitation of the alphabet —and the entire, wacky tale is told in 253 different words, all (except for Voom) culled from primers used by beginning readers.

The Cat in the Hat Comes Back exemplifies Dr. Seuss's best plots, as well as some of his convictions about crafting a book for children. A simple, straightforward situation unfolds, step by rational step, into a cumulative uproar that is then suddenly, easily, and satisfyingly resolved—just before tragedy strikes, or Mom walks in the front door. "Logical insanity," Geisel says of his plots. And though he despises what he calls "preachments," many of his stories have a moral. In *Horton Hears a Who!*, an elephant protects a colony of creatures so tiny that they have built an entire city—complete with town hall, mayor, tennis courts, and a bubbling fountain—on a single speck of dust. "After all," says Horton, "a person's a person. No matter how small." A reviewer for the *Des Moines Register* described *Horton* as "a rhymed lesson in the protection of minorities and their rights." And the Grinch—as most of us will remember from the televised version, if not the book—experienced a change of heart and returned all the presents he had stolen when he discovered that Christmas for the Whos down in Whoville consisted not in receiving things, but in expressing their love for each other.

As to technique, Geisel believes in pairing words and pictures: everything mentioned in the text must be illustrated, and there must be no more than one illustration to a page. Though all the words in his books for beginning readers were originally taken from approved lists, he has since dispensed with a list, both for his own work and that of the authors he guides as president and editor of Beginner Books, a division of Random House. "We just try to say what we have to say simply and concisely," he explains. "Adults minimize the speed and the desire children have for learning. Children can do at three or four what is expected from them at six or seven." Television, he believes, has vastly expanded children's vocabularies, making it possible for authors to use words that rarely appear in primers.

Drawing for a Living

Geisel found his work in life through a roundabout route—and a lucky accident. Born in Springfield, Massachusetts, in 1904 to parents of German descent—his mother's maiden name was Seuss—Geisel attended the local public schools and entered Dartmouth with the class of 1925. While in college, he edited the Dartmouth humor magazine and drew cartoons for it— many involving weird animals. He initially planned to go into teaching, but abandoned the idea after a year at Oxford convinced him that he had little interest and no future in scholarship.

At Oxford, too, he met another American student, Helen Palmer. Observing his enthusiasm for cartooning, she convinced him that his real calling lay there, not in the classroom. After selling two cartoons to *Judge*, a humor magazine of the time, Geisel returned to the United States, married Miss Palmer, and took the plunge into drawing for a living.

He was soon doing well enough, selling cartoons to various magazines, to support himself and his bride in an apartment on Park Avenue. His income was further boosted when he drew a cartoon for *Judge* depicting a knight whose bedroom had been invaded by a dragon. "Darn it all," says the knight, "another dragon. And just after I'd sprayed the whole castle with Flit!"

Nothing uproarious today, certainly—but an advertising man for Standard Oil, which produced the insecticide, spotted the cartoon, and signed Geisel to a contract. For seventeen years he drew advertisements for Standard, most with the caption—famous in the 1930s and 40s—"Quick, Henry! The Flit!"

Successful as he was commercially, however, Geisel still had a yen to do something more than ephemeral cartoons. He wanted to produce a book, drawings *and* text. His inspiration came in 1936 when, returning from Europe, his attention was captured by the rhythm of the ship's engines—much as the rest of us hear a song, start humming it in our minds, and then can't get rid of it. In an effort to chase the annoying beat from his head, Geisel put words to it.

The result was *And to Think That I Saw It on Mulberry Street,* a tale about a boy named Marco who—under orders from his father to observe what he sees on the way home from school, and then report—notices only a horse pulling a broken-down wagon. Since that's not much of a sight, the boy begins embellishing, so that he will have a *real* tale for his father; by the time he arrives home, the horse and wagon have become a brass band drawn by an elephant and two giraffes, led by a police motorcycle escort past a reviewing stand filled with applauding city officials, while an airplane dumps out bushels of confetti.

But after twenty publishing houses rejected the manuscript, Geisel had just about abandoned it when, walking down the left side of Madison Avenue one day, he encountered a friend from Dartmouth. The friend, Geisel learned, had just been appointed editor of juvenile books for Vanguard Press—and he was looking for manuscripts.

Dr. Seuss was on his way. "If I'd been walking down the *right* side of Madison Avenue," Geisel has pointed out, "I'd be in the dry-cleaning business today."

Though *Mulberry Street* appeared in 1937 and was followed by a number of other well-known Seusses in the 1940s and early 50s—including *Horton, The Grinch,* and *The 500 Hats of Bartholomew Cubbins*—the popular success of the books was far from matching the critical acclaim they had received. As late as 1954, Geisel was earning less than $5,000 a year from royalties, and wondered if he could ever improve on that so-so figure.

But in 1954, too, John Hersey, author of *A Bell for Adano* and several other books, wrote an article in *Life* magazine, complaining about the dreariness of children's primers. Someone like Dr. Seuss—whose books had so far been written for children who had already learned to read—should take a crack at producing livelier fare for beginning readers, Hersey argued.

Geisel accepted the challenge—and found it more formidable than he had anticipated. He had not realized until then that primers had limited vocabularies, and he initially doubted that he could put together a tale within such verbal confines that would still be good verse. But he made lists of words that appeared in the primers of the day, arranged them in rhymed ranks, and started.

Three years later, in 1957, *The Cat in the Hat* appeared—and Geisel had a swift answer to his doubts about earning more than $5,000 a year. By 1961, *The Cat* had sold a million copies, and had produced a gross financial return rivaled until then by only two paperbacks: *God's Little Acre* and *Peyton Place.* Moreover, *The Cat* pulled up sales of the other Dr. Seuss books; *Horton Hatches the Egg,* which sold only 5,801 copies when it appeared in 1940, sold 27,000 copies the year after *The Cat* was published, and quickly hit the 200,000 mark.

Today, forty-five years after the thrumming of a ship's engines nagged him into writing his first book for children, Theodor Geisel lives in La Jolla, California, with his second wife, Audrey, whom he married in 1967, after the death of Helen Palmer Geisel. Though Mrs. Geisel has two children by a previous marriage, Geisel has never had any. Which is just as well, he has always claimed: it would be difficult to write books for children if you had a bunch of them looking over your shoulder. "You have 'em, I'll amuse 'em."

And, at 78, Geisel is still trying to amuse them. Though he long ago earned more than enough money to sit back and enjoy his Grinch-gotten gains, he continues fighting his perfectionist's battle at his drafting table in an old observatory on the top of a mountain overlooking the Pacific. A new Dr. Seuss, titled *Hunches in Bunches,* will appear this fall.

Geisel's successes exceed even those mentioned here. He won an Academy Award in 1946 for a film documentary written while serving in the Army Signal Corps during World War II, received another in 1947 for a documentary on the Japanese people, written in collaboration with Helen Palmer Geisel, and yet another in 1951 for *Gerald McBoing-Boing,* an animated cartoon featuring a child who could not speak, but could only emit sound-effects. In typical happy-ending fashion, the problem child, who has worried his parents and baffled psychiatrists, goes to Hollywood and wins fortune and fame by producing the sounds of pounding hooves, creaking doors, and gunshots for Westerns.

In all Geisel's career, in fact, it is hard to find any endeavor at which he has failed.

Yet there was one—a book called *The Seven Lady Godivas,* published in 1937. The tale, about seven nude Godivas pursued by seven brothers whose last name was Peeping (and one, of course, whose first name was Tom), sold only 2,500 copies. The problem, Geisel concluded, may have been draftsmanship. "I tried to draw the sexiest-looking women I could, and they came out just ridiculous."

The real problem, of course, lies much deeper than that. *The Seven Lady Godivas* is the one and only book Geisel has ever written for adults, and adults don't interest him. "Adults are just obsolete children, and to hell with 'em."

His father was an international rifle champion, and Geisel has on the wall of his home beneath the observatory tower a framed target that his father fired at in a 1902 competition; the bull's-eye is virtually obliterated by holes. "That," Geisel says, "is to remind me of perfection."

One feels sure that Geisel *père* would have admired his son's marksmanship.

Jonathan Cott traces the history of children's literature and ends at Geisel's La Jolla doorstep for an enchanting visit with Dr. Seuss.

Cott's book Pipers at the Gates of Dawn *contained lengthy chapters about "six extraordinary creators of children's literature": Seuss, Maurice Sendak, William Steig, Astrid Lindgren, Chindua Achebe, and P.L. Travers.*

"Pipers at the Gates of Dawn" *was a chapter title in Kenneth Grahame's* The Wind in the Willows.

12

The Good Dr. Seuss

JONATHAN COTT

from *Pipers at the Gates of Dawn: The Wisdom of Children's Literature*, 1983

On June 18, 1744, the following advertisement appeared on the back page of the *Penny London Morning Advertiser:*

> This Day is publish'd According to Act of Parliament (Neatly bound and gilt) A LITTLE PRETTY POCKET BOOK, intended for the Instruction and Amusement of little Master Tommy and pretty Miss Polly; with an agreeable Letter to each from *Jack the Giant-Killer;* as also a Ball and Pincushion, the Use of which will infallibly make Tommy a good Boy and Polly a good Girl.
> To the Whole is prefix'd, A Lecture on Education, humbly address'd to all Parents, Guardians, Governesses, etc.; wherein Rules are laid down for making their Children strong, hardy, healthy, virtuous, wise, and happy ...
> Printed for J. Newbery, at the *Bible and Crown*, near Devereux Court, without Temple Bar. Price of the Book alone 6d., with Ball or Pincushion 8d.

In England up until the eighteenth century, most reading matter for children consisted of grammars, primers, catechisms, lesson and courtesy books, and other edifying works emphasizing religious, moral, and scholastic concerns. But what boys and girls loved most of all, of course—then as now—were the fables, romances, ballads, and old wives' tales that children shared with adults as part of an irrepressible oral and popular literary tradition. "Keep them from reading of fayned fables, vayne fantasies, and wanton stories and songs of love, which bring much mischiefe to youth," advised Hugh Rhodes in his *Boke of Nurture* (1545), foreshadowing similar types of warnings that were to be promulgated during the following four centuries by innumerable educators, moralists, and critics.

After the excrescence in the seventeenth century of the malignant "Joyful Deaths" tradition of life-denying Puritan children's books ("Are the Souls of your Children of no Value?" asked the children's author James Janeway. "They are not too little to die, they are not too little to go to Hell"), it is a comfort to be able to point to the publication of *A Little Book for Little Children* (c. 1705) by a certain "T.W."—a short reading and spelling book, meant to instruct "in a plain and pleasant way," which featured verses, riddles, and tiny woodcuts illustrating, for example, the famous nursery rhyme beginning: "A was an Archer, and shot at a frog,/ B was a Blindman, and led by a dog." Then, in the early 1740s, there appeared Thomas Boreman's *Gigantick Histories* (a series of two-inch high books for children that, among other things, told the story of Gog and Magog, the two giants of the Guildhall, and described the Tower of London, St. Paul's, and Westminster Abbey), as well as works such as T. Cooper's *The Child's New Play-thing* (which featured alphabet rhymes, fables, songs, proverbs, and shortened versions of medieval tales about St. George and Guy of Warwick), and Mary Cooper's *Tommy Thumb's Song-Book* (the first nursery rhyme collection for children).

Although it drew heavily on the innovative form and content of its predecessors, *A Little Pretty Pocket-Book* is today regarded as an historic milestone in the development of children's literature. Its creator was a clever entrepreneur. Born in 1713, John Newbery was the son of a Berkshire farmer, and when he was about sixteen he was apprenticed to a printer whose widow he eventually married and with whom he moved to London in 1744. From then until his death in 1767, he designed, produced, marketed, and sold about thirty books for children—all issued anonymously or under alliterative pseudonyms (Abraham Aesop, Tommy Trapwit, Tom Telescope). Some of the books, it is surmised, were written by persons such as Oliver Goldsmith, Christopher Smart, and, perhaps, Newbery himself. Conjointly with his publishing ventures, Newbery was merchandising gingerbread for children, as well as nostrums and remedies—Cephalic Snuff, Dr. Hooper's Female Pills, and Dr. James's Fever Powder for adults. (In Newbery's children's novel *Goody Two-Shoes* the heroine's father, we are informed, dies for lack of Dr. James's Powder!)

A Little Pretty Pocket-Book was Newbery's first publication; like most of those that followed, it was small (about four by two-and-a-half inches) and attractively attired with a cover of Dutch floral paper. Unlike Boreman's or the Coopers' books, Newbery's little volume was "profusely illustrated," as we would say today (it contained fifty-eight rough woodcuts in a text of ninety pages); in content, it was a kind of gallimaufry, consisting of a letter from Jack the Giant-Killer, an advertisement, an alphabet, verses about games and play, proverbs, four Aesopian fables, and a "Poetical Description of the Four

Seasons." Following the educational theories of John Locke (who vowed that children should "play themselves into what others are whipp'd for"), Newbery insisted that learning be made pleasurable, not onerous. It was obviously an idea whose time had officially come. For with this book—which was in its twelfth edition by 1767—Newbery single-handedly created (or discovered) the children's book market. And, as with most pioneers, he ingenuously set the patterns—in terms of subjects, themes, and approaches—that children's book creators and publishers would later develop.

Among Newbery's publications were alphabet, spelling, and riddle books; collections of fables and poems; histories; novels—especially the popular *The History of Little Goody Two-Shoes;* a ten-volume compendium of knowledge for boys and girls known as *The Circle of Sciences;* a science text containing fact and fiction entitled *The Newtonian System of Philosophy;* and possibly the first children's magazine, *The Lilliputian Magazine.* His books are filled with amusingly named characters like Tommy Trip, Zig Zag, and Giles Gingerbread; and with friendly animals like Tippy the lark, Jouler the dog, and Willy the lamb. But aside from his informal publishing approach, John Newbery could barely disguise his Lockean-derived notion that amusement and delight were simply the sugar-coated ingredients of a cachet (think of Giles Gingerbread, who learned his letters by eating them!),the medicinal purpose of which was to foster an acceptance of a conservative social order and a mercantile ideology. And Newbery's books do nothing less than idolize, as they help define, middle-class values. He advised young boys to learn to read well so that they might be rewarded with a "Coach and Six"; to young girls he promised that virtuous behavior would result in their becoming "Ladies of the Manor." The qualities and virtues he valued and promoted were those of dutifulness, moderation, self-control, rationality, sobriety, prudence, and industry. His motto: "Trade and Plumbcake forever, Huzza!"

Almost two hundred years later, in 1936, a cartoonist, illustrator, and writer named Theodor Geisel was walking along Madison Avenue, carrying the manuscript of a children's book that had already been rejected by twenty-seven publishers, when he ran into a Dartmouth schoolmate, one year his junior. Marshall McClintock had just the day before become juvenile editor of Vanguard Press, and this fortuitous reunion resulted in the publishing of *And to Think That I Saw It on Mulberry Street* (1937), a book credited to Geisel's nom de plume "Dr. Seuss" (Seuss was Geisel's middle, and his mother's maiden, name; the "Dr." his self-appointed title, saving his real name for his "still forthcoming"—as he laughingly puts it—Great American Novel).

John Newbery—great admirer of pseudonyms and of commercial enterprise that he was—would have undoubtedly admired the panache with which Theodor Geisel entered the publishing marketplace. But he would have been appalled by Dr. Seuss's first children's book, and would certainly have identified himself with the father of the book's imaginative hero, Marco:

When I leave home to walk to school,
Dad always says to me,
"Marco, keep your eyelids up
And see what you can see."
But when I tell him where I've been
And what I think I've seen,
He looks at me and sternly says,
"Your eyesight's much to keen.
"Stop telling such outlandish tales.
Stop turning minnows into whales."

"Now, what can I say/ When I get home today?" Marco asks himself. And in the course of his walk home from school, he notices a now-immortalized dumpy horse and wagon—"That *can't* be my story. That's only a *start*"—and transforms it into what, added detail by added detail, eventually becomes a howdah-caparisoned blue elephant marching astride two crocked-looking yellow giraffes pulling a seven-piece brass band and attached pixilated-old codger-inhabited trailer to the admiring salutes and cheers of flag-waving governmental dignitaries—the entire police-escorted parade entourage showered by brightly colored confetti emptied from red and white baskets by two jaunty men on the top of a low-flying, whirring motor plane.... But when Marco gets home and his frowning, prosaic father asks him what he has seen that day, he gives his only possible reply: "'Nothing,' I said, growing red as a beet,/ 'But a plain horse and wagon on Mulberry Street'."

"Useless trumpery" is the way John Locke condemned fairy tales, ballads, and chapbook romances in the eighteenth century; his disciple John Newbery might have applied the same epithet to Marco's Mulberry Street hallucinations, as well as to the book that preserves them. But just as *A Little Pretty Pocket-Book* opened up new possibilities for children's literature in its time, so did *Mulberry Street* in ours. One could say that while Newbery created the children's book industry in England, Dr. Seuss—two centuries after its inception—has, astonishingly, been able to create his own microcosmic publishing universe: Walk into most children's bookstores today and you will find sections devoted to "Fairy Tales," "Picture Books," and "Dr. Seuss." He has become a genre, a category, an institution; more than eighty million of his books have been sold around the world.

"What exactly is it that makes this stuff immortal?" asked Rudolf Flesch (author of *Why Johnny Can't Read*) about Dr. Seuss's work. "There is something about it," Flesch tried to explain. "A swing to the language, a deep understanding of the playful mind of a child, an undefinable something that makes Dr. Seuss a genius pure and simple."

And to Think That I Saw It on Mulberry Street immediately provides several other answers to Flesch's question, striking as it does the characteristic Seussian chord and rhythm, and ringing their changes. There is, first of all, the unflagging momentum, feeling of breathlessness, and swiftness of pace, all together acting as the motor for Dr. Seuss's pullulating image machine that brings to life—through rhymes and pictures—what William James describes as our earliest experiences of the world ("The baby, assailed by eyes, ears, nose, skin, and entrails at once, feels that all is one great blooming, buzzing confusion"), as well as what, more specifically, Selma G. Lanes calls "Marco's rapidly expanding universe." All of this expansiveness expresses itself through Seuss's unique, children's-drawing style of illustration and through a theme-and-variations technique (the theme is usually that of searching for, discovering, or inventing something *new*) that the author uses in many of his books, including *Scrambled Eggs Super!* (in which the hero cook searches for new and different birds whose eggs will create a unique mélange) and *On Beyond Zebra!* (in which the hero creates a new alphabet beyond the letter Z with invented animals representing each new letter). It is a technique that features the use of visual exaggeration. "I think that when ideas are first differentiated by children," says Brian Sutton-Smith—professor of education and folklore at the University of Pennsylvania—"they have to be caricatured. There has to be an exaggerated form of a thing in order to get it out of the background, in order to differentiate the figure from the ground—whether you're talking about an idea or a picture. You can't, for example, do jigsaws unless you make the edges really clear. And Dr. Seuss uses exaggeration all the time."

In *Mulberry Street,* Dr. Seuss's illustrations are less exaggerated than they would become several years later—as in the books mentioned above—but you can already observe incipient signs of this tendency in the way he portrays the bibulous faces of his animals—zebras, reindeer, giraffes, and elephants. (His creatures, as poet and critic Karla Kushin aptly observes, all have "slightly batty, oval eyes and a smile you might find on the Mona Lisa after her first martini.") Indeed, more than any other children's book artist—except perhaps for Edward Lear (think of the Dong with a Luminous Nose and the Quangle Wangle)—Dr. Seuss has created the most extraordinary variety of ingeniously named, fantastical-looking animals and composite beasts. (One might have imagined that it could *only* have been Dr. Seuss who had thought up and named the zedonk—the animal produced when a male zebra mates with a female donkey!) Looking at preternatural creations such as Seuss's Foona-Lagoona Baboona and the Nutches—as well as his elephant-bird (*Horton Hatches the Egg*) and fish-cow (*McElligot's Pool*)—one is reminded of the zoomorphic creatures universally imagined by artists in all parts of the world. Seuss-like animals are suggested by, for example, the tao-tieh of the Chinese Bronze Age, and by the hybrid creatures known as the shen—the ancient Chinese mountain gods; by the ant-lion (lion in front, ant in back) and the eales or yales (with tails like an elephant's and the jowls of a boar) of the fourth-century *Physiologus,* medieval bestiaries, and Topsell's seventeenth-century *The Historie of Fourefooted Beastes;* and by the imaginary animals of the sixteenth century Father André Thevet and of the six-year-old English girl, Sybil Corbet, who, in 1897, published them in a book entitled *Animal Land Where There Are No People.*

Also extremely characteristic of Seuss's work—in this and almost all of his other books—is his habitual use of anapestic tetrameter verse. Geisel claims that in 1936, when he was returning from Europe on an ocean liner, he became entranced by the rhythm of the ship's engines: "Da da *da,* da de *dum* dum de *da* de de *da.*" The words that to him seemed to match the boat's beat were: "And to think that I saw it on Mulberry Street"—the line that set him off writing and illustrating the book, and was a promise of the musical energy and excitement to be found in all of Dr. Seuss's poetry. For the anapest line embodies movement and swiftness, as in: "Oh, he flies through the air with the greatest of ease" and "O who rides by night thro' the woodland so wild?"

This last line is Sir Walter Scott's translation of the opening words of Goethe's famous "The Erl-King" (Scott used anapestic tetrameter to imitate Goethe's anapest-weighted *Knüttelvers).* It is a poem, both in the original German and in Scott's translation, that acts on its readers and listeners like a dream, with its forceful depiction of a father embracing his dying son as they ride feverishly through the woods. Yet what is worth mentioning here is that, as their journey progresses, the son and his father engage in a dialogue much like that between Marco and *his* father:

> "O father, see yonder! see yonder!" he says;
> "My boy, upon what dost thou fearfully gaze?"
> "O, 'tis the Erl-King with his crown and his shroud."
> "No, my son, it is but a dark wreath of the cloud."...
>
> "O father, my father, and did you not hear
> The Erl-King whisper so low in my ear?"
> "Be still, my heart's darling—my child, bet at ease;
> It was but the wild blast as it sung thro' the trees."...
>
> "O father, my father, and saw you not plain
> The Erl-King's pale daughter glide past thro' the rain?"
> "O yes, my loved treasure, I knew it full soon;
> It was the gray willow that danced to the moon."...

Although the poem resonates on many levels, it might be taken to suggest that the denial of one's powers of fantasy and imagination (both share the same image-generating roots) is a form of death. John Newbery and his contemporaries, one remembers, wished to crush children's imaginative powers and the literature that nourished them. One eighteenth-century writer even boasted that writing for children required one "to restrain a lively imagination," a "sort of heroic sacrifice of gratification to virtue, which I cannot doubt is acceptable to the Supreme Being."

In this century, of course, many artists, educators, and psychologists have adamantly taken a stand strongly in favor of fantasy ("Whenever we are caught in a literal view," states the depth psychologist James Hillman, "a literal belief, a literal statement, we have lost the imaginative metaphysical perspective to ourselves and our world"). But such disparate figures as Einstein and Lenin have also affirmed the important of fantasy. As the former once said: "When I examine myself and my methods of thought, I come to the conclusion that the gift of fantasy has meant more to me than any talent for abstract, positive thinking." And as the latter stated: "It is incorrect to think that fantasy is useful only to the poet. This is an insipid prejudice! It is useful even in mathematics—even differential and integral calculus could not have been discovered without it. Fantasy is a quality of the highest importance." And it was another Russian—the children's poet and educator Kornei Chukovsky—who spoke of the child's "rights" to fairy tales and nonsense verse. "Fantasy," he said, "is the most valuable attribute of the human mind, and it should be diligently nurtured from earliest childhood." And he offered the following little case study:

> The well-known children's author, T. A. Bogdanovich, was brought up by another children's author, Aleksandra Annenskaia. Under the influence of the "enlightenment" of the Sixties [of the nineteenth century], she so zealously protected the little girl from the *skazka* [the folk tale] that she even hesitated to hire a *niania* for her, fearing that the nurse would tell the child fairy tales. Only educational books were read to the child—mainly books on botany and zoölogy. But, at night, when the governess finally fell asleep, the child, at last free from the constant supervision, filled her room with all kinds of creatures. Monkeys scampered all over her bed. A fox and her babies suddenly appeared on her table. Strange birds nested in her clothes left folded near her bed, and she talked to these visitors for a long time.

And this last nighttime scene might well be the prototype for the plot of *There's a Wocket in My Pocket!*—a book featuring the appearance of some of Dr. Seuss's most outrageous bedtime companions.

"It is central to the Seuss formula," writes Selma G. Lanes in *Down the Rabbit Hole*, "that the action of all his books with children as protagonists takes place either (1) in the absence of grownups, or (2) in the imagination"—usually in both at the same time, one might add. In *If I Ran the Circus*, the young hero Morris McGurk finds that "the most wonderful spot" for imagining his circus is behind Sneelock's Store "in the big vacant lot"—confirming Iona and Peter Opie's suspicion that "the places [children] like best for play are the secret places 'where no one else goes'." As the Opies write in *Children's Games in Street and Playground:* "The literature of childhood abounds with evidence that the peaks of a child's experience are not visits to a cinema, or even family outings to the sea, but occasions when he escapes into places that are disused and overgrown and silent. To a child there is more joy in a rubbish tip than a flowering rockery, in a fallen tree than a piece of statuary, in a muddy track than a gravel path."

Imagination, said Wordsworth, "Is but another name for absolute power/ And clearest insight, amplitude of mind,/ And Reason in her most exalted mood." He also knew that it was an "awful Power" which "rose from the mind's abyss/ Like an unfathered vapour," usurping the light of the senses. In the story "The Glunk that got Thunk," for example, from *I Can Lick 30 Tigers Today! and Other Stories,* the heroine uses her Thinker-Upper to create the monstrous and obstreperous green Glunk and finds that she can't easily "unthunk" him. "Our true element extends without shores, without boundaries," asserts the Italian writer Italo Calvino, affirming what both artists and scientists have always known. (As the hero of *On Beyond Zebra!* says: "In the places I go there are things that I see/ That I *never* could spell if I stopped with the Z.") But imagination, in the mind of an obliquitous or greedy person (like the king in *Bartholomew and the Oobleck* who brings down ruin from the sky in the form of an all-entangling, sticky, gluey, viscous slime), can be a dangerous power. Yet it is a necessary one. Imagination allows for and creates the possibility for things to happen and to change, freeing us from the genetic programming of specific behavior patterns (and making life less boring in the process). As Brian Sutton-Smith remarked in a conversation with me:

> I think that Dr. Seuss is packaging flexibility and possibility, and it's a new kind of thing in children's literature, which used to be much more staid. His books reflect a recognition—at least implicitly by intelligent people—that flexibility of thinking and brightness and associations and combinations, etc., are what mental development is about these days—it's as much a part of achievement as anything else. The notion that you can capture people's souls just by pressing the basics on them is nonsense and terrifying and stupid.... Seuss breaks barriers. What happens is that some person like him comes along who's intuitively a bit more in touch with the younger generation, he's nearer to his childhood and he expands the danger zones a little; and because kids love it, gradually parents come to accept it. It's the *adults* who have to be confronted.

And as Theodor Geisel has often said: "Adults are only obsolete children, so the hell with them!"

"You're going to see the good Doctor?" asked the cabdriver cheerily as we drove up the La Jolla hills to Theodor Geisel's home. "He's full of character and brings joy—unlike most doctors!" the driver adds. "My children love his books, and so do I."

It was July of 1980, and a typically beautiful southern California morning—sunshine, warm breezes, and a perfect blue sky—the kind of weather that makes you feel as if you've finally arrived in Dr. Seuss's mythical city of Solla Sollew, "where they *never* have troubles! At least, very few" (*I Had Trouble in Getting to Solla Sollew*).

The good Doctor met me at the gate, with a twinkle in his eye and sporting a white beard that reminded me of the high-spirited, white-bearded figure pictured in the trailer in *Mulberry Street*, who oversees the wondrous, multi-spangled parade scene with exorbitant delight. I told Geisel about the cab-driver's exuberant characterization of him, which he appeared pleased by, saying modestly and with a smile, "I'm probably just a good tipper."

He led me through the front door of his spacious, pink-stucco house built around a converted watchtower overlooking La Jolla and the Pacific—a house he shares with his second wife, Audrey, and Sam (short for Samantha), a twelve-inch Yorkshire terrier almost as tiny as a Who. Geisel took me into the living room, and we sat down and began to chat.

He pointed through the window to the dozens of sailboats out on the Pacific below, saying, "Those are some of my retired friends down there, but retirement's not for me! [Geisel was seventy-six when I saw him in 1980.] For me, success means doing work that you love, regardless of how much you make. I go into my office almost every day and give it eight hours—though every day isn't productive, of course. And just now," he added, putting on a pair of glasses, "I've slowed down because of my second cataract operation. It was impossible for me to mix a palette—I didn't know which colors were which. With my cataract I had two color schemes—red became orange, blue became slightly greenish: my left eye was like Whistler and the right one was like Picasso—seeing things straight and clear in primitive colors."

"I was just thinking of your book *I Can Read with My Eyes Shut!*" I said, "with those lines: 'If you keep/ your eyes open enough,/ oh, the stuff you will learn!... Keep them wide open.../ at least on one side'."

"That book was dedicated to my surgeon, by the way," Geisel replied, smiling. "Now I have to learn to focus my pen—it'll take about a month.... I realized I was getting blind when I was at the Hilton Hotel in Las Vegas. It has this tremendous runway, and forty naked women on Harley-Davidsons came right by us; my friend asked me what I thought of the women, and I could only see the motorcycles!"

"Your first published book was called *The Seven Lady Godivas*,"* I mentioned.

"It came out in 1937, in the Depression," Geisel said, "and nobody bought any copies at all—they were remaindered at Schulte's cigar store at a quarter a piece; today they go for about three hundred dollars. It's a book that proved that there were seven Lady Godivas who happened to be engaged to the seven Peeping brothers. The seven daughters weren't frivolous or anything like that ... they just happened not to have clothes on, and they couldn't marry the

---

* The Seven Lady Godivas *was published in 1939, but there were two, or possibly three, Seuss books published previously.* And to Think That I Saw It on Mulberry Street *was published in 1937;* The 500 Hats of Bartholomew Cubbins *was published in 1938 and* The King's Stilts *was published the same year as* Godivas, *1939. —T.F.*

Peeping brothers until each of the girls had discovered a horse truth: you shouldn't put the cart before the horse, you shouldn't change horses in midstream, et cetera.... The book was embarrassing to many librarians—it got onto the children's bookshelves, and they had to take it out."

"I'd imagine children would have loved it!" I commented.

"They did! That was the problem."

"You once said that your career began at the zoo. What did you mean by that?" I asked.

"When I was young," Geisel explained, "I used to go to the zoo a lot, and when I returned home I would try to draw the animals.... You see, my father, among other things, ran a zoo in Springfield, Massachusetts. He was a guy who became president of a Springfield brewery the day Prohibition was declared (this was wartime prohibition). So he became very cynical and sat for days in the living room saying 'S.O.B., S.O.B.' over and over—he didn't know what to do with himself. But he had been honorary head of the Parks Department, and there had been a mix-up with the books and he had to straighten them out. At that time the superintendent left the park system, so my father took the job permanently. And at a salary of five thousand dollars a year he became a philanthropist. He built tennis courts, trout streams, three golf courses, bowling greens—he changed people's lives more than he would have done if he'd been a millionaire; he used WPA funds and government money to put people to work. So he ended up as a very worthwhile guy."

"Imagine what you might have conceived in that position!" I said.

"I would have been fired if I'd had that job!"

"Would your father have been critical or approving of Marco's imaginative powers in *Mulberry Street*?" I wondered.

"My mother would have loved it," he said. "My father would have been critical. But he was a remarkable man. Let me tell you a story: My father's hero was a person named Cyril Gaffey Aschenbach, who had been captain of the first Dartmouth football team that beat Harvard. When I lived in New York City, I mentioned to my father that Cyril lived near me. So one night we all had dinner together. My father would ask all night long: Tell me how you scored that winning touchdown. And Cyril would say: 'Look at these sconces, they're two hundred and fifty years old'—all he talked about was antiques. So when my father was heading back to Springfield, he said, 'I'm going to send you an antique that will shut Cyril Gaffey Aschenbach up forever!' He found a dinosaur footprint—a two-hundred-and-fifty pound slab showing three toes—which is hanging outside next to the swimming pool— you can see it through the window. It was found around Holyoke, Massachusetts, near a shale pit. My father sent it to me in New York in a truck, but on the way down he stopped off at Yale and had it appraised—and he found out that it was a hundred and fifty million years old.

"My father, as you see, had an unusual sense of humor. And every time

I've moved I've taken that footprint with me: It keeps me from getting conceited. Whenever I think I'm pretty good, I just go out and look at it. Half the people I show it to think I've made it myself."

"The Glunk might have made a similar footprint," I suggested.

"I think they're related," Geisel was happy to agree. He pointed to a shelf across the room on which were resting various baked-clay imaginary animals. "They were made a couple of hundred miles from Kabul, Afghanistan," he told me, "at a place the American diplomats call Dr. Seussville—they've had this craft going on for a thousand years. Someone at the embassy sent me these weird animals—a lot of two-headed beasts."

"'Where *do* you suppose he gets things like that from?/ His animals all have such very odd faces./ I'll bet he must hunt them in rather odd places!'" I said, quoting from *If I Ran the Zoo*. "What is it with you and the animals?" I asked him.

"Let's just say I find them more compatible than most people," he said, smiling.

In reading a number of articles about Geisel, I'd discovered that he had been drawing "his" animals since his childhood days at the zoo; had done animal cartoons for Dartmouth's humor magazine *Jack-o-Lantern*, which he edited for a while, as well as for magazines such as *Judge, Vanity Fair,* and *Saturday Evening Post*; had doodled winged horses in his class notebooks at Oxford; had painted pictures of donkeys for a month in Corsica after leaving academia; had used animals for his political cartoons for *P.M.* magazine—depicting a Nazi as a dachshund, Pierre Laval as a louse on Hitler's finger—as well as for his famous advertising cartoons that accompanied his "Quick, Henry! The Flit!" insect-spray caption; and had created many bizarre animals for Standard Oil billboards, including the Moto-Munchus, the Oilio-Gobelus, and the Zerodoccus. As a child once wrote to him: "Dr. Seuss, you have an imagination with a long tail!"

"My style of drawing animals," Geisel now explained, "derives from the fact that I don't know how to draw. I began drawing pictures as a child—as I mentioned before—trying, let's say, to get as close to a lion as possible; people would laugh, so I decided to go for the laugh. I can't draw normally. I *think* I could draw normally if I wanted to, but I see no reason to re-create something that's already created. If I'd gone to art school I'd never have been successful. In fact, I did attend one art class in high school. And at one point during the class I turned the painting I was working on upside down—I didn't exactly know what I was doing, but actually I was checking the balance: If something is wrong with the composition upside down, then something's wrong with it the other way. And the teacher said, 'Theodor, real artists don't turn their paintings upside down.' It's the only reason I went on—to prove that teacher wrong.

"I'm fascinated by all kinds of animals. When I was at Oxford, I read

The Travels of Sir John Mandeville, which describes weird animals and a race of people who lived in a desert; they had enormous feet, which they put up in the air over their heads to give them shade. I was bogged down in Old High German, and Mandeville sort of opened up a door for me. That's one reason I left Oxford—in order to go in that direction.

"I met a professor there who suggested that I leave Oxford and come study with him in Paris. He was a Jonathan Swift scholar, and I thought he had a bright, original mind. So I packed up and went to the Sorbonne. I had fifteen minutes with him in his study, and I almost went crazy; instead of the wild, exciting things I expected to be studying, he asked me to investigate whether Swift wrote anything between the ages of sixteen and a half and seventeen—something like that—and I was to research all the obscure libraries in England, Scotland, and Ireland to find out. And, I said, supposing I found out that he didn't write anything? Well, the professor said, you will have had a lovely time in Paris and in traveling. That was when I booked myself on a cattle boat to Corsica—it was my final revolt against academicism."

"I wanted to bring up a slightly 'academic' point of my own"—I hesitated—"about the possibility of *Mulberry Street* and Goethe's 'The Erl-King' being somewhat similar, for both of them are about a father and a son and about the exigencies and power of the imagination."

"It's interesting you say that," Geisel replied, as he broke into German: "*Wer reitet so spät durch Nacht und Wind?/Es ist der Vater mit seinem Kind....* I was brought up in a German-speaking home, I minored in German in college, and I learned 'The Erl-King'—I still remember those first two lines—when I was still in high school. It could tie up, though I never thought of it before. It's very odd that you discovered that ... I've learned something. Back to the psychiatrist's couch!"

"I was wondering what books you read as a child," I said. "I've brought along a few pages from two books about freedom-loving creatures that I thought might have influenced you a bit—Palmer Cox's *Brownies: Their Book* and Gelett Burgess's *Goops and How to Be Them.*"

"Both books were very popular when I was a kid," Geisel replied. "My parents bought them and I read and loved them, though I haven't seen them for years. They bring back a lot. The Goops were a little too moralistic for me, but I loved the Brownies—they were wonderful little creatures; in fact, they probably awakened my desire to draw.

"I also remember liking Wilhelm Busch's *Max and Moritz;* and when I was six or seven years old I read Peter Newell's *The Hole Book,* which I remember very well. It had a die cut through the whole thing, from the cover to the end, and it began: 'Tom Potts was fooling with a gun/ (Such follies should not be),/ When—bang! the pesky thing went off/ Most unexpectedly!' And it followed the course of that bullet, which went through a hot-water boiler—and the house got flooded—then through ropes people were swinging on ...

it just raised hell. And it ended with what was then considered to be one of the funniest things in the world: The bullet hit a cake made by a bride, and the cake was so hard that the bullet flattened out … which was very fortunate, because otherwise it would have gone completely around the world and come back and killed Tom Potts on the spot!"

"Aside from Newell and Cox—and, best of all, Carroll, Lear, and Busch," I added, "you've consistently written some of the greatest comic verse for children. Peter Slade, in his book *Child Drama*, states that 'after the age of six or so, this gift of rhythm appears naturally in child work, but the adult has to toil hard "for it" and often does not attain it. Those who are most successful in doing so are, for the most part, those who have actually retained it from childhood. We call them great artists.' And I wanted to know how you've managed to keep your rhythmic and rhyming impulses intact."

"It's so ingrained in me," Geisel replied, "that I now have trouble writing prose. I find that if I'm writing a short letter, it comes out in verse. It's become a normal method of expression.

"I hate making speeches, incidentally, but several years ago I solved my problem: In 1977, for a commencement address at Lake Forest College, I read an epic poem of fourteen lines entitled 'My Uncle Terwilliger on the Art of Eating Popovers.' The kids in the graduating class are probably still cheering because they thought I'd speak for hours. *The New York Times* picked it up and said that there should be a law that no commencement speech should be longer than that. And the *Reader's Digest* even 'digested' it by cutting out the three short introductory paragraphs."

"Is it easy or hard for you," I asked, "to write the kind of verse in your books—like the following stanza, say, from *On Beyond Zebra!*—a stanza, by the way, that sounds like a perfect description of the apartment situation in New York City:

> The NUH is the letter I use to spell Nutches
> Who live in small caves, known as Nitches, for hutches.
> These Nutches have troubles, the biggest of which is
> The fact there are many more Nutches than Nitches.
> Each Nutch in a Nitch knows that some other Nutch
> Would like to move into his Nitch very much.
> So each Nutch in a Nitch has to watch that small Nitch
> Or Nutches who haven't got Nitches will snitch.

"It's hard," Geisel said, laughing. "I'm a bleeder and I sweat at it. As I've said before: The 'creative process' consists for me of two things—time and sweat. And I've also said that too many writers have only contempt and condescension for children, which is why they give them degrading corn about bunnies. The difficult thing about writing in verse for kids is that you can write yourself into a box: If you can't get a proper rhyme for a quatrain, you not only have to throw that quatrain out but you also have to unravel the sock way back, probably ten pages or so.... You find that you're not driving the car, your *characters* are driving it. And you also have to remember that in a children's book a paragraph is like a chapter in an adult book, and a sentence is like a paragraph."

"In 1925," I mentioned, "the Russian children's poet Kornei Chukovsky wrote an important book that in English is called *From Two to Five,* and in it he formulated a set of rules for the composing of verse for children. I wanted to find out what you thought of these rules."

"I'd love to hear what they are!"

"Chukovsky's first rule is that poems for children must be *graphic,* and by that he meant that every stanza must suggest an illustration, since children think in terms of images."

"I agree," Geisel said, "and one should add the importance of eliminating the nonessentials."

"Two," I continued, "there must be a rapid change of images."

"He's talking about progression," Geisel responded, "and I agree entirely."

"Three, that this verbal painting must be lyrical—so that a child can sing and clap to the verse."

"I'll go along with that," said Geisel.

"Four, that there be a moving and changing of rhythm."

"Definitely a change of pace," Geisel allowed. "I'll get going at a certain pace and meter, and I'll turn the page and then have one line in prose to break up what I've been doing and then start building up again from there."

"Five, that there be a heightened musicality of poetic expressiveness."

"What does that mean?"

"He's referring to what he calls the flow and fluidity of sound—the avoidance of cluttered-up clusters of consonants, for example."

"O.K.," Geisel assented.

"Six, that there be frequent rhyming."

"Yes."

"Seven, that the rhyming words carry the meaning."

"That's *very* true," Geisel insisted. "I find that a lot of authors will use convenience rhymes and not positive thought rhymes. And the child's interest disappears entirely."

"Eight," I continued, "that every line must have a life of its own, with no internal pauses."

"Yes."

"Nine, that the author not crowd the poem with adjectives—*more verbs and fewer adjectives.*"

"He's definitely right about the adjectives," Geisel explained. "If I'm supplementing the words with pictures and if I can substitute the adjectives with a picture, I'll leave them out of the text."

"Ten, that the predominant rhythm be that of the trochee."

"That could be true in Russian," Geisel suggested, "it could come out of the way the Russian language sounds. In most of my work I use anapests. But in any case, I think the subject matter is more important than what meter you use."

"Eleven, that the verse be suitable for play and games."

"All of my books," said Geisel, "are informally dramatized in schools. And recently, the Children's Theater Company in Minneapolis did a wonderful adaptation of *The 500 Hats of Bartholomew Cubbins*—an amazing production."

"Twelve, that verses for children have the skill, the virtuosity, the technical soundness of poetry for adults."

"I think so," Geisel agreed.

"And thirteen," I concluded, "that through your verse you try to bring children within reach of adult perceptions and thoughts."

"I don't know how far you can bring them to it," said Geisel, "but you can try to initiate them.... I like this guy, and I think that what he says holds up."

About the first years of his life, Tolstoy wrote: "Was it not then that I acquired all that now sustains me? And I gained so much and so quickly that during the rest of my life I did not acquire a hundredth part of it. From myself as a five-year-old to myself as I now am there is only one step. The distance between myself as an infant and myself at five years is tremendous." And following Tolstoy's notion, Chukovsky states: "It seems to me that, beginning with the age of two, every child becomes for a short period of time a linguistic genius." Throughout his book, the author makes many fascinating observations, among them:

> Two- and three-year-old children have such a strong sensitivity to their language—to its many inflections and suffixes—that the words they construct inventively do not seem at all distorted and freakish but, on the contrary, extremely apt, beautiful, and natural.

> In the beginning of our childhood we are all "versifiers"—it is only later that we begin to learn to speak in prose. The very nature of an infant's jabbering predisposes him to versifying.

> Another quality of children's rhymes and nonsense verse is that they are saturated with joy. They do not show a trace of tears or a whisper of a sigh. They express the child's feeling of happiness with himself and his world which every healthy child experiences so much of the time. This is the reason that their rhymes and nonsense verse have such a zestful spontaneity.

> When the children sing, clap, play, or work out a project, I look with the greatest pleasure. When they begin to read me poems that have been taught to them in school or in boarding school, I often feel like a real martyr.... Together with the works of our classical poets, they have been taught hack-

neyed lines, absurd rhythms, cheap rhymes. There are times when I could cry with disappointment.

For some mysterious reason the child is attracted to that topsy-turvy world where legless men run, water burns, horses gallop astride their riders, and cows nibble on peas on top of birch trees.... The more aware the child is of the correct relationship of things, which he violates in his play, the more comical does this violation seem to him.

He is always in control of his illusions and knows perfectly well those limits within which it is important that he hold them. He is the strongest realist in his fantasies.... His main purpose, as in all play, is to exercise his newly acquired skill of verifying his knowledge of things.

It is high time to promote these "nonsense" verses into the category of educationally valuable and perceptive works of poetry.... With the help of fantasies, tall tales, fairy tales, and topsy-turvies of every type, children confirm their realistic orientation to actuality.

All of these observations make it clear that Chukovsky would undoubtedly have greatly approved of the works of Dr. Seuss, who has never severed his connection with the child's ways of being in and conceiving the world. As Goethe wrote: "Every child is to a certain extent a genius and every genius to a certain extent a child. The relationship between the two shows itself primarily as the naïveté and sublime ingenuousness that are a fundamental characteristic of true genius."

Geisel's illustrative style, for example, has its roots in the naive and sublimely ingenuous manner with which young children create their own drawings. Unlike the child, however—about whom André Malraux once wrote: "his gift controls him, not he his gift"—Geisel is always in command of his idiosyncratic style. As he once told Michael J. Bandler: "Schools send me hundreds of drawings each year, and I find most kids draw as I do—awkwardly. I think I've refined my childish drawing so that it looks professional. But kids exaggerate the same way I do. They overlook things they can't draw, their pencils slip, and they get some funny effects. I've learned to incorporate my pencil slips into my style." As he later told me: "Technically, I'm capable of doing more complicated things. But every time I try to do something sophisticated in a children's book, it fails—it doesn't attract kids. This is due to the fact that I work the way they work. A child's idea of art is a pen-and-ink drawing filled in with flat color, with no modulation and no subtlety. *McElligot's Pool*, which has modulation of tones, isn't as successful as the books with hard black outlines and flat color. That's just the way kids see things."

And concerning the little stories very young children themselves make up, Brian Sutton-Smith, in his essay "The Child's Mind as Poem," has noted certain recurring features in these stories—their verselike quality (rhythm, alliteration, and rhyme); their simplified syntax and use of nonsense; their expressive as opposed to referential features (melody preceding meaning);

their use of exaggeration and of emphatic and pantomimic effects; and their reliance on theme-and-variation, repetitive, and cyclical forms of organization. And Sutton-Smith concludes his discussion by affirming that "the child's mind is like a poem."

One might even suggest that the child's mind is indeed like many a Dr. Seuss book, for his poetic style—although more controlled—has its roots in these characteristic modes of children's storytelling; simply and unselfconsciously, Dr. Seuss has retained a fresh perceiving system, naturally communicating an understanding of children's energies, needs, and desires.

Nowhere is this more obvious than in *The Cat in the Hat* (1957). "It's the book I'm proudest of," Geisel told me, "because it had something to do with the death of the *Dick and Jane* primers. In 1954 John Hersey wrote an article in *Life* that suggested something to the effect that we should get rid of the boredom of Dick and Jane and Spot and hand the educational system over to Dr. Seuss! William Spaulding, who was then the textbook chief at Houghton Mifflin, read the article and asked me if I'd like to try to do a primer, and he sent me a list of about three hundred words and told me to make a book out of them.

"At first I thought it was impossible and ridiculous, and I was about to get out of the whole thing; then decided to look at the list one more time and to use the first two words that rhymed as the title of the book—*cat* and *hat* were the ones my eyes lighted on. I worked on the book for nine months—throwing it across the room and letting it hang for a while—but I finally got it done. Houghton Mifflin, however, had trouble selling it to the schools; there were a lot of Dick and Jane devotees, and my book was considered too fresh and irreverent. But Bennett Cerf at Random House had asked for trade rights, and it just took off in the bookstores."

It is not hard to guess what John Newbery would have thought of Dr. Seuss's first primer. In one of his prefaces to his own primer, *A Little Pretty Pocket-Book*, Newbery assumes the character of a moralizing Jack the Giant-Killer and in this guise addresses a letter to Little Master Tommy that begins:

My *dear* Tommy,
Your Nurse called upon me Today, and told me that you was [sic] a good Boy; that you was dutiful to your Father and Mother, and that, when you had said your Prayers in the Morning and the Evening, you asked their Blessings, and in the Day-time did every Thing they bid you. She says, you are obedient to your Master, loving and kind to your Play-fellows, and obliging to every body; that you rise early in the Morning, keep yourself clean, and learn your Book; that when you have done a Fault you confess it, and are sorry for it. And though you are sometimes naughty, she says you are very honest and good-humored; that you don't swear, tell Lies, nor say indecent Words, and are always thankful when any body gives you good Advice; that you never quarrel, nor do wicked Things, as some other Boys do.
This Character, my Dear, has made every body love you; and, while you

continue so good, you may depend on my obliging you with every thing I can. I have here sent you a *Little Pretty Pocket-Book,* which will teach you to play at all those innocent Games that good Boys and Girls divert themselves with: And, while you behave so well, you shall never want Play I assure you....

And just as Theodor Geisel, during his one and only art class, turned his painting upside down, so Dr. Seuss, in *The Cat in the Hat,* created one of the great *bouleversements* in the history of children's reading.

"The sun did not shine./ It was too wet to play./ So we sat in the house/ All that cold, cold, wet day" is the way the book begins, as two children—brother and sister—and a surprised goldfish in a bowl suddenly hear the *bump* that announces the dramatic arrival of the Cat in the Hat, who, in the absence of the children's mother, tells them: "I know it is wet/ And the sun is not sunny./ But we can have/ Lots of good fun that is funny!" To which the goldfish—a combination superego and what Geisel calls "my version of Cotton Mather"—warns: "No! No!/ Make that cat go away!/ Tell that Cat in the Hat/ You do NOT want to play./ He should not be here./ He should not be about./ He should not be here/ When your mother is out!" And the rest of the book is an unloosening of all sanctions and rules concerning "proper" children's behavior, as, in one rambunctious scene after another, the Cat and his blissed-out assistants—Thing One and Thing Two—run amok, create pandemonium, and tear the house apart—only to put everything back together just moments before the arrival home of Mother, who, like Marco's father, asks: "Did you have any fun?/ Tell me. What did you do?"

> And Sally and I did not know
> What to say.
> Should we tell her
> The things that went on there that day?
> Should we tell her about it?
> Now, what SHOULD we do?
> Well...
> What would YOU do
> If your mother asked YOU?

Like Coyote of many American Indian tribes and like Rabbit of Afro-American folklore, the Cat in the Hat is nothing less than an archetypal trickster hero, whose manifestation is perfectly suited—as is Bugs Bunny—for mid-twentieth-century children's appreciation and delight. As Brian Sutton-Smith describes this type of character: "The trickster figure does not just sit down and plan out logical maneuvers; he uses the most outrageous trickery. He does not simply make his way in the world independent of others' support; he baldly mocks authority figures and breaks all societal rules, which forces him to remain autonomous. Nonsense humor and the creation of ribald, regressive trickster figures give the child a more flexible grasp on what is and what is not possible."

John Hersey has called *The Cat in the Hat* a "gift to the art of reading" and a "harum-scarum masterpiece." Selma G. Lanes, in *Down the Rabbit Hole*, has perceptively written of Seuss's "clever and relentless piling on of gratuitous anxiety until the child is fairly ready to cry 'uncle' and settle for any resolution, however mundane, that will end his at once marvelous, exquisite, and finally unbearable tension.... The anxiety in Seuss's books," she adds, "always arises from the flouting of authority, parental or societal.... The child can sit back and experience genuine pleasure, knowing that the anxiety building up in him is vicarious and that no punishment will follow Seuss's forbidden pleasures." And Alison Lurie, in her essay "On the Subversive Side," has seen *The Cat in the Hat* as being part of the subversive tradition of children's literature represented by books such as *Huckleberry Finn* and *Alice's Adventures in Wonderland*. As she writes: "It is the particular gift of some writers to remain in one sense children all their lives: to continue to see the world as boys and girls see it, and take their side instinctively. One author who carries on this tradition today in America is Dr. Seuss, who like Twain and Carroll has adopted a separate literary personality."

"It's interesting," I mentioned to Geisel, "that after Samuel Clemens and Charles Dodgson, you are the most famous and most popular pseudonymous writer for children."

"I never thought of that," he replied. "Twain and Carroll are both a couple of phonies, masquerading under false colors. It's not bad company at all. I'm very flattered to be included. When I received an honorary Doctor of Humane Letters from Dartmouth in 1955, the president of the college, in his conferral speech, said that this would make an honest man of me, and no longer would I have to masquerade under a phony doctorate."

"You seem quite recusant yourself, and I think a lot of your books *are* subversive," I added. "Don't you?"

"I'm subversive as hell!" Geisel replied. "I've always had a mistrust of adults. And one reason I dropped out of Oxford and the Sorbonne was that I thought they were taking life too damn seriously, concentrating too much on nonessentials. Hilaire Belloc, whose writings I liked a lot, was a radical. *Gulliver's Travels* was subversive, and both Swift and Voltaire influenced me. *The Cat in the Hat* is a revolt against authority, but it's ameliorated by the fact that the Cat cleans everything up at the end. It's revolutionary in that it goes as far as Kerensky and then stops. It doesn't go quite as far as Lenin."

"Like many of your books," I suggested, "*The Cat in the Hat* is quite anarchistic."

"It's impractical the way anarchy is, but it works within the confines of a book," Geisel agreed.

"Without pushing you further down the revolutionary path," I said, laughing, "I've always wondered about the concluding lines of *Yertle the Turtle:* 'And today the great Yertle, that Marvelous he,/ Is King of the Mud. That is all he can see./ And turtles, of course … all the turtles are free/ As turtles and, maybe, all creatures should be.' Why 'maybe' and not 'surely'?"

"I qualified that," Geisel explained, "in order to avoid sounding too didactic or like a preacher on a platform. And I wanted *other* persons, like yourself, to say 'surely' in their minds instead of my having to say it."

"Within the confines of your books," I added, "you've written some very moral and political tales. The two books about Horton the elephant praise the virtues of loyalty and faithfulness. And you once said that the idea for *The 500 Hats of Bartholomew Cubbins* came about when you were 'taking a railroad train through Connecticut, sitting in a smoky, stuffy car, and ahead of me sat a smoky, stuffy Wall Street broker, wearing a derby and reading the *Wall Street Journal*. I was fascinated with his hat, and wondered what his reaction would be if I took his hat off his head. And then, half an hour later, I wondered how he'd react if there was still another hat on his hat.'"

"Yes," Geisel responded, "children's literature as I write it and as I see it is satire to a great extent—satirizing the mores and the habits of the world. There's *Yertle the Turtle* [about the turtle dictator who becomes the 'ruler of all that I can see' by sitting on the backs of hundreds of subject turtles, his throne brought down by the simple burp of the lowliest and lowest turtle],* which was modeled on the rise of Hitler; and then there's *The Sneetches* [about Star-Belly Sneetches who ostracize Plain-Belly Sneetches who pay to become Star-Belly Sneetches who then have to become Plain-Belly Sneetches, etc.], which was inspired by my opposition to anti–Semitism. These books come from a different part of my background and from the part of my soul that started out to be a teacher. Every once in a while I get mad. *The Lorax* [about a rapacious Once-ler who despoils the land of its Truffula Trees, leading to the total pollution and destruction of the environment] came out of my being angry. The ecology books I'd read were dull. But I couldn't get started on that book—I had notes but was stuck on it for nine months. Then I happened to be in Kenya at a swimming pool, and I was watching a herd of elephants cross a hill; why that released me. I don't know, but all of a sudden all my notes assembled mentally. I grabbed a laundry list that was lying around and wrote the whole book in an hour and a half. In *The Lorax* I was out to attack what I think are evil things and let the chips fall where they might; and the book's been used by ministers as the basis of sermons, as well as by conservation groups."

"Aside from works like *Yertle the Turtle* and *The Sneetches*, which have the power of the great fables," I said, "there's a certain folktale quality to a

---

* *In December 1981, New York City's Mayor Koch called the city's Council President, Carol Bellamy, "a horror show" who can be "just tremendously vicious." They made up in front of the press, but not before Bellamy presented Koch with a copy of* Yertle the Turtle, *saying: "Some days Ed Koch wakes up in the morning and decides he wants to be Yertle for the day. Whenever that happens, I find myself with a terrible case of indigestion."—J.C.*

few of your stories—I'm thinking particularly of "The Big Brag" in *Yertle the Turtle*—about the pomposity and egomania of a bear and a rabbit and of how they are cut down to size by a little worm—and "The Zax" in *The Sneetches*—about two Zaxs who bump into each other in the prairie and who each stubbornly refuse to let the other one pass until, eventually, highways are built over and around them. This last tale is similar to an African tale I recently read about two goats who bump into each other on a bridge and refuse to budge, each of them finally throwing the other into the water below."

"It just proves that there's nothing new," Geisel replied. "People are always reacting to the same stimuli. You could probably find duplications of all of my stuff. But I used to read a lot of Uncle Remus and a lot of Belloc, as I mentioned before, so maybe there's some influence there.

"Anyway, to get back to what we were talking about earlier," Geisel said: "*The Cat in the Hat* was an immediate best seller. And at that point Bennett and Phyllis Cerf of Random House conceived the idea of starting a publishing house just for the lower graders, which we called Beginner Books."

"It's interesting," I interrupted, "that a Zen Buddhist monk once said: 'If your mind is empty, it is always ready for anything; it is open to everything. In the beginner's mind there are many possibilities; in the expert's mind, there are few.... That is always the real secret of the arts: always be a beginner' [Shunryu Suzuki]."

"But to create a book," Geisel said, "you have to have an ability and a technique, which you don't have in an empty mind. So maybe we should change 'empty' to 'receptive.' ... Anyway, when we started Beginner Books we had no idea what we were doing—it was *really* an 'empty' mind. And when we began Beginner Books, we found out that *The Cat in the Hat* was at that time hard for first graders to read. It all depended, of course, on what experts you talked to—how many words a kid could read. But I realized that there was a level below Beginner Books, so we began making things simpler and simpler; and then we set up Bright and Early Books for younger and younger readers. At the moment I'm working on something I call Prenatal Books [laughing], but there are a few little difficulties we haven't yet solved. [N.B.: Theodor Geisel might have been kidding, but recently a number of persons have seriously suggested the educational importance of parents narrating to their womb-enclosed progeny; and many books—cloth and bathtime items among them—are being published for infants six months old and younger!]

"When I first started doing children's books I knew nothing about the market. But, obviously, parents read my earlier books to their kids. Did the parents like them? In his autobiography, Prince Rainer of Monaco says something like: 'My children insist that I read those silly Dr. Seuss books to them—I don't care for them, but my kids do.' In those earlier and regular-sized books I'm writing for people; into the smaller-sized Beginner Books I'm still writing for people, but I go over them and simplify so that a kid has a chance to handle the vocabulary. But, basically, I've long since stopped worrying about what exact ages the books are for—I just put them out. Sometimes the more complex books can be the simplest ones to read because the clues given in the pictures are stronger. You can't base it entirely on words."

Almost all the regular Dr. Seuss books have been widely praised by both children and adults—the most popular being *Horton Hatches the Egg, Horton Hears a Who!, Thidwick the Big-Hearted Moose, On Beyond Zebra!, If I Ran the Zoo, If I Ran the Circus, How the Grinch Stole Christmas*—though a book like *Dr. Seuss's Sleep Book* has its devotees (myself included).* Yet aside from *The Cat in the Hat* and its brilliant sequel *The Cat in the Hat Comes Back*, most of Dr. Seuss's Beginner and Bright and Early Books have often been overlooked, patronized, and undervalued.

One of the most difficult tasks is to create a book meant to be read by very young children that will prove instructive to the child and also exciting to adults who might be reading over their shoulders. John Newbery's books were pleasing in form and generally rigid and boring in content. Dr. Seuss's books perfectly mate form and content,† using nonsense, rhyme, and illustration to strengthen in the child's mind—and to confirm in the adults—a sense not of the "required" but of the "possible." (In Dr. Seuss's moral universe, what "should" happen is always connected to the heart's desires—as when Horton the faithful elephant hatches the elephant-bird, "it should be, it *should* be, it SHOULD be like that!"; and what "could" or "might" happen is limited only by one's patience and the powers of one's imagination—as when the hero of *McElligot's Pool* says: "*'Cause you never can tell/ What goes on down below!/* This pool *might* be bigger/ Than you or I know!*")

---

* *The most recent Dr. Seuss book,* Hunches in Bunches *(1982), is about a boy who, unable to make up his mind, follows all kinds of Hunches—one Hunch leading to another—in a thousand different directions at once.—J.C.*

† *Howard Gardner—the author of books such as* The Arts and Human Development *and* Artful Scribbles: The Significance of Children's Drawings—*is a research psychologist at the Boston Veterans Administration Hospital and the co-director of Harvard Project Zero. In a conversation with me, he expanded on and developed this point about form and content:*

"*Dr. Seuss really seems to be tuned into both the form and the content that constitute the child's world, and he can approach the world through the child's conscious and unconscious abilities or faculties.*

"*To fill that out a bit: There are some people who write works that appeal formally to children because they have certain rhythms, certain words, certain structures, certain visual patterns. You can enjoy Dr. Seuss's books, for example, even if you don't understand some of the words, even if you don't know English, and even if you don't follow the plots—some of them are fairly complicated. But there's enough regularity and sequence built into them so that even if you don't get all the words or all the points, it doesn't matter. You don't have to get the moral of* The Sneetches *in order to enjoy it.*

"*There are also people who can produce works which appeal to kids in terms of content—something little overpowers something big, for example, or somebody goes on an adventure and comes home and becomes secure. Or you can take a book like Robert McCloskey's* Make Way for Ducklings—*the content is something very close to kids (animals, mothers, etc.), but the form isn't the sort of thing kids produce themselves—there isn't that metrical wordplay. And what I think is special about Dr. Seuss is that he's exploited both of these things—form and content—at the same time.*

"*Now, as far as 'conscious' and 'unconscious' elements are concerned: I think that Dr. Seuss has read*

Dr. Seuss's ABC (one of the freshest additions to this centuries-old genre), *Hop on Pop* (subtitled "The Simplest Seuss for Youngest Use"), and *Fox in Socks* (a volume of mind-boggling tongue twisters) are among the most innovative, amusing, and audacious teaching books I have ever seen. *One Fish Two Fish Red Fish Blue Fish* and *There's a Wocket in My Pocket!* feature some of Dr. Seuss's most remarkable animal creations. And books like *Green Eggs and Ham, Mr. Brown Can Moo! Can You?* and *Marvin K. Mooney, Will You Please Go Now!* remind us that Dr. Seuss is one of the great creators of nonsense verse in the English language—verse in which you can almost hear an unmistakable musical accompaniment.

These last three books—along with *The Cat in the Hat Songbook* (which include titles like "My Uncle Terwilliger Waltzes with Bears," "Beeper Booper," and "Rainy Day in Utica, N.Y.")—are in fact part of the wonderful tradition of American nonsense songs represented by "Old Aunt Kate," "Chick-a-Li-Lee-Lo," and "Risselty-Rosselty." As Charles Wolfe—an authority on folk music and popular culture—has written: "Most traditional nonsense songs have been classified as children's songs ... and young children, for whom so much language is meaningless, doubtless delight in wordplay so full of assonance, consonance, and rhythm. Children's authors like Dr. Seuss often capitalize on this delight." And as composer Ruth Crawford Seeger points out in her excellent *American Folk Songs for Children:* "The adult faces numerous pitfalls when 'thinking up' words for children, such as affectation or over-conscientious attention to particular uses for a song, or preconceived notions as to child speech, understanding, or enjoyment." Dr. Seuss completely avoids these pitfalls, for he is especially sensitive to what Seeger calls the "sound-meaning" and "touch-meaning" of words, and is able to "play" with words like Chukovsky's two-to-five-year-old linguistic geniuses (and certain poets such as John Skelton and Edward Lear).

(continued) *his Freud, at least implicitly; I think his works are polymorphously perverse—they play with kids' desire to muck things up, to get dirty, to overpower authority. No kid would talk about this explicitly, but Dr. Seuss is sensitive to the unconscious strivings of kids in the same way that Bettelheim describes fairy tales as being responsive to kids' concerns.*

"But Dr. Seuss also writes about things and objects kids are consciously concerned with. In The Cat in the Hat, *for example, a mother goes away, and what do the kids do then? They play, but all the time are worrying about what their mother will think when she comes back and finds out what they've been doing. So he's right in the center of two very important intersections—the kinds of formal properties of work that children like and the kinds of content they're interested in, and kids' unconscious and conscious concerns.*

"Sesame Street could also be described in a similar way, though I don't think the program does very much with the child's unconscious because it's 'pro-social'—as is Mister Rogers' Neighborhood ... *they want to make kids behave well so they don't deal very much with kids' aggressive desires. And, in a way, Dr. Seuss can be said to capture not only this kind of* Sesame Street *approach but also things that you find in Saturday morning cartoons, which play a lot more with aspects of a child's unconscious.*

"In a way, of course, any good work of art has got to play with those two dimensions I spoke about before. And for society today—at least in the West—Dr. Seuss has been as effective as anybody in doing this."—J.C.

Along with "imagination," "play" is the cornerstone of Dr. Seuss's world. And its importance is specifically revealed in one of Seuss's early fairy tale-type prose works, *The King's Stilts* (1939), which seems to illustrate Nietzsche's comment that "in any true man hides a child who wants to play."

The Kingdom of Binn, we are told, is surrounded by mighty Dike Trees that hold back the sea from engulfing the land. But since the roots of these trees are extremely tasty to the rapacious Nizzard birds, King Birtram has gathered an army of a thousand Patrol Cats, who guard the kingdom both day and night. The Changing of the Cat Guard takes place at seven each morning; and once King Birtram reviews the Guard, he rushes off to a special castle closet where he keeps his beloved red stilts, grabs them and begins leaping around the palace grounds on them: "This was the moment King Birtram lived for. When he worked, he really worked ... but when he played, he really PLAYED!" ("The essence of kingship is childlikeness," wrote George Groddeck, adding: "The greatest monarch is the infant.")

The townsfolk do not really understand, but they approve of their king's playful ways, until one day the malicious, curmudgeonly Lord Droon ("Laughing spoils the shape of the face" is his motto) steals the stilts and has them secretly buried. King Birtram grows sadder and sadder and finds it impossible to take care of his Patrol Cats, who in turn become lazy and apathetic. The Nizzards, of course, start ravaging and destroying the roots of the trees, and the kingdom is in danger. But with the help of his courageous page boy Eric ("Quick, Eric! The stilts!" shouts the king—parodying Geisel's "Quick, Henry! The Flit!" insect-spray commercial), he regains his stilts and leads the Patrol Cats to victorious battle. And the book ends with Lord Droon imprisoned and Eric rewarded with his own pair of stilts, on which he races around the kingdom with King Birtram every afternoon: "And when they played they really PLAYED. And when they worked they really WORKED. And the cats kept the Nizzards away from the Dike Trees. And the Dike Trees kept the water back out of the land."

As Erik Erikson reminds us in *Toys and Reasons*, Plato's notion of playfulness recognized the need of young creatures—animal or human—to leap; and Erikson writes: "To truly leap, you must learn how to use the ground as a springboard, and how to land resiliently and safely. It means to test the leeway allowed by given limits; to outdo and yet not escape gravity" ... and, he adds, to leap into make-believe and yet be able to return to factual reality. ("True make-believe," he comments—as if to describe *Mulberry Street*—"may play with facts, but it cannot lie; while fake reality may, up to a point, seem to master the facts, but it never tells the truth"—which is what Beatrix Potter surely must have meant when she commented on "the natural truthful simplicity of the untruthfulness" of *Mulberry Street*.)

There are, of course, a great many theorists who have pointed to different (and, I think, equally valid) characteristics of play—the autonomous (Erikson), the cognitive (Piaget), the affective (Berlyne), and the communicational (Bateson), among many others. And today there certainly seems to be a consensus that the kind of adult-supervised or directed play that is supposed to instill the virtues of adult life has little to recommend it. (One is reminded of *A Little Pretty Pocket-Book's* moral about the children's money-tossing game called Chuck-Farthing: "*Chuck-Farthing*, like Trade,/ Requires great Care;/ The more you observe,/ The better you'll fare.") As Piaget wrote: "Every time we teach a child something, we keep him from inventing it himself. On the other hand, that which we allow him to discover for himself will remain with him." And as the hero of *McElligot's Pool* says: "If I wait long enough; if I'm patient and cool,/ Who knows *what* I'll catch in McElligot's Pool!"

Along with imagination, play allows us to innovate, test, accept, and reject; to explore and integrate different forms of behavior; and to envisage and to conceive of new ideas, new theories, new creations, new discoveries, and new societies. Imagination and play are at the basis of all our hope. In the words of the psychologist D. W. Winnicott: "One has to allow for the possibility that there cannot be a complete destruction of a human individual's capacity for creative living and that, even in the most extreme cases of compliance and the establishment of a false personality, hidden away somewhere there exists a secret life that is satisfactory because of its being creative or original to that human being."

In the words of the good Doctor Seuss: "There is no one alive who is you-er than you!"

13

Following the 1986 publication of an "adult" book, You're Only Old
Once, *Dr. Seuss suddenly became a worthy subject for
staid publications like business and news magazines.*
*Brevity might be a virtue in the news magazines, but this
engaging interview in* U.S. News *and* World Report
surely could have been much longer.

"Somebody's Got to Win" in Kids' Books
An Interview with Dr. Seuss on His
Books for Children, Young and Old

U.S. News and World Report, **April 14, 1986**

*Q Dr. Seuss, what prompted you to do a book for adults—*You're Only Old
Once!*—about the trials of medical treatment?*

I had some medical problems and found myself sitting in the vestibules
of hospitals rather more often than at my drawing board. The waits were
most unpleasant. I began to take sketch pads with me and amused myself by
thinking of the horrible things they were going to do to me next. Gradually
words came, too.

Now, kids are coming up with the book for autographs. I've said: "This
isn't a book for you." But they say that they've had their experience in hospitals with tonsillectomies and the like. They think it's amusing.

Q Your books tend to have a moral message—

I seldom start with one, but when you write a kid's book, somebody's
got to win. You find yourself preaching in spite of yourself. But sometimes
people find morals where there are none. People have read all kinds of things
into *Green Eggs and Ham,* including Biblical connotations. There's a teacher—
and this one nauseates me—who says the book's message is that you should-
n't make up your mind against anything until you've tasted it. I'm getting
blamed for a lot of stuff I haven't done.

Q Where did you get the idea for Green Eggs and Ham?

People write essays and deliver lectures about the meaning of that book. The only meaning was that Bennett Cerf, my publisher, bet me 50 bucks I couldn't write a book using only 50 words. I did it to show I could.

Q Are your books designed to introduce youngsters to only a limited number of new words?

My first book with a controlled vocabulary was *The Cat in the Hat,* but that was 30 years ago for an educational publishing house which said that it was impossible for a first grader to comprehend more than 250 words at a time. They sent me a list, and I was forbidden to use any words beyond it. I almost threw the job up. I finally gave it one more chance and said, "If I find two words that rhyme and make sense to me, that's the title." That's how educationally wise I was. So I found *cat* rhymed with *hat.* And like a genius, I said, "That's the name."

I did only a few books after that from a controlled list. I changed the rules, based on my belief that a child could learn any amount of words if fed them slowly and if the books were amply illustrated. We began to concentrate our efforts on linking the artwork with the text.

Q How important is rhyming to your books?

Rhyming forces recognition of words. You also establish a rhythm, and that tends to make kids want to go on. If you break the rhythm, a child feels unfulfilled.

Q Do rhymes come easily to you?

The agony is terrific at times, and the attrition is horrible. If you're doing it in quatrains and get to the end of four lines and can't make it work, then it's like unraveling a sock. You take some of your best stuff and throw it away.

Q Does it take long to come up with a rhyme that works?

The Lorax was a son of a gun. I worked almost two years and got nowhere. And my wife said, "We'll get out of the country." She was finding me a little bit difficult to live with.

We went to Africa. We were at an inn in Kenya, and I was sitting near a swimming pool. About a mile away, a herd of elephants came over a hill. I don't know what happened. I grabbed a laundry list that I had beside me and wrote the whole book in 45 minutes.

I've looked at elephants ever since, but it has never happened again.

Q Do you first write the story and then draw the pictures?

There's no pattern. When I start a new book, I'll noodle things over and develop some characters. Most of them go in the wastebasket, but a couple get in conflict. Then words begin to come. If I get stuck mentally in a story,

I'll draw my way out. Other times, as in the case of *The Lorax*, I wrote the whole thing without any illustrations.

Q　What are your favorite children's books by others?

I'll give you one name, Maurice Sendak. I'm going to duck the rest because no matter how I do this I offend confreres by leaving them out. Sendak has the courage not to be influenced by editors. Everybody said his book *Where the Wild Things Are* would drive kids crazy, and they love it. Like me, he isn't writing for kids; he's writing for all people.

Q　Do you try to stay in touch with kids?

Not especially. I keep getting asked the question, "Do you like children?" I like children in the same way that I like people. There are some stinkers among children as well as among adults. I like or dislike them as individuals.

In my early days, I was forced by the publisher to do a certain amount of dropping in at schools. I finally said "No" because youngsters expect you to be wearing a hat, and I'm a disappointment.

In an autographing line, it's different. You just have a short contact. But I had a horrible thing happen recently. A mother brought a child in who was about a year and a half. The child had his hand all the way in his mouth. And the mother said, "Take your hand out of your mouth and shake hands with Dr. Seuss." I looked around, and I tried to get out of the store. I was able to grab the child somewhere up on the arm. You get that about once every year or so.

There's a mother who will say, "Osbert, don't you want to kiss Dr. Seuss?"

Q　And what do you do?

Usually I'm on a platform and can't escape. You sometimes get kissed.

*How Dr. Seuss—with an assist from Art Buchwald—chased
Richard Nixon from office, and why a good children's book has to
"sound like you knocked it off on a rainy Friday afternoon."*

14

The Private World of Dr. Seuss:
A Visit to Theodor Geisel's
La Jolla Mountaintop

HILLIARD HARPER

The Los Angeles Times Magazine, **May 25, 1986**

Imagine Dr. Seuss, beloved writer of wry and whimsical children's fables, stepping into the public forum to take sides in the country's greatest crisis of government. Unlikely? Nothing is unlikely in the land of Dr. Seuss, where what he calls "logical insanity" rules.

During the Watergate scandal, the man best known for his fanciful books about oobleck and grinches publicly called for the President of the United States to resign. In July 1974, he sent newspaper columnist Art Buchwald a copy of his book *Marvin K. Mooney, Will You Please Go Now!* In the text, Dr. Seuss had scratched out each reference to Marvin and substituted "Richard M. Nixon."

This typically Seussian book tells of a pestilent brat who has overstayed his welcome. The narrator's demands that the kid scram escalate in fury until the conclusion:

> You can go by balloon ...
> Or broomstick,
> Or
> You can go by camel
> in a bureau drawer.
> You can go by Bumble-boat
> ... or jet.

129

> I don't care how you go.
> Just GET!
> Richard M. Nixon!
> I don't care HOW.
> Richard M. Nixon
> Will you please
> GO NOW!

And Nixon did, just a week after Buchwald ran Seuss' revision in his nationally syndicated column. Seuss would say it was just coincidence.

In real life, the good doctor is Theodor Seuss Geisel, a man whose private world seems as full of contradictions as the notion of an author of gentle children's books firing off a tirade against the nation's chief executive.

With more than 100 million of his books sold, and with kids all over the globe disciples of the Cat in the Hat and the Grinch who stole Christmas, Seuss at 82 has uncharacteristically leaped into books for adults. Published in March, his 45th book, *You're Only Old Once!: A Book for Obsolete Children*, quickly sold out a first printing of 200,000 copies and shot to the top of the New York Times best-seller list—for *nonfiction*.

Now comes a retrospective at the San Diego Museum of Art that covers almost 60 years of Dr. Seuss' work and highlights aspects of his personality not easily discerned from such mainstays as *Horton Hears a Who!* and *Green Eggs and Ham*.

The exhibit, which runs through July 13, includes a well-doodled notebook the future author kept while studying at Oxford University in England (he dropped out before earning his doctorate), as well as early illustrations for humor magazines. The exhibit also showcases his book art, with one section following, step by step, the process used to illustrate "You're Only Old Once!"

But fans of his quirky drawings might be surprised to find among his early work a more baldly commercial Seuss, in addition to the one with a decidedly political bent. There amid the likes of Horton the elephant and Yertle the turtle are Seuss' advertising campaigns for motor oil (with the slogan, "Foil the Moto-raspus!" and a drawing of an engine-wrecking creature) and bug spray ("Quick, Henry! the Flit"), next to tough-minded editorial cartoons from his days at the long-defunct New York newspaper *PM*.

These are sides of Geisel familiar to the tight social circle that knows him not as the recluse often depicted by the media but rather as a playful raconteur and something of a screwball. But these faces of Geisel emerge less often from his mountaintop perch above the Pacific in La Jolla, where the nation's most renowned children's author toils amid yet another contradiction: no children or grandchildren. "You have 'em, I'll amuse 'em" has long been his curmudgeonly motto.

It is almost easier to get to Dr. Seuss' mythical land of Solla Sollew than to Geisel's real life lair on Mt. Soledad. A narrow road corkscrews up the mountainside; rounding a bend, one almost expects to meet an outrageous figure careening downhill astride a one-wheeler wubble, or at least to spot some of the author's imaginary menagerie: loraxes, yopps, grinches grouching in grickle grass, sneetches lurking in lerkims or a covey of green-headed Quilligan quail.

Tall, slim and energetic, with eyes that really do twinkle, the white-bearded Geisel suggests an attenuated Cat in the Hat as much as someone's kindly grandfather. By turns droll and gracious, he welcomes visitors, who on this day arrive at the same time as the mailman. "God, what do you suppose is in my mail today?" he says, warily eyeing stacks of packages and fan letters, including several hundred birthday cards from children around the country.

Each spring, birthday greetings ranging from hand-lettered cards to rolls of decorated butcher paper pour in, littering the floor of his study between twice-weekly visits of his secretary. ("Don't ever have a birthday," he grumps good-naturedly.) This room—he refers to it as "The Office"—is the nerve center of his world. Its walls are covered with cork, on which he pins book illustrations as he completes them. Bookcases filled with the mysteries and biographies he devours late at night stand against one wall. But the focus on the room is his draftsman's desk and reclining chair, from which he commands a spectacular 180-degree view of the coastline from Oceanside to Mexico.

"I can't imagine Ted really being productive without that view, and the way his seat knocks back and his feet go up and he gets a thought and slaps forward," says his wife Audrey. "That all is part of his creativity."

It is a life far removed from Prospect Street in downtown La Jolla below, with its gridlock of trendiness. And it seems well suited to an author who insists on the privacy of home instead of cross-country book tours or even the occasional trip to his publisher's office in New York. Yet for all their privacy, the Geisels hardly shirk from San Diego society—their social calendar often keeps them out and down the hill until 2 A.M. Audrey has cut it back a bit in the wake of Geisel's heart surgery and cataract operations of the last few years. But still they go out—"to stay rounded," she says.

"Ted works very hard and has more discipline than anyone I know," says the Geisels' friend, nutrition writer Jeanne Jones. "And yet when he cuts loose and walks out of that office, he plays hard. He is the silliest person in my life and my favorite playmate, along with Audrey. I look at him as the kid on the block I most like to play with."

That "kid" is Dr. Seuss' inspiration, his wife says. "He maintains something terribly worthwhile that most other people no longer have after maturity.... After the children's hour, the crazy little kid grows up, and he's a crazy grown-up. [Ted's] mind just keeps flipping out ... getting kind of crazier all the time."

But age has inevitably taken its toll. That's reflected in *You're Only Old Once!* a charming guide through the daunting maze of geriatric medicine, which Geisel knows well. A former chain smoker, he was forced to give up cigarettes five years ago. And the author of *Green Eggs and Ham* can no longer eat his favorite breakfast. Says Audrey: "Ted once was an egg man, with all the accouterments that go with eggs." Now, she adds, he is getting used to life as a cereal man. "He rants and rails at the change, but man does not live by cholesterol alone, although he sometimes dies by it."

Illness has also slowed Geisel's literary output. Accustomed to turning out one book annually, he has published three in the last six years. Even so, he continues to maintain a disciplined schedule. After a 9:30 breakfast, he opens "The Office" and works steadily—with a break for lunch—until 5:30 P.M.

"Some days he's in a state of flux, on his back looking at the ceiling," his wife observes. Geisel calls that process "puzzling my puzzler." It is often interrupted by calls to and from his publisher, Random House (Geisel is also president of Random House's Beginner Books division). He conducts virtually all of his business by telephone from his mountaintop.

The La Jolla aerie is both workplace and retreat. Geisel and his first wife, Helen, moved there from Los Angeles in 1948. They built the home, which sits on 6½ acres, around what he facetiously calls "a derelict observation tower used by the Marine Corps as a seduction chamber for innocent *Maedchen.*"

The tower, actually built by a real estate firm, is now part of the living room wall. In it are mounted stuffed Seussian creatures, often wearing horns of real animals—animals that died in the zoo Geisel's father ran in Springfield, Mass. Just off the study is a closet bulging with a collection worthy of Bartholomew Cubbins, the Seuss hero who owned 500 hats. And there may be that many here, ranging from an Ecuadorian fire chief's helmet to a top hat that Geisel swears was a gift from the Duke of Luxembourg.

Within a year of Helen's death in 1967, Geisel married Audrey Stone Dimond, a nurse about 20 years his junior. She and her ex-husband, a cardiologist, had been close friends of the Geisels. "The feeling was that at his age you grab for the gusto. You don't wait," Audrey said. "You don't think you have much time. Now we've had 17 glorious years."

The two complement each other. Audrey, a gracious hostess who devotes much of her time to San Diego area charities, is an easy conversationalist. Geisel brightens noticeably when she enters the room. Although friends describe him as garrulous, he tends to be reticent with strangers, shooting pithy one-liners often punctuated with a questioning "Hmmph?"

Geisel suffers interviews politely, but carefully steers clear of controversy. "I stay out of politics because if I begin thinking too much about politics, I'll probably ... drop writing children's books and become a political cartoonist again." But he freely acknowledges that, from time to time, his books veer in that direction. *The Lorax* (1971) was "propaganda" for environmental concerns, he says. And *The Butter Battle Book* (1983) was an attack on the arms race. But those are exceptions, he insists, and any social messages that emerge are simply byproducts of a workable plot.

He attributes most of his success to the rhyming format of his books, and, in general, avoids analyzing the muse that drives him. "I prefer to look at things through the wrong end of the telescope," he offers. "I see things more clearly with a little astigmatism." He bridles at people who accost him at parties and say they could knock out a kids' book in a few hours.

Geisel's breezy style just makes it look easy. His success affords him an autonomy rare in publishing: He writes, designs, lays out and selects the colors and paper of each book.

But when a visitor asks Geisel to draw a self-portrait, he refuses, protesting that he "can't draw things the way they are. I just get at the soul of things, like that sculpture." He points to a small, bosomy figurine in his bathroom. Geisel sculpted it when he was a young man, and although the face does not resemble the woman who inspired it, the figure must have caught her essence—because when his employer found Geisel working on the sculpture, he recognized it and cried, "You're doing my wife!" The future children's author was out of a job.

But the illustrating is fun compared to the writing, he says: "The problem with writing a book in verse is, to be successful it has to sound like you knocked it off on a rainy Friday afternoon. It has to sound easy. When you can do it, it helps tremendously because it's a thing that forces kids to read on. You have this unconsummated feeling if you stop. You have to go right through to the end—to the final beat.

"The main problem with writing in verse is, if your fourth line doesn't come out right, you've got to throw four lines away and figure out a whole new way to attack the problem. So the mortality rate is terrific."

At 5:30 P.M., the publishing phenomenon leaves these travails behind and ends his workday. "I have now left the office; now hear this," Geisel announces, ignoring his ringing telephone. It's the cocktail hour, and with great relish he settles down with Audrey and a vodka to watch the evening news. His wife says that he has a great deal to say about each item.

He also has several ideas for his 46th book, but balks at saying just what it will be. "It might be on chipmunks," he says. Or it might be an autobiography or a musical adaptation of his single publishing failure, *The Seven Lady Godivas*, written almost 50 years ago. "It has occurred to me that it would make a good musical, if I could solve the problem of the naked women and the horses. The naked women are easier today; the horses make more of a problem."

He has a Pulitzer Prize (a special citation in 1984), three Oscars (for two documentaries he made in the 1940s and for the 1951 animated short subject, *Gerald McBoing-Boing*), an Emmy and a Peabody Award, and the adoration of millions of children. But the owner of these laurels is characteristically terse in assessing his life's greatest satisfaction: "I think I had something to do with kicking Dick and Jane out of the school system. I think I proved to a number of million kids that reading is not a disagreeable task. And without talking about teaching, I think I have helped kids laugh in schools as well as at home. That's about enough, isn't it?

"Hmmph?"

15

Maurice Sendak and
Dr. Seuss: A Conversation

GLENN EDWARD SADLER
The Horn Book, **September/October 1989**

NARRATOR: How do you get your ideas for books?

DR. SEUSS (DR): This is the most asked question of any successful author. Most authors will not disclose their source for fear that other less successful authors will chisel in on their territory. However, I am willing to take a chance. I get all my ideas in Switzerland near the Forka Pass. There is a little town called Gletch, and two thousand feet up above Gletch there is a smaller hamlet called Uber Gletch. I go there on the fourth of August every summer to get my cuckoo clock repaired. While the cuckoo is in the hospital, I wander around and talk to the people in the streets. They are very strange people, and I get my ideas from them.

N: Mr. Sendak, I know a four-year-old who is afraid of your books. Should she be encouraged to work through those feelings and read the books aloud with us?

MAURICE SENDAK (MS): I think you should leave her alone. I mean there's absolutely no reason why, if the child is frightened, that you would frighten the child still further by trying to make her read the book. Obviously this is a child with a problem. But taking that into consideration, I would not torment the child.

N: Mr. Sendak, were you Pierre as a child?

MS: No, I was never Pierre at any point in my life. Perhaps I harbored his thoughts, but I would not have dared speak to my parents in such a way. That's why I wrote the book.

N: Dr. Seuss, how do you handle the nonsense words in translation?

DR: The books have been translated into about fifteen foreign languages. I have no idea how they handled it in the Japanese. Oddly enough, the Germanic and Nordic languages—German, Norwegian, Swedish, Danish—are much more successful for translating the nonsense words than the romance languages are. Why that is, I don't know. The Germans will take a name like *Bartholomew Cubbins* and turn it into *Bartel Lugepros,* which I think is a very beautiful approximation.

N: Mr. Sendak, when you illustrate books for other authors, do you become closely involved with them? Who do you admire most, and how have they influenced your work?

MS: Well, I've worked with many, many writers. A good many of them don't want to be involved in the illustration process. They have written the book; the illustrator gets it; and that's the end of the relationship. That is, of course, the least interesting way to work. But I've had some half dozen or so writers—such as Randall Jarrell, Ruth Krauss, and Isaac Singer—who were intensely involved with the business of illustrating the book. The work is much better for that involvement. There's the joy of collaboration. One would assume that the writer would want to be involved because, after all, it is primarily his book. I'm just there to adorn and decorate.

N: How would you motivate the child who does not like to read?

DR: That is the job of the mother, I think. The motivation of the child is not Maurice's or my responsibility. It falls to the school and the parents. All we can do is create books and hope that someone steers them into children's hands.

MS: I think Ted is right. We're often confused with being sociologists and psychologists and teachers and parents. We're not. Primarily we are artists. We cannot urge children to read books. I don't know how one goes about doing that.

N: Mr. Sendak, do you ever draw for your own diversion? What do you like to draw?

MS: Occasionally portraits of friends which I never show except to the people who posed. Mostly I draw to music as an imagination exercise. I put some favorite piece on the record player. I start with my hand at the top of the paper, and the whole point of the exercise is to finish that page by the end of the first movement. Needless to say, you get very few good drawings. It is a kind of pleasure drawing I do for myself for the most part.

N: Have the responses of critics made it easier or more difficult for you to accomplish the task of achieving your goals?

MS: It's made no difference whatsoever, alas. It just causes irritation and migraine. If one could learn something from criticism, it would be a marvelous thing. Reading criticism has been a grave disappointment in terms of what one doesn't learn. The process is hurtful for the most part, and in a sense the good reviews are no better than the bad because they don't tell you anything.

DR: I think about the only positive thing is that a good review sells more books than a bad review.

MS: It makes you more cheerful that morning.

DR: It wakes you up.

MS: Your friends, who are waiting for you to get the bad review, don't call you up to commiserate with you.

DR: And you always agree with the good reviews.

MS: You always agree with them. That person has hope for a long life.

N: Do you think there will still be a place for the traditional fairy tale in twenty years?

DR: I would like to see it come back, but I don't think the average child is going to fall for it. No, I miss it, don't you?

MS: Well, there's almost not a place right now for the old-fashioned fairy tale or fantasy. It's hard to imagine where children's literature is going; it's gotten so slippery and glitzy at this point. One almost feels that children's books are going to slide off the face of the earth. The old-fashioned fairy tale at this point, I think, has already slid off. It is not considered seriously. It's already out of date, and most fairy tales, when they are done, are watered down considerably. So we are not getting the real thing.

N: Do your characters live with you all the time?

MS: Well, I hope not. I think we would all be in the madhouse at this point. Is that true for you?

DR: Yes, that's so.

MS: We rid ourselves of these characters by writing them out of our lives.

DR: Yes, we expunge them.

MS: Then new horrors keep springing up all the time. If I ran into these people in my social life, I would flee. I think we are always being chased by these people, and we keep creating books to get rid of them.

DR: If I were invited to a dinner party with my characters, I wouldn't show up.

N: Would you comment on the effect of the media on children today?

MS: Well, it always aggravates me when people get colossally worked up about certain things in my books that supposedly will upset children or upset librarians or parents or teachers. But there seem to be no restrictions on what children can watch on television. Children see massacres continuously on the news—how do you control that? Books are quite controllable. The media is totally uncontrollable and vastly disgusting for the most part, and children are watching it all the time. I wonder how anybody's going to solve that problem. To make a great fuss over an odd word in a Dr. Seuss book or a naked child in a Sendak book seems so fatuously simple-minded in relation to television, where children are being poisoned.

N: Mr. Sendak, do you have a preference for writing or illustrating?

MS: I have a preference for writing. Writing is very difficult and gives me a great deal of pleasure, partly because it is so difficult. Illustrating is very automatic. I have a Polaroid kind of brain. I have to stem the tide of pictures. I don't get those writing images quickly; I have to struggle for them. So naturally I like writing better. When I do achieve something, it feels more victorious. I know I'm going to get illustrations if I just hang in long enough, and that's less challenging at this point in my life.

N: Dr. Seuss, was your first book, *And to Think That I Saw It on Mulberry Street* (Vanguard), rejected by many publishers before it was accepted?

DR: Twenty-seven or twenty-nine, I forget which. The excuse I got for all those rejections was that there was nothing on the market quite like it, so they didn't know whether it would sell.

MS: Publishers are always nervous about original work. They are worried about financial aspects, which corrupt their consideration of a new work. When *Wild Things* (Harper) came out, there was a concern about the effect of this book on the public. It was a natural nervousness about publishing an odd book.

N: Would each of you comment on how much your own early childhood has influenced your work?

DR: Not to a very great extent. I think my aberrations started when I got out of early childhood. My father, however, in my early childhood, did, among other things, run a zoo, and I used to play with the baby lions and the antelope and a few other things of that sort. Generally speaking, I don't think my childhood influenced my work. But I know Maurice's did.

MS: I have profited mightily from my early childhood.

DR: I think I skipped my childhood.

MS: I skipped my adolescence. Total amnesia.

DR: Well, I used my adolescence.

MS: Isn't that interesting, because you get your inspiration from young manhood, and I go all the way back to the crib days for mine.

N: Mr. Sendak, how did your parents feel when you told them you wanted to be a book illustrator?

MS: They were relieved. They had no idea that I could do anything. I did so badly in school. I had a very brilliant sister who skipped grades. I hated her. I had a brother who was dutiful and serious, so I hated him, too. But I could draw, which seemed to be my salvation. In fact, when I could earn a living from that, my father was tearfully content.

N: Do your ideas for books spring forth from free drawing you might be doing, and do you have a direction for your books?

MS: There is a vague sense of a direction; there is no formulated plot. There are certain elements I want to get into the book, and I just dive off and don't know if there's any water in the pond. I find a kind of pleasure in that process. With perseverance I will gradually evolve a book. Creating is a kind of groping in the dark procedure. Yet, when the book is finished, it should have all those elements that satisfy some part of me.

DR: Mine always start as a doodle. I may doodle a couple of animals; if they bite each other, it's going to be a good book. If you doodle enough, the characters begin to take over themselves—after a year and a half or so.

MS: Sometimes that happens quite accidentally. In 1969 I was doing a Mother Goose book, and I found that I was picking out poems that had to do with food, like bread and milk. It seemed a peculiar obsessive interest; "Little Jumping Joan, She ate so much, She went bananas." I finally decided that under the guise of preparing a Mother Goose, my own book was being written. It ended up being called *In the Night Kitchen* (Harper), and I even stole one of the verses. "I see the moon, and the moon sees me" because "I'm not the milk and the milk's not me." So my homage to the original project was in that book. But I had no knowledge that my book was sneaking in.

DR: Sometimes you have luck when you are doodling. I did one day when I was drawing some trees. Then I began drawing elephants. I had a window that was open, and the wind blew the elephant on top of a tree. I looked at it and said, "What do you suppose that elephant is doing there?" The answer was: "He is hatching an egg." Then all I had to do was write a book about it. I have left that window open ever since, but it's never happened again.

N: Dr. Seuss, I understand that much of your work contains actual figures from history and some political commentary. Could you identify these figures?

DR: Not in their actual form. Yertle the Turtle is Adolf Hitler. In *Yertle* (Random), the turtle Mack was on the bottom of the pile until he solved the problem by burping. It makes me realize how much children's book publishing has changed to recall that they had a meeting at Random House to see whether I could use the word *burp*, and that was in the late 1950s. The other historical characters, I don't know about.

N: How do you shut out the reality of the world when you're creating your books? Do nuclear weapons, cancer, unemployment, and pollution affect you?

MS: Well, there is no way you can shut out those facts unless you're insane. Perhaps they permeate the work and color in some particular way, but there is no magic way you can shut the door on all these things. We don't work in "airy fairy land" when we're doing books for children. We are dealing with real life, even though we're using forms that are nonsensical or funny or bizarre. In fact, real life should be in the book. It has to permeate the work. I live in this world.

DR: They're all there, but we look at them through the wrong end of the telescope. We change them in that way.

N: I encountered several discourses concerned with the underlying psychological meanings of your books, Mr. Sendak. How do you feel about that?

It doesn't sound like you had those things in mind when you were writing books.

MS: Well, I didn't. Of course, it's always fun to read about them. There are so many variations, some of them may be quite accurate; I don't know. As an artist you cannot consciously construct a book psychologically because it would not be a work of art. But such interpretations are fun to read.

N: As a closing note, I'd like to leave you with a little quote, something to take with you: "Ninety-nine zillion,/ Nine trillion and two/ Creatures are sleeping!/ So ... / How about you?"

This article shows us what and how children learn from And to Think
That I Saw It on Mulberry Street, The Cat in the Hat,
The 500 Hats of Bartholomew Cubbins, The Lorax,
The Butter Battle Book and other Seuss books.

16

"We need to encourage children to identify and consider issues raised in
Seuss' books, think about the way his characters resolve the issues, and
consider the impact these resolutions have on others," Rita Roth writes.

On Beyond Zebra with Dr. Seuss

RITA ROTH

The New Advocate, **Fall 1989**

There's no end to the things you might know
Depending how far beyond zebra you go.
(Dr. Seuss, 1955, *On Beyond Zebra*)

Like his character who leads a friend beyond "Z for Zebra" and the confines of the conventional alphabet, Theodor Geisel (alias Dr. Seuss) goes
beyond well established boundaries to provide a voice of opposition and possibility—opposition to the established order and possibility for social change.
For more than 50 years the stories of Dr. Seuss have delighted children with
predictable cadence and rhyme, with invented words and cartoon-like illustrations.

Teachers can build upon children's interest in Dr. Seuss by providing
opportunities that encourage them to reflect upon and express their reading
of his books and to connect them to their own lives. In this way students can
move closer to realizing the emancipatory possibilities that Dr. Seuss holds.
His stories are emancipatory in the sense that they provide alternative views
of the way things are and the way they might be, as well as alternative courses
of action to bring about change. Issues of empowerment and control are played
out through the use of imagination and common sense in ways that expand
and enrich lives.

My interest in Dr. Seuss began as an elementary school teacher in the
late sixties. It was apparent that my students were attracted to his books in
a way that was different from their response to most other books for children.
Yet, I never took Dr. Seuss seriously. Was it the careless whimsy that char-

141

acterizes his illustrations and texts that kept me from seeing these stories as "literature"?

I remember feeling puzzled and a little annoyed by the strong preference my students showed for Dr. Seuss. However, there was no way I could ignore their enthusiasm as they read and reread *The Cat in the Hat* (1957) nor their foot-dragging as they approached the basal reader. Whatever the reason for his attraction, it seemed clear to me then that Dr. Seuss, like comic books, provided a kind of frivolity that was not appropriate for school. "Let the children read Dr. Seuss at home," I thought, "not in my classroom." Still, there was no denying the impact of his work and its popularity. I wondered who this Dr. Seuss was and why children were perennially tuned-in to his tales.

Twenty years later, I teach children's literature, language arts, and reading to teachers and prospective teachers. With a less narrow view of what constitutes school language learning and a wider base of experience, I find Dr. Seuss more than a peddler of mere nonsense. Geisel deserves serious attention because his work is replete with social commentary and critique. A "smasher of conventional boundaries," he explores oppression in many forms (Mensch & Freeman, 1987, p. 30). A kind of "non-sense with basic sense" (Sutherland & Arbuthnot, 1986, p. 256), these stories present useful insights into our culture and the experience of childhood.

I look at the writings of Theodor Geisel as a cultural discourse about power relations, as a kind of rhetoric of opposition and possibility. Because these stories call into question ideologies that reinforce the established society, they illustrate the view that the way things are is not necessarily how they must be. What meanings could children take from this perspective? These delightfully zany tales provide children an alternative voice, a voice that turns away from passive conformity and encourages active engagement and a sense of community. In order to place his work in context, let us begin with a look at Geisel himself.

Who Is Dr. Seuss?

In the children's room of a suburban branch of a large, metropolitan public library system, the librarian jokingly responds to my question about Geisel's books. "Dr. Seuss? Oh, we hide Dr. Seuss ... well, not really. We keep him over there on a *special* shelf ... We'd really rather they read something better—something more like A. A. Milne." Upon examining the "special shelf," I find that nearly all Dr. Seuss books have been checked out.

This incident exemplifies one of a number of contradictions surrounding Dr. Seuss: beloved by his audience, yet, until comparatively recently, he was held at arm's length by the children's literature establishment. Although he has become as common a part of elementary classrooms as crayons, it is uncommon to see Dr. Seuss taken seriously. Some children's literature specialists do not see beyond rhyme schemes that admittedly can be taken as trite and contrived, thus closing the door to possibilities that grow out of the rich content of Geisel's work. Others, largely outside the children's literature establishment, disagree. For example, Mensch and Freeman, who are professors of law, say:

> What the snobbish may dismiss as Dr. Seuss' doggerel is an incessant, bouncy anapestic rhythm punctuated by lively, memorable rhymes. In opposition to the conventional—indeed, hegemonic—iambic voice, his metric triplets offer the power of a more primal chant which quickly draws the reader in with its relentless repetition. Moreover, what seems to be the silly whimsy of his books—the made-up words, the outlandish creatures and machines—carries an empowering message [p. 30].

In *Children's Literature in the Elementary School* (Huck, *et al.*, 1987), Geisel is said to be "following a formula of exaggeration" (p. 231), and the reason given for excluding Dr. Seuss books from its 'Guide to Selected Read-Alouds' list is that "Children will have read them on their own" (p. 646).

While his *McElligot's Pool* (1947) was cited as a runner-up for the Caldecott medal in 1948, it was not until 1980—43 years and more than 40 books after his first publication—that Geisel was named the first-place winner of a major award. He received the prestigious Laura Ingalls Wilder Award for making a lasting contribution to children's literature.

In contrast, the film/TV industry has recognized Geisel's work from the start. His *Gerald McBoing-Boing*, made soon after World War II, received an Academy Award. The Peabody Award was given to Geisel for two TV animated films of his books. *How the Grinch Stole Christmas* (1957) and *Horton Hears a Who!* (1954). For the animated version of *The Lorax* (1971) he received the Curtis Award from the International Animated Cartoon Association.

Contradictions abound in the life of Theodor Geisel/Dr. Seuss. His use of a pseudonym is a case in point. "I really don't know why," he says. "Is it shyness? Am I hiding?" (Freeman, 1969, p. 168). Except for an occasional departure, such as Theo. LeSieg (Geisel spelled backwards), Dr. Seuss remains his alter ego.

Another possibility exists: anonymity provides a comfortable separation from Geisel's oppositional discourse. As Dr. Seuss, he speaks outside the establishment; as Geisel, he functions within it. Geisel's description of his father's work experience reveals another contradiction. "After working thirty-five years to run a brewery, the day he [Geisel's father] was appointed president, Prohibition was declared" (Geisel quoted in Wilder, 1979, p. 23).

The irony of his father having done all "the right things" diligently following the work ethic—all for naught—left its mark on Geisel. His father "became very cynical and sat for days in the living room saying, 'S.O.B., S.O.B.' over and over—he didn't know what to do with himself" (quoted in Cott, p. 16). Eventually, he turned what previously had been an honorary position with the Parks Department into a new career, and while the pay was meager, it proved to be meaningful work. Through the use of WPA funds, he built tennis courts, golf courses, and a zoo. Geisel's father "became a philanthropist ... a very worthwhile guy ... changed people's lives more than he would have done if he'd been a millionaire" (quoted in Cott, p. 16). Much of Geisel's boyhood was spent behind the scenes at the zoo his father built where he developed a love for animals, and perhaps, inspiration for his *If I Ran the Zoo* (1950).

Witnessing the elder Geisel's disillusionment with the business world may have had a profound effect on young Geisel. He may have reasoned: "Why conform when conformity is no guarantee for success? Nonconventional work is not only more fun, it is more useful. Perhaps, after all, the best of all possible worlds would be success in the business world without having to conform." It is this kind of logic that tends to surface in Geisel's life and recur throughout Dr. Seuss' writings.

From his school days onward, Geisel has been engaged actively in some form of public comment—school magazine writer, editor, ad man, political cartoonist, film maker, and children's literature innovator. Asked if he considers himself recalcitrant or even a bit subversive, Geisel replied, "I'm subversive as hell!" (quoted in Cott, p. 28).

Dr. Seuss seems to have suffered from well intentioned efforts to apply high standards to the literary form and content of children's literature. Indeed, Geisel experienced the same frustration endured by many writers whose work falls outside commonly accepted conventions and standards for form, content, and illustration. His first book was rejected by 27 publishers (Freeman), and it was not until a chance meeting with a former schoolmate who had just become an editor at Vanguard that *And to Think That I Saw It on Mulberry Street* (1937) was accepted for publication.

To pass over a work that does not fit certain conventions and expectations can be the result of a hidden as well as more easily recognizable censorship. Censorship, according to Shannon (1989):

> is an act of both negation and affirmation because at the same time that censors are removing information, values, and language from children's consideration, they are confirming what knowledge they think is valid, valuable, and virtuous for school curricula and library shelves. In a similar way, those who oppose censorship negate the removal of information and affirm what they think is important for children to know [p. 97].

In other words, rejection can be the indirect result of affirmation. Efforts to ensure the *inclusion* of literary works seen as "highly literate" in terms of style or form, or even literature containing content considered "highly desirable" (such as race or gender) can result in the *exclusion* of literature that moves in new directions. While such literature may not fit established conventions for a genre, it has the potential to expand the field of possibilities. As Shannon says, "covert censorship" is "censorship wherein our collective biases prevent us from considering alternative futures."

The enormous success of *The Cat in the Hat* surprised everyone. Random House was so impressed that it opened a new division, Beginner Books, expressly for the young reader's market with Geisel as president and chief editor. This placed him in the unique position of being author, illustrator, chief editor, and president all rolled into one. Geisel soon learned about marketing. "[W]hen we started Beginner Books we had no idea what we were doing ... I realized there was a level below Beginner Books ... [so] we set up Bright and Early Books for younger and younger readers" (Geisel in Cott, p. 31). His marketing program now supplements traditional library and bookstore sales with ads in magazines like *Woman's Day* and in direct mail packets along with discount coupons for laundry soap and pet food.

Since the spectacular economic success of Beginner and Bright and Early Books, as well as those not targeted for the younger reader (published by Random House, the parent publisher), Geisel has maintained complete control over his work.

As Geisel, then, he has become a publishing magnate, achieving economic success and total authority over his work by operating safely within the status quo. As his anonymous self, Dr. Seuss, he has become a subversive who questions authority and poses imaginative alternatives to the status quo.

The following discussion of selected works by Geisel suggests that the meanings children are invited to take from reading Dr. Seuss center around two themes: first, seeing that the way things are is not necessarily the way they must be; and second, that active engagement in our own lives can involve us in the lives of others. Children are exposed to meaningful models of action through the antics of characters who deal with issues of autonomy, control, resistance, and possibility. They can see that imagination may be a useful tool in dealing with these issues; in finding and carrying out alternatives.

A Discourse of Resistance and Possibility Through Imagination

In Dr. Seuss, children read about authority as disconnected from virtue (Mensch & Freeman). The typical Dr. Seuss protagonist is a nonconformist, a young boy who defies authority and not only survives but who, along with others, is better off for it. While the bulk of Dr. Seuss stories center around an individual rather than a collective response to disempowerment (Shannon,

1986), they typically illustrate the potentially positive effect of an individual's action upon the community.

Dr. Seuss' characters use imagination to develop new possibilities in their lives. This points readers toward themselves and each other as resources. Imagination becomes a means to accommodate, resist, or create transformative ways to deal with the controlling demands of childhood.

Children frequently hear parent and teacher admonishments to "stop daydreaming." But when children read Dr. Seuss they see imagination being prized as a source of power and autonomy in an adult-controlled world. Geisel's first book, *And to Think I Saw It on Mulberry Street*, presents a young boy who receives a double message from his father: Be observant, but don't fantasize.

> When I leave home to walk to school,
> Dad always says to me,
> "Marco, keep your eyelids up
> And see what you can see."
> But when I tell him where I've been
> And what I think I've seen,
> He looks at me and sternly says,
> "Your eyesight's much too keen.
> Stop telling such outlandish tales.
> Stop turning minnows into whales..."

The boy cautiously protects this imaginary world, choosing not to say that his imagination has turned a plain horse and wagon into one more delightful outlandish sight after another:

> There was so much to tell, I JUST COULDN'T BEGIN!
> Dad looked at me sharply and pulled at his chin.
> He frowned at me sternly from there in his seat,
> "Was there nothing to look at ... no people to greet?
> Did *nothing* excite you or make your heart beat?"
> "Nothing," I said, growing red as a beet,
> "But a plain horse and wagon on Mulberry Street."

The boy's decision projects an understanding that, for the powerless child in a world of powerful adults, a private imaginary space is one worth preserving.

The Cat in the Hat and *The Cat in the Hat Comes Back* (1958) exemplify Dr. Seuss' use of imagination as a way to resist authority. This familiar favorite tells of a boy and his sister who dream up a mischievous cat when they are left alone. Children reading or listening to this story understand the implicit message: "Don't get into mischief," and the strong temptation to get into as much mischief as possible. The cat invites the reluctant children to let go; to risk an imaginative venture free from adult-established rules and expectations.

When the Cat's helpers, Thing One and Thing Two, make a complete mess of the house, he miraculously provides a pick-up machine that restores things to normal, just as mother returns. The book ends asking the reader,

> Should we tell her
> The things that went on there that day?
> Should we tell her about it?
> Now, what *should* we do?
> Well ...
> What would *you* do
> If your mother asked *you?*

The question poses the possibility of withholding the incident—of preventing adult intrusion into a promisingly empowered world of imagination.

The 500 Hats of Bartholomew Cubbins (1938), *The King's Stilts* (1939), and *Bartholomew and the Oobleck* (1949) are concerned with power—a king's misuse of power, a resulting problem, and its resolution by a young boy. *The 500 Hats* introduces us to Bartholomew, who

> In the beginning ... didn't have five hundred hats. He had only one hat.
> It was an old one that had belonged to his father and his father's father
> before him.

It is a story of a boy's fantasy meeting with the king and the resolution of the crisis that follows.

His inability to conform to the rule that all must remove their hats to the king is a great a surprise to Bartholomew as it is to everyone. Each time he takes it off another hat pops up on his head. Thus, Bartholomew's innocent defiance infuriates the king. While climbing to the highest turret where he is to be pushed to his death, the boy tries his darnedest to conform. As he pulls off one hat after another, they begin to change, culminating with the irresistible 500th hat. In the end, Bartholomew goes home wealthy, bareheaded, and bereft of innocence.

In *Bartholomew and the Oobleck* readers see Bartholomew in a more direct challenge to authority. Written 11 years later, the book returns the reader to the Kingdom of Didd, King Derwin, and Bartholomew, who now lives in the castle as a trusted page boy. No longer an "innocent," he has complete run of the castle and is privy to the king's deepest thoughts. The king's boredom leads to a demand for "something NEW to come down!" from the sky. Soon everything is covered with green, sticky "Oobleck." As the king struggles to remember magic words to stop the Oobleck, Bartholomew rebels. He speaks out disapprovingly in a reversal of roles:

> YOU ought to be saying some plain, *simple* words! ... this is all *your* fault!
> Now, the least you can do is say "I'm sorry."

Once again, it is a child who provides a resolution to consequences of power-hungry actions. Tampering with nature has its consequences, and technology (modern-day magic) has its limitations. Moreover, youth has a clearer vision of these consequences than those in control—those whose vision is limited by whim, self-interest, and power. It is a reminder that earth's natural heritage is to be valued; that it is possible for authority to be challenged.

Dr. Seuss addresses the theme of environmental preservation in *The Lorax* and *The Butter Battle Book* (1984). Both show the strong cadence, predictable rhyme, invented words and images, and full use of color that typify Dr. Seuss. Both call into question ideologies that are deeply rooted in our culture: the celebration of entrepreneurship and technology. Both speak to the need for critique, for dialogue, and for transformative action.

The Lorax provides the reader a worst-case scenario of greed superseding environmental responsibility. A young boy seeks out a recluse, the Once-ler, to learn about the way things were long before the Lorax was "lifted," when the world had trees and birds. The Once-ler remembers how he ignored the Lorax's pleas to attend to the needs of the environment only to tell the Lorax that "Business is business! And business must grow." Eventually, the Lorax disappears, leaving one puzzling word etched in stone: UNLESS

> But *now*, says the Once-ler,
> Now that *you're* here,
> the word of the Lorax seems perfectly clear.
> UNLESS someone like you
> cares a whole awful lot,
> nothing is going to get better.
> It's not.

In *The Butter Battle Book* Dr. Seuss examines the folly of xenophobia and dehumanization that can grow out of an overdependence on technology. We see two groups, the Yooks and the Zooks, trapped in differing ideological positions: the Zooks, that bread should be eaten with the butter side down; the Yooks, with the butter side up. Here a young boy's grandfather tells the history of this quarrel. Over the years the weapons developed by each group's respective "Boys in the Back Room" become more and more complex. As Yooks enter bomb shelters, the Chief Yook gives the boy's grandfather the newest bomb and says:

> You just run to the wall like a nice little man.
> Drop this bomb on the Zooks just as fast as you can.

The grandfather had always done what was expected of him. Will he now? The last page shows the boy shouting to his grandfather who is face to face atop the wall with a Zook, each holding his newest "bomb":

"Grandpa!" I shouted. "Be careful! Oh, gee!
Who's going to drop it? Will *you* ... Or will *he*..."
"Be patient," said Grandpa. "We'll see. We will see..."

The ideological stance readers could challenge here is clear: adults know best; leaders make reasoned judgments for the good of society and these judgments are above question; technology resolves all problems; cultural difference is to be abhorred and nationalism supersedes all other considerations.

Children can also read how power may be resisted in *King Looie Katz* (1969). The king's preference for having his tail held up to prevent it from dragging on the ground makes this a status establishing practice. Soon every cat has another cat holding up his/her tail—except for Zooie, the last cat in the line:

Poor Zooie got so awfully mad
So mad he could have split.
But he did a far, far braver thing ...
He simply yelled, "I QUIT."

After the initial shock at this unexpected behavior, everyone began to notice Zooie's newfound self-confidence. Soon they all take pride in being able to hold up their own tails.

In *On Beyond Zebra!* (1955) children read about alternatives to what appears to be an indisputable limitation: the alphabet. When a young boy brags about knowing the alphabet all the way to Z, an older boy tells him:

If you stay home with Zebra.
You're stuck in a rut.
But, on beyond Zebra
You're anything but ...
You can stop, if you want, with the Z
Because most people stop with the Z
But not me!
My alphabet starts where your alphabet ends!

The balance of the book presents 20 new, enchantingly different letters that make it possible to say extraordinary things, to break away from what appears to be the way things must be, and to create new options.

Classroom Applications

Increasing numbers of teachers demonstrate daily in their classrooms that children's literature holds great potential to expand and enrich the school curriculum. It can facilitate connections across disciplines, among and within students. It touches us.

Because of its potential, children's literature can be a strong vehicle in the effort to stretch our students, to move them toward critical literacy—a literacy that goes beyond decoding and comprehending, what the author says (Freire, 1973, 1974, 1985). Critical literacy entails reflection—connecting the printed text to our personal experience and prior knowledge. It entails relating the meanings evoked by a text to the practical world; questioning, confirming, rejecting.

Giroux describes critical literacy as a form of cultural politics. He suggests that teachers:

> create classroom conditions necessary for identifying and making problematic the contradictory and multiple ways of viewing the world that students use in constructing their view of the world; [Giroux in Freire & Macedo, 1987, p. 22].

When children become aware of alternatives, when they learn to challenge, accept, adapt, and generate new options, they begin to tap their own voices— to learn what Giroux calls a language of empowerment. "Students need a language of empowerment that permits thinking about community life as possibility" (p. 21).

The works of Dr. Seuss discussed in this article provide an ideal medium in which to engage children in precisely the sort of critical reading, discussion, and reflection called for by Giroux. We need to encourage children to identify and consider issues raised in Seuss' books, think about the way his characters resolve the issues, and consider the impact these resolutions have on others.

What classroom conditions would foster response to themes found in Dr. Seuss? Providing students risk-free opportunities to respond is one necessary ingredient. Building opportunities that go beyond individual response would be another (Freire). That is, students need to identify the themes and possible implications of these themes not only for themselves as individuals, but as members of a community.

To develop the notion of different perspectives, children can engage in role playing. For example, one child, as King Derwin (in *Bartholomew and the Oobleck*), could respond to questions from the group, as members of his kingdom who had tried to deal with the sudden appearance of Oobleck covering their land. Perhaps the problem of his boredom could be resolved in a way that would not only satisfy the king's need but also the needs of his subjects.

After reading a story or having a story read to them, children could retell it, putting themselves into the story as a new character. For example, a student could become Bartholomew's best friend who witnesses the scene where he is confronted by the king. Or, perhaps the child could become a secret friend of the boy or the grandfather in *The Buttler Battle Book* who lives on the other side of the wall. What resources might be gathered to assist a friend? What new resolutions might be imagined? What could be the implications of these resolutions for all Zooks and Yooks, for the whole kingdom of Didd, as well as for the main characters? Perhaps children could work in small groups or with a partner and retell [the story] into a tape recorder. After hearing the story in its retold form, children could compare it to the original, discuss the various forms and the possibilities opened up by the changes.

Expanding discussion circles to include opportunities through the visual arts provides additional avenues for expression (Woodhouse, 1987). A strategy such as "Sketch to Stretch" (Harste & Burke, 1979) invites readers to create images reflecting their perception of a text and its meaning to them. Such a switch to another mode of expression could reveal something new about their own understanding of the text, as well as expose them to understandings of others not previously considered.

To stimulate a tie between the reader and the story, teachers could ask students to consider whether a character's actions make sense to them and why; whether they would have acted differently, and, if so, how; what similar or dissimilar experiences they have had. Using an adaptation of the "Click/Clunk" strategy (in Weaver, 1988, p. 298) students could read with a partner or in small groups and respond, "click" if the story is making sense to them or "clunk" if it is not. They could, for example, consider the way the Zooks and Yooks go about resolving their differences (*The Butter Battle Book*). They could say "click" or "clunk" about the effect of Zooie's decision to stop conforming and start behaving differently than others (*King Looie Katz*).

By modeling response (Singer, 1978) teachers can support the imaginative creation of new possibilities. Modeling ways of thinking about stories can demonstrate the process of reflecting we seek to encourage, show how the issues in these stories are connected to our lives, to the school community, and to the larger community. A teacher or another student thinking out loud provides this kind of model.

> I wonder how Bartholomew was feeling when he could not get his hat off. I know I would be worried. Maybe he will come up with a magic word or maybe someone in the town will help him. Maybe he will become the king's official provider of hats. Maybe he will see to it that everyone in the town has a hat. I wonder what else could happen?

Strategies such as these can facilitate the articulation of alternative viewpoints. The absence of such alternatives, Shannon (1989) noted, narrows our sense of the possible and serves as a conservative force in society. By fostering the construction of collective responses built on the views of the individuals that comprise our classrooms, we can help children gain a greater sense of their connection to one another and the possibility of developing communities that serve the needs of all of their members.

Conclusion

Theodor Geisel provides stories that are populated by characters drawn in cartoon-like style who speak in predictable narrative or verse while providing a rhetoric of opposition and possibility. During a productive half-century, Theodor Geisel has played out two contradictory roles successfully. As Geisel, he is a savvy businessman who knows the rules of the establishment and operates by these rules successfully enough to turn his stories into a multi-million dollar publishing business. As Dr. Seuss, the lighthearted author of children's books, he seeks to subvert the same establishment. Dr. Seuss can help us help our children develop a language of empowerment. By providing varied opportunities for response to his stories, and others like them, we can move children beyond the mere decoding and comprehension of texts and toward a critical literacy that will provide a model of active engagement and a route toward a development of the sense of community our society so sorely needs.

References

Cott, J. (1983). The good Dr. Seuss. *Pipers at the gates of dawn.* New York: Random House, pp. 3–37.

Freeman, D. (1969, 15 June). Parade. *San Jose Mercury News,* pp. 12–13.

Freire, P. (1973). *Education for the critical consciousness.* New York: Seabury Press.

Freire, P. (1974). *Pedagogy of the oppressed.* New York: Seabury Press.

Freire, P. (1985). *The politics of education.* South Hadley, MA: Bergin & Garvey.

Giroux, H. (1987). Literacy and the pedagogy of political empowerment. In P. Freire & D. Macedo (Eds.), *Literacy: Reading the world and the word.* South Hadley, MA: Bergin & Garvey.

Harste, J.C., & Burke, C.L. (1979). Understanding the hypothesis: It's the teacher that makes the difference. *Reading horizons: Selected readings.* Kalamazo, MI: Western Michigan University Press.

Huck, C., Hepler, S., & Hickman, J. (1987). *Children's literature in the elementary school,* fourth edition. New York: Holt, Rinehart & Winston.

Mensch, B., & Freeman, A. (1987). Getting to Solla Sollew: The existentialist politics of Dr. Seuss. *Tikkun,* 2, 30–34, 113–117.

Shannon, P. (1986). Hidden within the pages: A study of social perspective in young children's favorite books. *The Reading Teacher,* 39(7), 656–663.

Shannon, P. (1989). Overt and covert censorship of children's books. *The New Advocate,* 2(2), 97–104.

Singer, H. (1978). Active comprehension: From answering to asking questions. *The Reading Teacher,* 31, 901–908.

Sutherland, Z., & Arbuthnot, M. (1986). *Children and books.* Glenview, IL: Scott Foresman.

Weaver, C. (1988). *Reading process and practice.* Portsmouth, NH: Heinemann Educational Books.

Wilder, R. (June 1979). Catching up with Dr. Seuss. *Parents Magazine,* 60–64.

Woodhouse, M. (1987). A big book and poetry emphasis. In J. Hancock & S. Hill (Eds.), *Literature-based reading programs at work*. Portsmouth, NH: Heinemann, pp. 77–81.

DR. SEUSS BOOKS MENTIONED IN THIS ARTICLE

And to Think That I Saw It on Mulberry Street (1937)

The 500 Hats of Bartholomew Cubbins (1938)

The King's Stilts (1939)

McElligot's Pool (1947)

Bartholomew and the Oobleck (1949)

If I Ran the Zoo (1950)

Horton Hears a Who! (1954)

On Beyond Zebra! (1955)

The Cat in the Hat (1957)

The Cat in the Hat Comes Back (1958)

How the Grinch Stole Christmas (1957)

King Looie Katz (1969)

The Lorax (1971)

The Butter Battle Book (1984)

Novelist Alison Lurie (The War Between the Tates) shows how Seuss went from his early books of wild invention to the later books, such as The Lorax, The Butter Battle Book, You're Only Old Once! *and* Oh, the Places You'll Go!, *which offer more profound lessons for the young—and the not-so-young.*

17

The Cabinet of Dr. Seuss

ALISON LURIE

The New York Review of Books, **Dec. 20, 1990**

Theodore [sic] Seuss Geisel, known to millions as Dr. Seuss, is the most popular living juvenile author in America today. Almost everyone under forty was brought up on his books and cartoons, and even those who didn't hear the stories read aloud or see them on TV probably met his fantastic characters at school. Beginning with *The Cat in the Hat* in 1957, Seuss revolutionized the teaching of reading, managing to create innovative, crazily comic tales with a minimum vocabulary (*The Cat in the Hat* uses only 220 words). The inventive energy of these books and their relative freedom from class and race norms made middle-class suburban Dick and Jane look prissy, prejudiced, and totally outdated.

What made it all the more wonderful was that Dr. Seuss's life was a classic American success story. He began as a cartoonist and advertising artist; his "Quick, Henry, the Flit!" drawings showing a citizen attacked by giant insects, half-comic and half-threatening, were widely reproduced. But his first children's book, *And to Think That I Saw It on Mulberry Street,* was rejected by forty-three publishers; it was finally printed in 1937 only as a favor by a friend.*

An interesting variation on the "first publication" story. The number of rejections in this story usually hovers around 27, the number Geisel most often cited. Forty-three is by far the highest number ever offered. Also, to say the book was "printed ... only as a favor by a friend" harks back to George Kane's mistaken conclusion (in the Rocky Mountain News) that the book was published by a vanity press. It seems very unlikely that Marshall McClintock, as a newly hired editor, would have offered him a Vanguard contract had he not believed the book would sell. —T.F.

Why didn't editors see at once what a winner Seuss would be? Partly because of his artistic style, which was unabashedly cartoon-like and exaggerated in an era when children's book illustration was supposed to be pretty and realistic. Perhaps even more because of the content of his stories, especially their encouragement of wild invention and, even worse, the suggestion that it might be politic to conceal one's fantasy life from one's parents. Children in the Thirties and Forties were supposed to be learning about the real world, not wasting their time on daydreams, and they were encouraged to tell their parents everything.

Marco, the hero of *And to Think That I Saw It on Mulberry Street*, is warned by his father at the start of the book to "stop telling such outlandish tales" about what he sees on the way home from school. Yet the very next day his imagination turns a horse and wagon, by gradual stages, into a full-blown parade with elephants, giraffes, a brass band, and a plane showering colored confetti—all portrayed by Seuss with immense verve and enthusiasm. Marco arrives home in a state of euphoria:

> I swung 'round the corner
> And dashed through the gate,
> I ran up the steps
> And I felt simply GREAT!
> FOR I HAD A STORY THAT NO ONE COULD BEAT!

Then he is quizzed by his father about what he has seen. His reply is evasive:

> "Nothing," I said, growing red as a beet,
> "But a plain horse and wagon on Mulberry Street."

The message that it is sometimes, perhaps always, best to conceal one's inner life reappears in *The Cat in the Hat*.

Here "Sally and I," two children alone and bored on a rainy day, are visited by the eponymous Cat. He proceeds to totally destroy the house, causing first excitement and then panic. (What will their mother say?). Finally he puts everything back in place. The kids—and not only those in the story, but those who read it—have vicariously given full rein to their destructive impulses without guilt or consequences. When their mother returns and asks what they've been doing, there is a strong suggestion that they might not tell her:

> Should we tell her about it?
> Now, what SHOULD we do?
> Well …
> What would YOU do
> If your mother asked YOU?

In these tales the children whose imagination transforms the world are abashed or secretive when confronted with possible adult disapproval. More often, however, Seuss lets fancy run free without equivocation or apology. A whole series of books from *McElligot's Pool* through *On Beyond Zebra!* and *If I Ran the Circus* celebrates the wildest flights of fantasy. They usually begin in familiar surroundings, then move into an invented world where the scenery recalls the exotic landscapes of *Krazy Kat* comics. There, just as Seuss's Elephant-Bird, Tufted Gustard, and Spotted Atrocious defy natural history, so his buildings and roads and mountains defy gravity, seeming always to be on the verge of total collapse.

Though these stories are full of euphoric vitality, there is occasionally something uneasy and unsatisfying about them. Seuss's verbal inventions can become as shaky and overblown as the structures in his drawings. At the end of these books the elaborate language always does collapse. There is an abrupt return to simple diction, and a simple, realistic illustration implicitly declares that Seuss's protagonist was only fantasizing.

Innovative as he was, Seuss can also be seen as squarely in the tradition of American popular humor. His strenuous and constant energy, his delight in invention and nonsense recall the boasts and exaggerations of the nineteenth-century tall tale, with its reports of strange animals like the Snipe and the Side-Winder. Seuss brought this manner and these materials up to date for a generation raised on film and TV cartoons. And, though most of the time he addresses himself almost exclusively to children, he includes occasional jokes for adults. In *If I Ran the Zoo*, for instance, the hero plans to bring a Seersucker back alive; he will also "go down to the Wilds of Nantucket / And capture a family of Lunks in a bucket." According to the illustrations, the Seersucker is a foolish, shaggy, flower-eating animal with what looks like a red bow tie, while Lunks are pale, big-eyed creatures with blond top-knots, captured with the help of beach buggies.

Parents as well as children seem to be addressed in *One Fish, Two Fish, Red Fish, Blue Fish* (1960), in which two kids find a very large uncomfortable-looking tusked sea monster. They exult:

> Look what we found
> in the park
> in the dark.
> We will take him home.
> We will call him Clark.
>
> He will live at our house.
> He will grow and grow.
> Will our mother like this?
> We don't know.

But Seuss is not only in favor of the free-ranging imagination: in many of his books there is a strong liberal, even anti-establishment moral. As in the classical folk tale, pride and prejudice are ridiculed, autocratic rule overturned. In *Yertle the Turtle*, Mack, who is bottom turtle on the live totem pole that elevates King Yertle, objects to the system:

> I know, up on top you are seeing great sights,
> But down at the bottom we, too, should have rights....
> Besides, we need food. We are starving!

So he burps and upsets the whole stack, turning Yertle into King of the Mud. In *Bartholomew and the Oobleck* another overreaching ruler, dissatisfied with the monotony of the weather, commands his magicians to cause something more interesting than rain or snow to fall from the sky. He gets a sticky, smelly substance which, though it appears as green, is clearly excrement ("You're sitting in oobleck up to your chin"); it does not disappear until he admits that the whole thing was his own fault.

In *Horton Hatches the Egg* and *Horton Hears a Who!*, a charitable and self-sacrificing elephant protects the rights of the unborn and of small nations and obscure individuals in spite of the ridicule and scorn of his friends, because "A person's a person, no matter how small." There are limits to charity in Seuss, however. *Thidwick the Big-Hearted Moose* allows his horns to become the refuge of an overwhelming number of immigrant animals and bugs, repeating wearily that "A host, above all, must be nice to his guests." Luckily, just when he reaches the limits of his endurance and is being pursued by hunters, his antlers moult and he escapes. His guests end up stuffed and mounted on the wall of the Harvard Club, "as they *should* be."

For years Seuss's tales were hailed by experts as a wonderful way to teach children not only reading but moral values. Recently, however, a couple of them have run into opposition. Last year loggers in northern California went after *The Lorax* (1971). In this story, a greedy Once-ler and his relatives move into an area of natural beauty and proceed to chop down all the colorful Truffula Trees in order to manufacture Thneeds, which resemble unattractive hairy pink underwear. Soon the sky is choked with smog and the water with something called Gluppity-Glup. Though Seuss said the book was about conservation in general, the loggers saw it as blatant propaganda and agitated to have it banned from the school's required reading list. "Our kids are being brain washed. We've got to stop this crap right now!" shouted their ad in the local paper, taking much the same belligerent anti-environmentalist tone as the Once-ler himself does when criticized:

> I yelled at the Lorax, "Now listen here, Dad!
> All you do is yap-yap and say 'Bad! Bad! Bad! Bad!'

Well, I have my rights sir, and I'm telling you
I intend to go on doing just what I do!
And for your information, you Lorax, I'm figgering
  on biggering
    and BIGGERING
    and BIGGERING
    and BIGGERING
turning MORE Truffula Trees into Thneeds
which everyone, EVERYONE, EVERYONE needs!"

The Butter Battle Book (1984), a fable about the arms race, also provoked unfavorable comment. Like Swift's tale of the Big- and Little-Endians who went to war over how to open an egg, it begins with a meaningless difference in domestic habits. Two groups of awkward looking flightless birds, the Yooks and the Zooks, live side by side; the Yooks eat their bread butter side up, the Zooks prefer it butter side down. They become more and more suspicious of each other, and finally a member of the Zook Border Patrol with the rather Slavic-sounding name of VanItch fires his slingshot. Escalation begins: more and more complicated weapons are developed by the Boys in the Back Room ("TOP-EST, SECRET-EST, BRAIN NEST" says the sign on their door), until both sides possess the means of total destruction. Unlike most of Seuss's books, this one doesn't end reassuringly, but with the child narrator asking anxiously, "Who's going to drop it?/ Will *you*...? Or will *he*...?" *The New York Times Book Review* considered the story "too close to contemporary international reality for comfort," while *The New Republic*, somewhat missing the point, complained that the issues between our real-life Zooks and Yooks were more important than methods of buttering bread.

Other, perhaps more relevant criticisms might be made today of Seuss's work. For one thing, there is the almost total lack of female protagonists; indeed, many of his stories have no female characters at all. The recent *You're Only Old Once!*, a cheerfully rueful tale about the medical woes of a senior citizen, which was on the best-seller list for months, is no exception. It contains one female receptionist (only her arm is visible) and one female nurse, plus a male patient, a male orderly, and twenty-one male doctors and technicians. There is also one male fish.

The typical Seuss hero is a small boy or a male animal; when little girls appear they play silent, secondary roles. The most memorable female in his entire *oeuvre* is the despicable Mayzie, the lazy bird who callously traps Horton into sitting on her egg so that she can fly off to Palm Beach. Another unattractive bird, Gertrude McFuzz in *Yertle the Turtle and Other Stories*, is vain, envious, greedy, stupid, and fashion-mad. She gorges on magic berries to increase the size of her tail, and ends up unable to walk.

Seuss's little girls, unlike his boys, are not encouraged to exercise and expand their imagination very far. In "The Gunk That Got Thunk," one of the tales in *I Can Lick 30 Tigers Today!*, this is made clear. The narrator relates how his little sister customarily used her "Thinker-Upper" to "think up friendly little things / With smiles and fuzzy fur." One day, however, she gets bored; she speeds up the process and creates a giant Gunk:

> He was greenish.
> Not too cleanish.
> And he sort of had bad breath.

She tries to unthink him, but fails; meanwhile the Gunk gets on the phone and runs up a $300 long-distance bill describing recipes. Finally he is unthunk with the help of the narrator, who then gives his sister

> Quite a talking to
> About her Thinker-Upper.
> NOW ...
> She only
> Thinks up fuzzy things
> In the evening after supper.

Moral: Woman have weak minds; they must not be ambitious even in imagination.

Seuss' most recent book, which has been on the *New York Times* best-seller list for thirty-nine weeks, also has a male protagonist. But in other ways *Oh, the Places You'll Go!* is a departure for him. "The theme is limitless horizons and hope," Seuss, now eighty-six years old told an interviewer, and the blurb describes the book as a "joyous ode to personal fulfillment"; but what it really reads like is the yuppie dream—or nightmare—of 1990 in cartoon form.

At the beginning of the story the standard Seuss boy hero appears in what looks like a large clean modern city (featureless yellow buildings, wide streets, tidy plots of grass). But under this city, as an urbanite might expect, are unpleasant, dangerous things—in this case, long-necked green monsters who put their heads out of manholes. Seeing them, Seuss's hero, "too smart to go down any not-so-good street," heads "straight out of town."

At first everything goes well; he acquires an escort of four purple (Republican?) elephants, and rises in the world, joining "the high fliers / who soar to high heights." The narrative is encouraging:

> You'll pass the whole gang and you'll soon take the lead.
> Wherever you fly, you'll be best of the best.
> Wherever you go, you will top all the rest.

In the accompanying illustration Seuss's hero is carried by a pink and yellow balloon high over fields and mountains; his competitors, in less colorful balloons, lag behind at a lower altitude.

Then comes the first disaster: the balloon is snagged by a dead tree and deflated. The boy's "gang" doesn't stop for him—as presumably he wouldn't for them—and he finds himself first in a Lurch and then in a Slump, portrayed as a dismal rocky semi-nighttime landscape with giant blue slugs draped about. Doggedly, he goes on and comes to a city full of arches and domes which looks rather Near Eastern,

> where the streets are not marked.
> Some windows are lighted. But mostly they're darked.

Turning aside (in the light of recent events, an excellent choice), he continues "down long wiggled roads" toward what Seuss calls The Waiting Place. Here the sky is inky black and many discouraged-looking people and creatures are standing about:

> ... waiting, perhaps, for their Uncle Jake
> or a pot to boil, or a Better Break.

For the energetic, ever-striving young American, this is a fate worse than death, and it is vigorously rejected:

> NO!
> That's not for you!
>
> Somehow you'll escape
> all that waiting and staying.
> You'll find the bright places
> where Boom Bands are playing.

Seuss's hero is next seen riding another purple elephant in a procession of elephants, on his way to further solitary triumphs.

> Oh, the places you'll go. There is fun to be done!
> There are points to be scored. There are games to be won...
> *Fame!* You'll be famous as famous can be.
> with the whole wide world watching you win on TV.

In the accompanying picture, some kind of fantasy football or lacrosse is being played—our hero kicking off from the back of his elephant, the other contestants on foot. But almost immediately this success is undercut:

> Except when they don't.
> Because, sometimes, they won't.

> I'm afraid that *some* times
> you'll play lonely games too.
> Games you can't win
> 'cause you'll play against you.

The most dangerous enemy of the celebrity is his own doubt and self-hatred. The illustration shows a totally insecure-looking fantasy version of a Hollywood hillside mansion, where the protagonist is shooting baskets alone. Seuss assumes, no doubt quite properly, that in any career devoted to success, competition, and fame, "Alone will be something / you'll be quite a lot." and that often "you won't want to go on."

But his hero, of course, does go on, meeting a number of comical and/or frightening monsters.

> You'll get mixed up
> with many strange birds as you go...

Seuss predicts. The strange birds, who all look alike, are shown against another totally black background, some marching upward to the right with smiles, others plodding downward to the left with depressed expressions. The message here seems to be that it is a mistake to commit oneself to any organization; instead one must

> Step with care and great tact
> and remember that Life's
> a Great Balancing Act.

This is followed by the happy climax, in which Seuss's hero is even more triumphant than before:

> And will you succeed?
> Yes! You will, indeed!
> (98 and ¾ percent guaranteed.)
> KID, YOU'LL MOVE MOUNTAINS!

This promise is depicted literally in the illustration; if we chose to take it that way, we might assume that Seuss's "kid" has become a property developer, like so many California celebrities.

In one or two of Seuss's earlier books, similar dreams of money and fame occur. Gerald McGrew, for instance, imagines that

> The whole world will say, "Young McGrew's made his mark.
> He's built a zoo better than Ñoah's whole Ark!...

"WOW!" They'll all cheer,
"What this zoo must be worth!"
(If I Ran the Zoo)

This was written in 1950, when Seuss's own imaginary zoo had just begun to make his fortune. Today life has wholly imitated art; his wild inventions, like those of his boy heroes—and of course in the end they are the same thing—have made him fantastically rich and famous. It is difficult to estimate what Seuss's own zoo much be worth now: according to his publishers, over 200 million copies of his forty-two books have been sold worldwide, and many have been animated for TV.

Gerald McGrew and Seuss's other early heroes were content simply to fantasize success. *Oh, the Places You'll Go!* has a different moral. Now happiness no longer lies in exercising one's imagination, achieving, independence from tyrants, or helping weaker creatures as Horton does. It is equated with wealth, fame, and getting ahead of others. Moreover, anything less than absolute success is seen as failure—a well-known American delusion, and a very destructive one. There are also no human relationships except that of competition—unlike most of Seuss's earlier protagonists, the hero has no friends and no family.

Who is buying this book, and why? My guess is that its typical purchaser—or recipient—is aged thirty-something, has a highly paid, publicly visible job, and feels insecure because of the way things are going in the world. It is a pep talk, and meets the same need that is satisfied by those stiffly smiling economic analysts who declare on television that the present recession is a Gunk that will soon be unthunk, to be followed—On Beyond Zebra!—by even greater prosperity.

BOOKS DISCUSSED IN THIS ESSAY

And to Think That I Saw It on Mulberry Street (Vanguard, 1937; Random House, 1988), $9.95

Horton Hatches the Egg Random House (1940), $10.95

McElligot's Pool Random House (1947), $9.95

Bartholomew and the Oobleck Random House (1949), $9.95

Thidwick the Big-Hearted Moose Random House (1949), $9.95; $3.95 (paper)

Yertle the Turtle and Other Stories Random House (1950), $12.95

If I Ran the Zoo Random House (1950), $9.95; $3.95 (paper)

Horton Hears a Who! Random House (1954), $10.95

On Beyond Zebra! Random House (1950), $8.95; $3.95 (paper)

If I Ran the Circus Random House (1956), $9.95; $3.95 (paper)

The Cat in the Hat
Random House (1957), $6.95

One Fish Two Fish
Red Fish Blue Fish
Random House (1960), $6.95

I Can Lick 30 Tigers Today!
Random House (1969),
$9.95; $3.95 (paper)

The Lorax
Random House (1971), $11.95

The Buttler Battle Book
Random House (1984), $9.95

You're Only Old Once!
Random House (1986), $12.95

Oh, the Places You'll Go!
Random House (1990), $12.95

While this article only briefly mentions Seuss, it is important to know what lies on the edges of Dr. Seuss's pages. Writing in The New York Times, *Karla Kuskin explains why many children's books are full of illustrations with characters at the edges of the pages ("bit players" Kuskin calls them) that adults often miss seeing.*

18

The Mouse in the Corner, the Fly on the Wall: What Very Young Eyes See in Picture Books

KARLA KUSKIN

The New York Times Book Review, November 14, 1993

A funny-looking bird in a tree smiles down at the young hero in a Dr. Seuss classic, *The 500 Hats of Bartholomew Cubbins,* as Bartholomew, wearing a red-feathered topper, strides along on a journey that will bring him face to face with King Derwin and 499 more hats. If you are older than 7 or 8 you probably did not notice the bird. That means that you did not notice it either 39 pages later when Bartholomew returns, toting a big bag of gold. So why is that bird there? He's there to interest younger, sharper eyes than yours.

The illustrations of picture books are alive with bit players like that bird, or the two cats who romp through the opening chapters of Attilio Mussino's illustrations for the big 1911 edition of *Pinocchio.* Although they are not mentioned in the text, such actors often play significant roles. The cats in *Pinocchio,* for example, serve as tour guides, especially for nonreaders who follow the story through the pictures. The artist David Small contributes a contemporary cousin of Mussino's cats in Arthur Yorinks's *Company's Coming.* The time is 1988, the place is the suburb of Belmore, and while all eyes are riveted on the U.F.O. that has just landed in Moe and Shirley's backyard, a thin white cat sits tensed at the edge of the scene. As the jokes grow and spin off one another, the cat acts out a running commentary. At the sight of two aliens its eyes widen; the hair on its back stands up when the spacemen enter the house; and while all those around the cat are losing their heads at the thought of an alien invasion, it delicately licks up a deviled egg that has dropped from Shirley's hors d'oeuvre tray.

Who has not longed to be a fly on the wall, a bird on a branch, a mouse in the shadows watching an adventure unfold? When William Hazlitt wrote about being "a silent spectator of the mighty scene of things" he might have been describing the minor players in picture books. Cats, born to watch from the sidelines, wander in and out of Edward Ardizzone's books about Tim at sea *(Tim and Ginger, Tim in Danger)*. The author-artist uses them to establish a wonderful balance between a great adventure and a child's view of the world. When Tim survives a terrible storm and his ship sinks in *Tim All Alone* he is not, in fact, all alone, because the ship's cat is with him. In six pages they wash up on land together, walk the streets of a convenient seaside town together, and together find Tim's lost mother crying in a coffee shop. After a joyous embrace Tim and his mother settle down to tea and talk while the cat laps milk from a dish at their feet.

When I mentioned this scene to a middle-aged Ardizzone fan recently she said, "Cats? I didn't know he did cats." No child could have overlooked them or the other domestic animals that enliven Ardizzone's English countryside. With that special appeal of small, familiar creatures they draw non-readers into a story.

The dachshund in Tomi Ungerer's *Mellops* books beguiles in a similar way. A loyal pet who keeps a low profile, he follows that very charming family of pigs high (flying) and low (spelunking). Mr. Ungerer's art is filled with witty details: tiny mice, interesting pictures on the walls, a lizard here, a turtle there. But the faithful dog becomes the reader's friend and finding him becomes a game, so that a double page without him is disappointing.

Spotting initially minor characters in the picture-book underbrush can be such sport that some minor characters have become stars. In 1964 Hilary Knight's *Where's Wallace?* made a treasure hunt out of a search for an orangutan. Every time the child-sized Wallace escapes from the zoo he loses himself in a crowd at the beach, the circus, the natural history museum. In each crowd scene one not only hunts for Wallace but other recognizable characters who keep showing up. This is a perfect game for a 4- to 6-year-old. In 1987, Martin Handford's *Where's Waldo?* began mining fame and riches from a similar lode. In that book and the five that have followed it, a hiker spends his time getting lost precisely so that we can find him in very crowded scenes like the museum or the beach.

Mitsumasa Anno creates a subtler game of hide and seek in *Anno's Britain, Anno's Italy* and others of this series. In each of them a medieval page on horseback rides through lightly penned town- and country-scapes richly populated with myriad figures to identify from history and literature. Because these are wordless books the silent horseman, like the narrator in a pantomime, sets the pace and leads the way.

The rhythm in a picture book—the way words and pictures move from page to page—is often paced theatrically. In the planning stage a picture book, like film, particularly animated film, is done in storyboard form. The rough illustrations are laid out and matched to the appropriate words: These storyboards resemble comic strips, usually minus the word balloons. A baby crawling from frame to frame or a dog playing hide and seek from page to page contribute to the rhythm a picture book needs to keep readers involved and turning the pages. It is not surprising that such minor characters are also common in animated film and comic strips; they may not say much but they catch young eyes and move things along. The littlest animal tumbling after all the others is almost a Disney trademark. Pogo had a puppy. And Snoopy, who over time made the jump from bit player to the big leagues, has Woodstock, his own silent observer, who in turn has his own groupies, that bunch of birds.

Sometimes the bystander's role goes to a human. In her 1968 version of *The Scroobious Pip*, by Edward Lear, the illustrator Nancy Ekholm Burkert cast two children as the onlookers to the Pip's tour of world wildlife. The Pip, patterned after Lear's original sketches, is a natural conglomerate, parts bird, beast, insect and fish, who introduces readers to each of those groups. Only human beings are left out of the verse, so the children in the illustrations become their representatives as well as ours.

Randolph Caldecott (1846–86), the English artist who set the modern picture book in motion, employed a human family of four as the silent observers in the miniature drama he constructed out of *A Frog He Would A-wooing Go*. Father, mother and two daughters are first seen from afar as the elegantly attired Mr. Frog sets out on his wooing. The artist, working a bit like a camera, gradually brings the family into closer focus until at the end of the tale they stand marking the site of Mr. Frog's demise. The children cling to their parents, the father reflects gravely on the sad event and the mother points with her umbrella at Mr. Frog's last remains: his flattened top hat. The formal solemnity of the human observers adds one more layer of humor to the tale.

Maurice Sendak uses a faithful German shepherd to indicate the passage of time in his 1988 edition of the Grimms' tale "Dear Mili." In a series of three paintings of the child Mili and the old man (who is St. Joseph), the shepherd ages from puppy to young dog to grizzled old dog. Because the people remain unchanged we realize that they are immortal. Like Caldecott, Mr. Sendak is a master of what the author and editor Charlotte Zolotow refers to as "visual subplots." In his 1965 *Hector Protector* and his new *We Are All in the Dumps with Jack and Guy* he has quarried English nursery rhymes and come up with fully illustrated dramas. In the verse in *Hector Protector* that begins "As I went over the water," a sea beast with bangs rises from the waves, determinedly swallows an ocean liner and then slowly and happily regurgitates it in a solo turn worthy of a very large Esther Williams. We see the creature, the creature sees all, yet it is never mentioned in the verse.

But an illustrator's work is not simply to echo words, Mr. Sendak has explained. In *We Are All in the Dumps with Jack and Guy* a group of children forms a Greek chorus of witnesses that is mirrored by a chorus of multi-colored kittens. Above them the moon, which is not mentioned in that rhyme, not only looks on from on high but also descends to earth to play a starring role in the book's climax.

Observers are everywhere in *Komodo!* by Peter Sis. They peer from jungly flora that, when examined with care, begins to resemble fauna of the lizard persuasion. By creating this watchful green world, Mr. Sis makes a child's imagination visible. This child is in love with dragons. He has come to visit Bali and see a real Komodo dragon. When the time comes to leave, the ship passes the tiny island of Komodo. If you are under 8 you will look closely at that island. It lies in the sea curled around its own tail, watching.

"Pick any Seussian invention, and nature will equal it.... It is important to remember that the world of science is a made-up world, a world of let's pretend, no less so than the strange flora and fauna of Dr. Seuss," Chet Raymo explains.

In fact, as Raymo demonstrates, for every improbable beast in the world of Seuss, there is an equally improbable creature in nature.

Raymo's article is valuable for the perspective he brings—that of a scientist examining Seuss.

19

Dr. Seuss and Dr. Einstein: Children's Books and Scientific Imagination

CHET RAYMO

The Horn Book, September/October 1992

A few years ago, when an insect called the thrips—singular and plural—was in the news for defoliating sugar maples in New England, I noted in my Boston *Globe* science column that thrips are very strange beasts. Some species of thrips give birth to live young, some lay eggs, and at least one species of switch-hitting thrips has it both ways. Not even the wildest product of Dr. Seuss's imagination, I said—the Moth-Watching Sneth, for example, a bird that's so big it scares people to death, or the Grickily Gractus, a bird that lays eggs on a cactus—is stranger than creatures, such as the thrips, that actually exist.

As if to prove my point, a reader sent me a photograph of a real tropical bird that does indeed lay eggs on a cactus.

What about the Moth-Watching Sneth? Well, the extinct elephant bird of Madagascar stood eight feet tall and weighed a thousand pounds. In its heyday—only a century or so ago—the elephant bird, or Aepyornis, probably scared many a Madagascan half to death.

Pick any Seussian invention, and nature will equal it. In Dr. Seuss's *Mc-Elligot's Pool* (Random) there's a fish with a kangaroo pouch. Could there possibly be such a fish in the real world? Not a fish, maybe, but in South America there is an animal called the Yapok—a wonderfully Seussian name—that takes its young for a swim in a waterproof pouch.

Dr. Seuss, who died last year at age eighty-seven, was a botanist and zoologist of the first rank. Never mind that the flora and fauna he described were imaginary. Any kid headed for a career in science could do no better than to start with the plants and animals that populate the books of the madcap master of biology.

One thrips, two thrips, red thrips, blue thrips. The eggshell of an elephant bird, cut in half, would make a splendid salad bowl. Is it Seuss, or is it reality? You see, the boundary between the so-called "real" world and the world of the imagination begins to blur. And that is just as it should be if a child is to grow up with a proper attitude toward science.

Do black holes, those strange products of the astronomer's imagination, really exist? What about electrons, invisibly small, fidgeting in their atomic shells? How about the dervish dance of DNA as it unzips down the middle to reproduce itself? No one has ever seen these things, at least not directly. Like the Gractus and the Sneth, they are wonderful inventions of the imagination.

Of course, we are convinced—for the time being at least—that black holes, electrons, and unzipping DNA are real, because of the way those things connect with other things we know about the world and because certain experiments turn out in certain ways. But it is important to remember that the world of science is a made-up world, a world of let's pretend, no less so than the strange flora and fauna of Dr. Seuss. The physicist Michael Faraday once said, "Nothing is too wonderful to be true." To be a good scientist, or to have a scientific attitude toward the world, one must be able to imagine wonderful things—even things that seem too wonderful to be true.

Creative science depends crucially upon habits of mind that are most readily acquired by children: curiosity; voracious observation; sensitivity to rules and variations within the rules; and fantasy. Children's books that instill these habits of mind sustain science. I am not talking about so-called "science books for children." I am not talking about "fact" books. I would argue that many science books written especially for children may actually diminish the very habits of mind that make for good science.

I occasionally review children's science books for a splendid journal called *Appraisal.* Most of the offerings I have been sent for review are packed full of useful information. What most of these books do not convey is the extraordinary adventure story of how the information was obtained, why we understand it to be true, or how it might embellish the landscape of the mind. For many children—and adults, too—science is information, a mass of facts. But facts are not science any more than a table is carpentry. Science is an attitude toward the world—curious, skeptical, undogmatic, forward-looking. To be a scientist, or simply to share the scientific attitude, one must be like the kid in Dr. Seuss' *On Beyond Zebra!* (Random) who refused to be limited by the fact of the alphabet: "In the places I go there are things that I see/ That I *never* could spell if I stopped with the Z."

We live in an age of information. We are inundated by it. Too much information can swamp the boat of wonder, especially for a child. Which is why it is important that information be conveyed to children in a way that enhances the wonder of the world. For example, there are several fine information books for children about bats. But how much richer is that information when it is presented this way:

> A bat is born
> Naked and blind and pale.
> His mother makes a pocket of her tail
> And catches him. He clings to her long fur
> By his thumbs and toes and teeth.
> And then the mother dances through the night
> Doubling and looping, soaring, somersaulting—
> Her baby hangs on underneath.

There is every bit as much information in Randall Jarrell's *The Bat-Poet* (Macmillan) as in the typical informational book. But, oh, what information!

If a child is led to believe that science is a bunch of facts, then science will not inform the child's life, nor will science enhance the child's cultural and imaginative landscape. Every September I meet a new crowd of students who have the dreariest impressions of science. For many of them, science is a dull, even painful, subject to be gotten out of the way as a general education requirement, then quickly replaced in life by astrology, parapsychology, or some other pseudoscience. By all means let's have books for kids that communicate what we know—or think we know—about the world; the more factual information we accumulate about the world, the more interesting the world becomes. But the scientific attitude—ah, that's something else. There is no better time to communicate the scientific attitude than during childhood, and no better way than with quality children's books. Consider these lines of Jarrell's *The Bat-Poet:*

> The mother eats the moths and gnats she catches
> In full flight; in full flight
> The mother drinks the water of the pond
> She skims across.

That wonderful line—"In full flight; in full flight"—conveys the single most important fact about bats: their extraordinary aviator skills. By repeating the phrase, Jarrell not only teaches us a bat fact but also helps us experience what it means to be a bat.

Curiosity, voracious seeing, sensitivity to rules and variations within the rules, and fantasy. These are habits of mind crucial for science that are best learned during childhood. Let us consider them one by one.

Curiosity. Albert Einstein wrote: "The most beautiful experience we can have is the mysterious. It is the fundamental emotion which stands at the cradle of true art and true science." At first, this might seem a strange thought as it applies to science. We are frequently asked to believe that science takes mystery out of the world. Nothing could be further from the truth. Mystery invites curiosity. Unless we perceive the world as mysterious, we shall never be curious about what makes the world tick.

My favorite books about curiosity are the children's books of Maurice Sendak, precisely because of their successful evocation of mystery. Sendak's illustrations convey the spooky sense of entwined order and chaos, good and menace that we find in nature. In *In the Night Kitchen* (Harper) Mickey hears a *thump* in the night. Down he falls, out of his pajamas, into the curious world of the night kitchen. The night kitchen is full of familiar things—the city skyline in the background consists of boxes and cans from the pantry—yet nothing is quite the same as in the daylight world. Mickey takes charge. He molds; he shapes; he rearranges. He contrives clothes from bread dough, and a dough airplane, too. He takes a dip in a bottle of milk. The night kitchen is the awake world turned topsy-turvy.

Mickey's adventure is a dream, of course, but so what? The American social philosopher Lewis Mumford said: "If man had not encountered dragons and hippogriffs in dreams, he might never have conceived of the atom." It is an extraordinary thought, that science depends upon the dreaming mind. The dreamer, says Mumford, puts things together in ways never experienced in the awake world—joining the head, wings, and claws of a bird with the hind quarters of a horse—to make something fabulous and new: a hippogriff. In the dream world, space and time dissolve; near and far, past and future, familiar and monstrous merge in novel ways. In science, too, we invent unseen worlds by combining familiar things in an unfamiliar fashion. We imagine atoms, for example, as combining characteristics of billiard balls, musical instruments, and water waves, all on a scale that is invisibly small. According to Mumford, dreams taught us how to imagine the unseen world.

In science we talk about "dreaming up" theories, and we move from the dreamed-up worlds of the night kitchen, Middle-Earth, Narnia, and Oz to dreamed-up worlds that challenge the adult imagination. An asteroid hurtles out of space and lays waste a monster race of reptiles that has ruled the earth for two hundred million years. A black hole at the center of the Milky Way galaxy swallows ten million stars. A universe begins in a blinding flash from a pinprick of infinite energy. How did we learn to imagine such things? Mumford believed that dreams released human imagination from bondage to the immediate environment and to the present moment. He imagined early humans pestered and tantalized by dreams, sometimes confusing the images of darkness and sleep with those of waking life, subject to misleading hallucinations, disordered memories, unaccountable impulses, but also animated now and then by images of joyous possibility. These are exactly the characteristics I admire in Sendak's works. As long as children are reading such books, I have no fear for curiosity.

Voracious observation. I love books that stretch a child's powers of observation. Graeme Base's *Animalia* (Abrams). The books of Kit Williams. Richly textured books. Books hiding secrets. Of these, my favorites are the books in Mitsumasa Anno's Journey series—Bayeux tapestries that hide a hundred observational surprises. The more you look, the more you see, ad infinitum. Texture is everything.

The texture of a book can be too simple, or too complex. It can be uninteresting, or hopelessly cluttered. The nineteenth-century physicist James Clerk Maxwell said: "It is a universal condition of the enjoyable that the mind must believe in the existence of a discoverable law, yet have a mystery to move in." Anno's books have a rich textural complexity, but they are structured by discoverable law. As often as I have perused these books, with children and alone, I have found new elements of law, subtly hidden, shaping the whole. With such books the child practices the very qualities of mind that led Maxwell to the laws of electromagnetism.

Rules and variations within the rules. If there is one thing that defines science, this is it. The Greeks called it the problem of the One and the Many. They observed that the world is capable of infinite variation yet somehow remains the same. And that's what science is—the discovery of things that stay the same in the midst of variation.

The human mind rebels from too much constancy and from too much chaos, preferring instead a balance of sameness and novelty. Endless variation within a simple set of rules is the recipe for the perfect game: patty-cake, ring-around-the-rosy, blackjack, chess, science. We learn this first in the nursery, with the rhyme on mother's or father's knee:

> Jack and Jill
> Went up the hill,
> To fetch a pail of water;
> Jack fell down,
> And broke his crown,
> And Jill came tumbling after.
>
> Then up Jack got,
> And home did trot,
> As fast as he could caper;
> To old Dame Dob,
> Who patched his nob
> With vinegar and brown paper.

The nursery song initiates the child into a kind of playful activity for which science is the natural culmination. Rhyme is a special activity marked off from ordinary experience by the parent's lap and the book. Presumably, the infant recognizes rhyme as a special use of language. The language of the rhyme is more highly structured than ordinary discourse, by rhyme, rhythm, and alliteration. In a chaos of unarticulated sound and dimly perceived meanings, the nursery song evokes a feeling of recognition and order. "Ah, this is familiar," is the emotion the child must feel. "This makes sense." The semantic aspect of the song is not the important thing. The rhyme creates order. Its perfection is limited and temporary, but it is enough to provide security and pleasure. The order of the rhyme is an end in itself, and the child will be quick to set even a minor deviation straight with, "That's not the way it goes." We do not begin to understand why the human mind responds this way, but in the nursery rhyme we are touching upon a quality of mind that drives science.

Tension between rules and the breaking of rules is a common theme of children's books. Chris Van Allsburg's award-winning *Jumanji* (Houghton) tells the story of a board game that two children find in the park. The game has three simple rules regarding the game pieces, rolling the dice to move through the jungle to the Golden City, and the object of the game. And a final rule: once the game is started, it will not be over until one player reaches the Golden City. And now comes the fun—and terror—as the children find themselves swept along by the rules of the game. Is it a dream? Is it life?

A side effect of those children's science books which stress factual information is a conviction on the part of the child that science is all rules, all order, all comprehensibility. Nothing could be further from the truth. The rules of science exist within a matrix of ignorance. The chaos and incomprehensibility of the natural world is not exhausted by science. As Thomas Huxley said, the point of science is to reduce the fundamentally incomprehensible things in nature to the smallest possible number. We haven't the foggiest notion what things such as electric charge, or gravity, or space, or time are. These are fundamentally incomprehensible. Why they exist we haven't a clue. We are content if we can describe a multitude of other things in terms of these fundamental incomprehensibilities. Science is an activity that takes place on the shore of an infinite sea of mystery.

Fantasy. The physicist Bruce Lindsay defined science this way: "Science is a game in which we pretend that things are not wholly what they seem in order that we may make sense out of them in terms of mental processes peculiar to us as human beings.... Science strives to understand by the construction of theories, which are imaginative pictures of things as they might be, and, if they were, they would lead logically to that which we find in actual experience." In other words, a scientific theory is a kind of fantasy which is required to match the world in a particularly strict sort of way. We have ample testimony from great scientists of the importance of fantasy to creative scientific thought. Einstein said: "When I examine myself and my methods of thought, I come to the conclusion that the gift of fantasy has meant more to me than any talent for abstract, positive thinking."

In the nineteenth century, educators often opposed encouraging a child's gift for fantasy. Knowledge imparted to children by Victorians was required to be "useful," as opposed to "frivolous." Victorian children who wanted to read romances, or fairy tales, had to do so by candlelight in the night closet or in the privacy of the park. What a sad, sad notion of what it means to grow up! I would more quickly welcome into my science classes the child who has traveled in Middle-Earth and Narnia than the child who stayed home and read nothing but "useful" information. In his most recent book of essays, *The Fragile Species*, Lewis Thomas says this of childhood: "It is the time when the human brain can set to work on language, on taste, on poetry and music, with centers at its disposal that may not be available later on in life. If we did not have childhood, and were able to somehow jump catlike from infancy to adulthood, I doubt very much that we would turn out human." And, he might have added, we would certainly not turn out to be scientists.

Let's not be too overly concerned about providing science facts to children. A child absorbs quite enough science facts from school and television, from computers and the other rich technologies at the child's disposal. If we want to raise the children who will grow up to understand science, who will be citizens who are curious, skeptical, undogmatic, imaginative, optimistic, and forward-looking, then let's turn the Victorian rule on its head and put into the hands of children books that feed imagination and fantasy. There is no better time to acquire scientific habits of mind, and no better instigator than quality children's books.

In my Boston *Globe* science column I have had occasion over the years to make reference to Dr. Seuss, Antoine de Sainte-Exupéry's *The Little Prince* (Harcout), Lewis Carroll's Alice books, Kenneth Grahame's *The Wind in the Willows*, Felix Salten's *Bambi*, and other children's books. In writing about science I have made reference to children's books far more frequently than to adult literary works. This is not an accident. In children's books we are at the roots of science—pure, childlike curiosity, eyes open with wonder to the fresh and new, and powers of invention still unfettered by convention and expectation.

How does a mother say good-bye when a grown son leaves home?
By turning to the good Dr. Seuss.

20

Turning Loose

Sue Monk Kidd

Guideposts, September 1991

Boxes are strewn across the floor of my son's room in various stages of packing. Two tan suitcases lie open on the bed. The drawers in his dresser jut out like stairsteps, almost empty. I stand in the doorway and watch Bob sort through the items in his room, deciding which ones he'll take to college and which ones he'll leave behind.

I can hardly comprehend this moment. Dear God, I think, I give birth to a baby and feed him carrots; I swoon when he says ma-ma and rock him all night when he gets a fever. I sing him silly songs and read him books and teach him to ride a bike and beam when he catches a fly ball in Little League. And now here I stand in the doorway, bewildered as he packs up to leave.

I watch as Bob picks up a book he got as a graduation gift. It's titled *Oh, the Places You'll Go!* and has a swirling rainbow on the cover. He ponders the book a moment, then puts it back on the shelf. I remember when he received it some weeks earlier. "Dr. Seuss?" he said a little indignantly. "That's for children!"

That was my sentiment too, until I read the book jacket. "It says here this book is for people of *all ages,*" I explained to Bob. "The perfect send-off for children starting out in the maze of life, be they nursery school grads or medical school achievers.'"

But he set the book on the shelf, unimpressed.

There was a time, of course, when my son would have done somersaults at receiving a Dr. Seuss book. Somewhere in the garage there's a whole box of them, along with all the other discarded remnants of his childhood.

I let out a sigh, wondering how this moment of life has arrived so quickly. Yesterday my child was sitting on my lap reading *The Cat in the Hat*. Tomorrow he is leaving home. I can't help it. I wonder if he's ready to be on his own. I wonder if *I'm* ready for him to be on his own. Sending a child off into the world is a new thing for me, and I don't much like the way it makes me feel.

Across the room Bob pulls his baseball glove from the closet. "I may need this," he tells me, dropping it in a box. "The university has intramurals."

"That sounds like fun," I say, hoping he doesn't notice that my voice is quivering.

He doesn't. "Mama, do you know where my baseball cleats are?" he asks.

"I'll look in the garage." I hurry off, glad to escape the sight of his room being stripped bare.

The garage is layered with all the stuff we can't bring ourselves to throw out. We're about a dozen garage sales behind. I look in several places for the cleats, without any luck. Finally I rummage through an old box in the corner. At the bottom of it is the minnow net that I bought four-year-old Bob when Sandy and I took him for a summer vacation at the beach. Suddenly my chest feels like something inside is being torn from me. I sink down onto the cool cement floor and stare at the net through a blur of tears.

That summer vacation Bob and I had a daily ritual. We would go to the beach first thing every morning. We would spread out our towel and read Dr. Seuss' *One Fish, Two Fish, Red Fish, Blue Fish*. When we finished I would say, "Ready to catch red fish and blue fish?" And off Bob would go along the shore with his new minnow net, skimming for fish, and I'd tag right behind him as if I were sewn to his shadow.

Fourteen years later I can see it clearly in my memory: the chrome-colored waves sliding in and out and Bob, small and tawny-skinned, with this little net flung over his shoulder. I clutch the net to my breast with shaking hands.

I have not cried once over this nest-emptying experience, but now my grief spills out, grief for the little boy chasing blue fish. I'm surprised it hurts this much. Tears drop off the end of my nose. "Please, God," I cry. "Help me turn loose."

Later that night I wander back into Bob's room. "Did you ever read that Dr. Seuss book you got for graduation?" I ask. He shakes his head.

"Me either," I say. I pull it off the shelf, plop down on the bed and open it, thinking of the way I read to him on the beach that long-ago summer.

I scan a few pages. It's filled with the inimitable Seuss rhymes and illustrations. "Listen," I say to Bob, who's playing a video game across the room.

He protests. "Aw, Mama."

But I read out loud anyway:

> Congratulations!
> Today is your day.

You're off to Great Places!
You're off and away!...
Oh, the places you'll go.

The rhymes are about a young fellow setting out into life with all its ups and downs, traveling to amazing places and experiencing amazing things, *all on his own*. Bob flicks off the video game and edges over. He peers across my shoulder at a picture of this fellow meeting up with several menacing gremlins that look an awful lot like frankfurters with green eyes. The verse says:

All alone!
Whether you like it or not,
Alone will be something you'll be quite a lot.
And when you're alone, there's a very good chance
you'll meet things that scare you right out of your pants.

But on you will go though the weather be foul.
On you will go though your enemies prowl.

As I read, Bob chuckles. Sometimes I chuckle too. The heaviness I've been feeling begins to fade a little.

One of the last pictures shows the dauntless adventurer single-handedly pulling a mountain behind him like a wagon.

And will you succeed?
Yes! You will, indeed!
(98 and ¾ percent guaranteed.)

When I close the book, I notice Bob's eyes are fired with eager anticipation. I stare at the title of the book, *Oh, the Places You'll Go!*, and a thought suddenly radiates in my mind as luminous as the swirling rainbow on the cover. *This time the shoreline Bob will walk is life itself, and if he's going to become truly whole and independent, he needs to walk it on his own, without me tagging behind like a hovering shadow.*

That night I do not sleep. I keep thinking about tomorrow. I keep trying to get the minnow net out of my dreams.

The next afternoon is warm and sunny as Bob, his father and I drive onto the campus, winding through redbrick, white-columned buildings and sprawling southern oaks. It's a nice place. Big, but nice.

It takes six trips, from the car and up three flights to Bob's dormitory room, to haul all the stuff he's brought. I help him put his clothes in the drawers. "Remember, wash the whites separate from the darks. And don't wash wool. It shrinks," I tell him.

"I *know*, Mama," he says. I look at him. Does he? Does he really know all these things?

There are suddenly about 50 other pieces of motherly wisdom I want to bestow on him. I have a particular urge to mention that he should not go around in short sleeves in 30 degree weather, or skip breakfast, or wait till the last minute to write his term papers, three things he's bad about doing. But then these are "gremlins" he's going to have to face on his own.

I arrange a blue rug across the tile floor of the dorm room, then tuck a blanket around his bed. His father helps him nail a poster on the wall. Finally, too quickly, it's all done.

We walk down the steps in silence. We pause on the sidewalk beside the car and stand there looking awkwardly at one another, trying to figure out how to say good-bye.

He's wearing his all-star baseball cap, grinning at us from under the bill. His daddy grabs him and gives him a hug. Then Bob turns to me. I reach for him and hold him. Then I turn loose. It is nearly the hardest thing I ever did in my life. "You'll be fine," I tell him.

Sandy and I stand still on the sidewalk and watch him walk away. At the corner of the dormitory he looks back over his shoulder and waves. I swallow real hard, then smile and give him the thumbs-up sign.

That night I go to the garage and take the minnow net from the box. I carry it into Bob's room, where I hang it on the wall beside his high school senior picture. In the lamplight the picture takes on a golden reflection, and the net seems to shine from the rays of a sunlit beach. I stare at them both a long while, pondering the seasons of love in a mother's life, knowing there's a time to hold and a time to let go, a time to tag along and a time to wave good-bye.

Then I turn to the window, my heart traveling far into the night. "Oh, Son, the places you'll go!" I whisper.

And finally, Daisy-Head Mayzie, *published posthumously,
the only Dr. Seuss book with a little girl as the main character.*

21

Dr. Seuss Finally Transcended the Gender Barrier

JAN BENZEL, *THE NEW YORK TIMES;*

published in the *Houston Chronicle,* January 20, 1995

My friend Harriet often calls to dissect movies, books, magazines and the news of the day. Because she is a speed reader, she somehow manages to digest mountains of publications even though she, like me, has two children under 5.

The phone rang one morning. "I've got a real problem with *One Fish Two Fish Red Fish Blue Fish,*" she said. "Have you read it? The only girl in the whole book is brushing hair."

Sure enough, on Page 46, accompanying Dr. Seuss's goofy drawing of a girl grooming a tiny yellow creature with big blue hair, is the offending verse:

> All girls who like
> to brush and comb
> should have a pet
> like this at home.

Not that I have anything against hairbrushing. In fact, I wish a little more of it happened in my house. And at this very moment, Harriet is very probably putting the finishing touches on a Cinderella birthday cake. But it was a shock to notice that even Dr. Seuss, that title of the preschool bookshelf, known and loved for his egalitarianism, feeds the cult of the preening princess.

As the Cat in the Hat, Sam I Am, Horton and the Grinch have re-entered my life, I've had to agree: Girls get short shrift in Seuss.

181

Of the 42 children's books Theodor Seuss Geisel published before his death in 1991, not one had a title character who was female. Not all the guys are model citizens, of course; there are wimps and sticks-in-the-mud, power mongers and party poopers, troublemakers and blowhards.

There are a couple of nasty mamas, like the kangaroo who taunts Horton in *Horton Hears a Who!*, and her counterpart, the bird who abandons her nest, in *Horton Hatches the Egg*. Horton, at least, is a sensitive New Age pachyderm. But the girls are mostly silent sidekicks, if they're there at all.

Until now. *Daisy-Head Mayzie* has hit the bookstores, with a television version coming next month on TNT. At last, a bona-fide girl star in a Dr. Seuss story.

Or is it pseudo-Seuss?

Daisy-Head Mayzie, it seems, was based on a screenplay that Geisel's widow, Audrey, found among his papers after his death. Random House, Geisel's longtime publisher, says the illustrations were "inspired by Seuss's sketches found in his original manuscript." The Cat in the Hat adds to the Seussian atmosphere with a guest appearance as the narrator.

Mayzie is no Joan of Arc. She's more victim than heroine. Here's what happens: A daisy sprouts on the top of her head. She becomes a celebrity, embraced by politicians, exploited by a sleazy agent who makes her piles of money in daisy-head spinoffs. But then poor Mayzie has a crisis. She doesn't know if anyone loves her. Think Forrest Gump meets Sally Field.

Still, even though the lines are no match for "I meant what I said, and I said what I meant.../ An elephant's faithful—one hundred percent!," they feed a hunger for fresh Seussian rhyme:

> Daisy-Head fever was gripping the nation.
> It had quickly become a world-wide sensation!
> Daisy-Head burgers and Daisy-Head drinks.
> Daisy-Head stockings,
> And Daisy-Head sinks.
> Daisy-Head buttons
> And Daisy-Head bows.
> Mayzie was famous
> The star of her shows.

And on one page, I found a nod to feminism that I point out each time I read the book to my girls: Mayzie's mother is a blowtorch-wielding welder.

Mayzie's hardly going to counter the forces of nature that hammer girls with the message that hair is important and the purpose of life is to marry a prince. But at least she is the star of her shows. It's a step.

It's hopeless to try to ward off the cultural behemoths that dominate the lives of even the preschool set these days.

So far I've managed to keep our apartment a Barbie-free zone, but I know it's just a matter of time. Most of the 4-year-old girls we know already have whole collections. My personal favorite is the one whose ample, pink-corseted chest detaches, revealing—what else?—a convenient mirror in which Barbie can check her lipstick. And even I would feel deprived in a life without Disney, but it rankles that for all its ballyhooed heroines, every movie still seems to end with a wedding.

At 4 and 2, my girls are soaking up the subtleties and puzzling over what girls are "supposed" to do when they grow up. Boys absorb the messages too: Girls aren't important, and they never get to do the fun stuff. Who would you rather be, Jasmine or Aladdin?

Denial is fruitless. All I can do is counterattack.

So I fill our shelves with alternative literature. Harriet introduced me to *The Paper Bag Princess* (by Robert N. Munsch, illustrations by Michael Marchenko; Annick Press, $4.95 and 99 cents), in which the resourceful Elizabeth, dressed only in a paper bag, outwits a dragon to save the helpless Prince Ronald. Ronald, a snappy dresser who never goes out without his tennis racket, tells her she's a mess. She blithely tells him he is a bum and skips off into the sunset.

I pass along paperback copies to my sisters and friends as if it were a subversive leaflet, along with *Tumble Tower* (by Anne Tyler, illustrated by Mitra Modarressi; Orchard Books, $14.95), in which Princess Molly the Messy teaches her neat family a lesson or two, and *My Working Mom,* (by Peter Glassman, illustrated by Tedd Arnold; Morrow, $15) about a little girl who is proud of her mother, a broomstick-riding witch. *Amazing Grace* (by Mary Hoffman, illustrations by Caroline Binch; Dial, $14) is there, too, the story of a young black girl, who, when she's told she can't play Peter Pan because she's not a boy and not white, triumphs in the audition and wins the role.

And my favorite, a gift from my sister: *Miss Rumphius* (by Barbara Cooney; Viking, $14.95), about a girl who grows up to travel to faraway places and rise to the challenge her grandfather set her: to do something to make the world more beautiful.

I've picked up tactics from other mothers: One young friend of ours was convinced that Mowgli, romping through Disney's *Jungle Book* with a pageboy haircut just like hers, was a girl. Her mother refrained from bursting that bubble.

And Dr. Seuss? I have a hard time holding a grudge against a guy who makes me laugh every time I open his books. His messages about humanity, delivered in his hilarious twists and turns of the tongue, apply to both sexes. Some of his characters look pretty androgynous, anyway. And my girls can't read yet, so I edit: I change the he's to she's. I'm sure he'd understand.

22

Theodor "Dr. Seuss" Geisel died in his sleep in La Jolla, California, September 24, 1991, at the age of 87.

Publishers Weekly, *the magazine of the book industry, followed Theodor Geisel's career for decades. Dr. Seuss had many friends at Random House and was widely admired throughout the book industry. It is fitting to reprint the memorial that appeared in the issue of* Publishers Weekly *immediately following Geisel's death.*

Dr. Seuss Remembered

Publishers Weekly, **October 25, 1991**

The world of children's books lost an incomparable talent on September 24, when Ted Geisel, better known as Dr. Seuss, passed away in his sleep at his home in La Jolla, Calif., at the age of 87. We asked a few of the people who knew him and worked with him to share some of their memories.

Gerald Harrison, president, Random House Merchandise Division

Trying to remember Ted in just a few words is like trying to cram a giant into a small bottle. This was a man who created a whole new world, a whole new way of viewing children's books and in doing so he left a legacy of delight for all children, for all time.

Ted was not only a brilliant master of word and rhyme, and an original and eccentric artist, but down deep, I think he was basically an educator. He helped teach kids that reading was a joy and not a chore; for children and adults he exposed the follies of war, of fascism, of wasting our natural resources. For those of us who worked with him, he taught us to strive for excellence in all the books we published.

We all miss Ted terribly, but we, and all the world, are a better lot because he gave us so much of his energy and his extraordinary talent.

Janet Schulman, publisher and division v-p, Random House Books for Young Readers

I had the great privilege of being Ted's editor for the last 11 years and I

can unequivocally say that he was the perfect author. He didn't require editing. He didn't need or want ego building. And he didn't believe that authors
should be paid for their work until the book had actually sold, so he never
accepted an advance against royalties. In short, he was old-fashioned in all
the best and most endearing ways.

He was an intensely private person but he did like to come to New York
to personally deliver a new book. He wouldn't let me read it or even tell me
what it was about until he presented the whole perfect word-and-picture
package. All he would tell me about *The Butter Battle Book* was that it was
about some people who ate their bread butter-side-up, and some others who
ate their bread butter-side-down. I had no idea that it was a book about
nuclear disarmament until he brought it all finished to New York. I say "all
finished," but actually, because of the method in which Ted's books are produced, there was still quite a bit of art decision-making to be done. Along
with the manuscript, Ted delivered black line drawings. Then he and our
executive art director, Cathy Goldsmith, would laboriously select the precise
ink percentages needed to obtain the color that Ted wanted for every tree,
umbrella, balloon, house, the whole works. No one but Ted made books that
way nowadays.

For years, whenever anyone would ask me, "What are you doing to find
a new Dr. Seuss?" I just laughed. There will never be another Dr. Seuss. We're
going to miss our friend as a person, but he will live on for us at Random
House and for future generations of readers through his wonderful books.

Cathy Goldsmith, executive art director, Random House Books for Young Readers

For more than 10 years, I had the honor—and the pleasure—of working
with Ted. I say "working with," because I've never known what label to give
to the work that I did for Ted. It certainly wasn't "art direction," because Ted
did not need any. Once a project left Ted's board, it was my job to see that it
came together the way that Ted wanted—that the color was right, the type
position correct, the printing sharp and clear.

Whatever the label, working with Ted was a lot like reading one of his
books. You had to be prepared for almost anything. Ted did things with words
and characters that no one else could. Just about the time that you thought
you had it all figured out, boom—he'd turn it all upside down and inside out
and make it even better than before. And, as if that weren't enough, there
were those colors, those wonderful unique Seuss colors.

This sense of the unexpected extended into his personal relationships as
well. In June 1989, I had just returned from California where I had been
working with Ted on *Oh, the Places You'll Go!* While there, I was quite taken
with a dwarf lime tree growing in the garden outside the house. A few days

later, a package arrived, looking for all the world like a black-velvet jeweler's box. That's exactly what it was, but there wasn't any jewelry inside. There was one perfect little lime. The note said that as recognition for all my help, I'd been voted a one-third share in the Meyer Lime Tree. (Ted and the Cat in the Hat held the other two shares.) That one lovely lime was my share of that year's crop. At the time, I thought it was a very special gift. It doesn't begin to compare, however, to the many wondrous books that Ted gave to all of us during his lifetime.

Robert Bernstein, advisor and editor-at-large at John Wiley; formerly president, chairman and CEO of Random House

Ted was above all a dear, loyal, and lovable friend. His books, both words and drawings, were so completely original that I believe as time goes on he will be recognized as a creative genius. Despite his enormous success he was modest, somewhat shy, and completely without greed.

My favorite times were when I would go to La Jolla as each book neared completion and he would wait for my opinion, actually nervous about what he had produced. A completed book was mounted on cork boards on three walls of his studio. When I expressed my complete delight, which was so easy to do, he would still challenge me to be sure I wasn't just being kind.

Once he was ready to throw out a book, *The Sneetches*, because a friend thought it had a note of prejudice. His relief when I told him this was nonsense was overwhelming. I always found it hard to believe that this amazing man had self-doubt even for a moment.

While always humorous, Ted was serious too, and concerned about the United States. He had invented, among other things, a law firm and constantly referred to it in short letters he would send me every month or so. The last one arrived July 12 and read as follows:

> *Dear Robert:*
>
> *I would not wish to be quoted on this and I have absolutely nothing whatever against Grimalken, Drouberhannus, Knalbner and Fepp, but as the Supreme Court moves further and further to the right, I am placing more and more of my litigation into the hands of Abernathy, Arbuthnot, Proudfoot and Cadwallader.*
>
> *Very Confidentially,*
>
> *Theodor S. Geisel*

Some people are hard to replace in one's life. Ted is impossible.

Christopher Cerf, writer, producer and composer

Among all his amazing talents, Ted Geisel was a consummate practical joker. My father, who became his publisher back in the '40s, used to delight me with the story of how Ted got even with a name-dropping acquaintance who constantly annoyed everyone by bragging about his connections in the world of avant-garde art. Ted greeted the offender one day with a piece of exciting, if contrived, good news: "I just had dinner with Seppälä, the great Finnish surrealist, and he's dying to meet you! I assume you know his work?" "Of course I do," Geisel's acquaintance replied impatiently—exactly the response Ted had counted on.

A meeting was hastily arranged at Seppälä's studio, and, as Ted escorted him there, he provided one small missing bit of information: "As you know, poor Seppälä is suffering from an extremely rare—and extremely contagious—disease. But you'll be fine as long as you don't let him touch you. To make sure this doesn't happen, Seppälä's painted a line down the middle of his studio. As long as you both stay on your own side of the line, there'll be no problem."

If the name-dropper was worried about this as he entered Seppälä's digs, he had little time to reflect on his fears: the "surrealist," actually a confederate of Ted's who had painted his face in what my dad described as "a range of colors wondrous to behold," rushed across the line and—with a cry of "My discoverer! My benefactor!"—embraced the hapless name-dropper in a vise-like hug. "It was a lesson that made a better man of him," Ted reported to my father with a self-effacing shrug.

Stan and Jan Berenstain

When our son, Leo, was four, he came home from day care with a request for a terrific book they had at school—it was called *McElligot's Pool* and could we buy it for him. We could and did, and were thus introduced to the uniquely wonderful words and the wonderfully unique illustrations of Dr. Seuss.

By dint of our submission of a manuscript to Beginner Books, a company that followed upon the extraordinary success of *The Cat in the Hat* and of which Ted was president and editor-in-chief, we were introduced to the great man himself. And great man he was: warm, charming and genially welcoming to a couple of neophyte children's authors, but also trenchant, dedicated and uncompromising about the serious business of being meaningfully funny for children. Over the next 13 years Ted was editor of 19 of our books. It is more than 30 years since we first met Ted in the eagle's aerie office at the top of the old Villard mansion that served at Random House's headquarters, but hardly a day passes that one or the other of us doesn't draw upon his wit, wisdom and *joie de vivre*.

And what of parents who read Dr. Seuss books to generations
of children? They, too, offered their tributes.

23

He Left Us Smiles

LEONARD S. MARCUS

Parenting, **December/January 1992**

When Theodor Geisel, aka Dr. Seuss, died eight weeks ago, front-page obituaries and network news broadcasts reeled off the author's numerous literary accomplishments (48 books translated into 20 languages), his many prestigious awards (a Pulitzer and two Emmys, among others), and a long list of his colorful creations (Sneetches, Zooks, and, of course, the Grinch). But while Geisel will be remembered for the respect he brought to the field of children's literature, his most lasting impact was his ability to address kids —tenderly and candidly—on their own fiercely imaginative terms.

Part playful jester, part hard-edged satirist, and part provocateur, the sharp-tongued Geisel rebelled against the delicate, protective approach taken by many writers, and the emotional squeamishness and sentimentality that characterized much of what had passed for kids' books. "... All the stories about fluffy little bunnies.... Terrible stuff," he told *Parenting* in one of his last major interviews, in 1987. Children want "the same things we want," he said. "To laugh, to be challenged, to be entertained and delighted."

In place of fluffy bunnies, Geisel created such vibrant characters as the Cat in the Hat and the Lorax—characters that celebrated children's innate curiosity, independent-mindedness, and love of boisterous mischief. From his first children's book, *And to Think That I Saw It on Mulberry Street,* published in 1937, to his last, *Oh, the Places You'll Go!* in 1990, he championed the incorrigible free spirits of this world, gently urging kids to embrace life as a wildly improbable, sometimes treacherous, but ultimately exhilarating adventure. Always one to eschew convention, he tackled some of the most troubling aspects of the modern world—including the threats of nuclear war and environmental disaster—because, he believed, kids not only can handle such difficult, sad, and scary subjects, but they are fundamentally curious about them.

Geisel never had any children of his own. "You make 'em, I amuse 'em," he often quipped. When asked to account for his work's universal appeal, he responded, "It's the verse, to a great extent. The absurdity, perhaps? And the fun." Equally important was his firm and quixotic resolution to "be a child" himself. And in so doing, he left shelvesful of captivating stories, and a wealth of wise, insightful messages to the world's children and parents, not the least of which is, "A person's a person no matter how small."

Typical of teachers' responses to Geisel's passing was this essay,
which appeared in The Reading Teacher *magazine.*

24

Oh, the Places You've Taken Us: *The Reading Teacher*'s Tribute to Dr. Seuss

Elizabeth B. Moje and Woan-Ru Shyu

The Reading Teacher, May 1992

And when things start to happen,
don't worry. Don't stew.
Just go right along.
You'll start happening too.
OH! THE PLACES YOU'LL GO!
You'll be on your way up!
You'll be seeing great sights!
You'll join the high fliers
who soar to high heights.

The above excerpt, taken from the most recent Dr. Seuss book, *Oh, the Places You'll Go!* (1990), is representative of the spirit and optimism Theodor Seuss Geisel offered to children of *all ages* for the last half century. When Geisel died on September 24, 1991, in his California home at the age of 87, he left many sad hearts, but he also left a rich legacy of "great sights and high heights." And what he also left us was the encouragement to explore life's journey with the same enthusiasm he had. Thus, we write this tribute to Dr. Seuss to acknowledge and celebrate his contributions to children's literature and to the lives of both adults and children around the world.

Beware of the Cat!

Dr. Seuss is a household name, but just who was the man behind the name? Dr. Seuss was a legendary author who lived in a converted lighthouse with a sign that read "Beware of the Cat." And, he was the creator of such well loved characters as Bartholomew Cubbins, the Lorax, Sam-I-Am, and the Cat in the Hat. More than 200 million copies of his 47 books have been purchased by parents, grandparents, and children in Japan, Israel, Norway, Sweden, Denmark, Germany, Holland, Italy, Brazil, and the countries of the British Commonwealth over the last 54 years.

However, the famous author was not always known as Dr. Seuss. Born in Springfield, Massachusetts, on March 2, 1904, he was known by his given name Theodor Geisel until he became involved in a minor infraction of school rules while attending Dartmouth College. After being dismissed from his post as editor-in-chief of the college humor magazine *Jack-o-Lantern* as a result of his shenanigans, he started using his middle name, Seuss, in order to continue writing for this magazine. When he dropped out of Oxford University in 1927, where he was studying English literature, he added "Dr." to his middle name because he did not want to disappoint his father. Even though he assumed various nicknames during the 1920s—such as Theo Seuss 2nd and Dr. Theophrastus Seuss—the name Dr. Seuss brought Theodor Geisel the most fame. A string of honorary doctorates, the first one from his alma mater, Dartmouth College, and the most recent from Princeton University, added academic credentials to the already world-famous doctor's reputation.

While attending Oxford, his attention was diverted by classmate Helen Palmer, who urged Geisel to pursue an art career. Her advice motivated him to leave the university and travel through Europe in 1926-27. During his travels, Geisel produced drawings representative of what he called his "Roman and Florentine Period." His travels completed, he returned to the United States in 1927, where his exotic animals doing the cocktail-party circuit were an uncommon subject for cartoons. A genius at creating a page crowded with images and spiced with a telling line of dialogue, he insightfully recorded the mores of society in popular humor magazines. He also expressed a political sensibility in his work from his earliest Dartmouth drawings of the 1920s to his explicit political cartoons of the early 1940s (Brezzo, 1986).

When his work was spotted by a Standard Oil advertising executive, Seuss was contracted to develop an ad campaign for the oil company. He also created other advertising campaigns for Schaefer Bock Beer, Ford Motor Company, Atlas Products, New Departure Bearings, NBC Radio, and Holly Sugar.

In 1927, Seuss married the former Oxford classmate, Helen Palmer, who had encouraged his art career. Palmer would remain his wife and business partner until her death 40 years later.

Seuss stumbled on the idea of writing children's books when he illustrated *Boners* (1931), a collection of schoolboy cartoons. He illustrated this publication in an attempt to circumvent his advertising contract which prohibited him from most commercial publishing ventures. Seuss did not want to be limited to illustrating, however, and in 1937 wrote, for his own amusement, his first full-length book *And to Think That I Saw It on Mulberry Street*. In the atmosphere of 1930s children's books, *Mulberry Street* became an instant hit once Seuss managed to convince publishers to accept it. "The Seuss style was born fully developed: looping, free-style drawings; clanging, infectious rhymes; and a relentless logic" (Kanfer, 1991, p. 71).

With the publication of *The Cat in the Hat* (1957), Random House (publisher of all the Dr. Seuss books since 1939) created a special division, Beginner Books, with Seuss as president. Best seller followed best seller; prize followed award. For example, Seuss was awarded an Oscar for the animated cartoon *Gerald McBoing-Boing* (1951), an Emmy for the *How the Grinch Stole Christmas* television special (1982), and a Pulitzer citation in 1984 for his overall contributions to the field of children's literature. His book *Green Eggs and Ham* (1960) was so successful that children actually mailed Seuss green eggs and ham as tokens of affection! In 1968 Seuss launched another learn-to-read concept with the creation of *The Foot Book*, and pioneered a new Random House division for preschool and kindergarten readers: Bright & Early Books.

Seuss created some of his most language-conscious works during the 1970s, including *There's a Wocket in My Pocket!* (1974), *I Can Read with My Eyes Shut!* (1978), and *Oh Say Can You Say?* (1979). These books helped establish the idea that children could experiment with language by reading humorous and appealing stories.

In 1984 the words of Dr. Seuss made headlines when *The Butter Battle Book* set a world's record by appearing for 6 months on *The New York Times* adult best-seller list. New York governor Mario Cuomo urged everyone to read this "magnificent little volume" for a clearer understanding of the issues surrounding nuclear war. And Seuss's final work, *Oh, the Places You'll Go!* (1990), approached life the way Geisel did, as a journey in which one could "move mountains."

"He Writes to Amuse Himself"

How did Dr. Seuss start writing? Why did he draw such wild pictures? And how did he think up those crazy places and names? In other words, as one 8-year-old fan wrote, "Dear Dr. Seuss, you sure thunk up a lot of funny books. You sure thunk up a million funny animals.... Who thunk you up, Dr. Seuss?" (Freeman, 1969, p. 12).

What was his answer? Seuss described his illustrations in this way: "My animals look the way they do because I can't draw" (Bunzel, 1959, p. 107). Seuss also claimed that he could think up and draw such unusual places with such crazy animals because he had been to most of those places before. The animals' names were no problem to spell, he said, because he kept a special dictionary with each animal listed in it for quick reference (Bunzel, 1959).

As for his stories, Seuss's first wife and business partner, Helen, explained, "Ted doesn't sit down and write for children. He writes to amuse himself. Luckily what amuses him also amuses them" (Bunzel, 1959, p. 113). Such amusement was usually inspired by conversations, overheard phrases, or as an accompaniment to some of his doodling. Sometimes rhythms would pop into his head, as the title of *And to Think That I Saw It on Mulberry Street* did. Seuss described the book as being written for "no lofty reason whatsoever."

> In the fall of 1936, while aboard the S.S. Kungsholm on a long rainy crossing of the Atlantic, I amused myself by putting words to the rhythm of the ship's engine. The words turned out to be *And to Think That I Saw It on Mulberry Street* [Hopkins, 1969, p. 255–256].

While *Mulberry Street* grew out of the rhythm of a ship's engines, *Bartholomew and the Oobleck* (1949) was inspired by something Seuss overheard a fellow G.I. say as they passed on a muddy street in France during World War II.

> "Rain! Always rain comes down!" one soldier was muttering as he passed me. "Why can't something new, something different, come down?" ... I stood there in the wet with an exciting idea running around and around in my head. Maybe something new could come down! [Commire, 1982, p. 113].

The Cat in the Hat, perhaps the most famous Dr. Seuss book, was, in contrast, the result of a concerted effort to write a particular kind of book. In the mid–1950s author John Hersey wrote an article in *Life* magazine condemning the Dick-and-Jane type of writing found in elementary school readers. Hersey challenged Dr. Seuss to use his skill to create books with controlled vocabulary which could still appeal to children. Seuss took up the challenge. He received a contract and a public school word list from a publishing company, and he started to write.

> Writing children's books is hard work, a lot harder than most people realize, and that includes most writers of children's books. And it never gets any easier. I remember thinking that I might be able to dash off *The Cat in the Hat* in two or three weeks. Actually, it took over a year. You try telling a pretty complicated story using less than two hundred and fifty words! No, don't, unless you're willing to write and rewrite [Commire, 1982, p. 114].

Writing such a book was apparently so difficult that Seuss almost gave up.

The popular story behind the writing of this book says that in frustration Seuss was looking through discarded sketches when he happened to spot one of a cat. Seuss took another look at the word list and two words which rhymed jumped out at him: cat and hat. At that moment, the infamous cat in the stovepipe hat was born (Freeman, 1969, p. 13).

The number-one selling Seuss book, *Green Eggs and Ham*, was written as a result of a bet with his publisher at Random House, the late Bennett Cerf (Clifford, 1991). Cerf bet Seuss that he could not write a book using only 50 words. Not only did Seuss manage to write such a book, but he wrote a best seller! According to Jane Clifford of the *San Diego Tribune* (1991), Seuss once said that *Green Eggs and Ham* was the only book he had written that still made him laugh.

Although Dr. Seuss described his work as being written for children, the meanings and purposes behind his books have long been a source of speculation. Critics often asserted that Seuss set out to write didactic moral lessons. According to children's literature critic E. J. Kahn, "In his books might never makes right, the meek inherit the earth, and pride frequently goeth before a fall, usually a pratfall" (cited in Clifford, 1991, p. C1).

Seuss, however, scoffed at the notion that he wrote to convey a moral message. The author claimed that he never wrote with a moral message in mind, but he did admit that morals developed naturally from the plots of his stories (Lingemann, 1976). Said Seuss in an interview, "Kids … can see a moral coming a mile off and they gag at it. But there's an inherent moral in any story" (Bunzel, 1959, p. 113).

One popular Seuss book often cited for its allegedly moral purpose is *Horton Hatches the Egg* (1940). According to Seuss, however, the book was written as a result of his doodlings of an elephant on a piece of transparent paper. The paper had been shifted about on his desktop when Seuss noticed it lying atop a sketch of a tree. "I stopped, dumbfounded. I said to myself, "That's a hell of a situation. An elephant in a tree! What's he doing there?'" (Kahn, 1960, cited in Commire, 1982, p. 111). Almost a month later, Seuss found himself in the midst of creating a story about an elephant playing surrogate for a duck.

Dr. Seuss was adamant about writing to have fun, which usually helped him produce books that children could have fun with, too. "My books don't insult their [children's] intelligence. Maybe it's because I'm on their level. When I dropped out of Oxford, I decided to be a child, so it's not some condescending adult writing" (*Parenting*, 1987, in Clifford, 1991, p. C2).

Apparently, Seuss drew a fine line between moralizing and examining issues. While Seuss denied sending moral messages, he never denied writing about issues. "It's impossible to write anything without making a statement in some way" (Freeman, 1969, p. 13). For example, Seuss wrote *Yertle the Turtle* (1958) as a reaction against the fascism of World War II, *The Lorax* (1971) in response to environmental concerns, and *The Butter Battle Book* (1984) to reflect on nuclear proliferation. *The Lorax* (which Seuss listed as his favorite) stirred up such negative feelings in the lumber industry in the northwestern United States that some schools considered banning its inclusion on school reading lists. Seuss argued that while the book was political, "propaganda with a plot," he also stated that it was a result of his frustration with the waste of natural resources in the world in general, not a direct attack against specific industries in the USA (Lamb, 1991).

Regardless of the meanings critics extended to Seuss books, his personal reason for writing was clear: Seuss wanted to write so children could have fun reading. "I'm trying to capture an audience. Most every child learning to read has problems, and I am just saying to them that reading is fun" (*New York Times*, 1968, cited in Commire, 1982, p. 116).

"You Make 'em, I'll Amuse 'em"

Whenever Seuss was asked about why he had remained childless throughout his lifetime, he consistently responded, "You make 'em, and I'll amuse 'em" (Freeman, 1969, p. 13). And amuse them, he did. Whatever critics may say about the messages Dr. Seuss's books convey, none can deny the immense popularity the legendary author enjoyed throughout his lifetime. All of the 47 Dr. Seuss books he wrote and illustrated during his 54-year career are still in print. In addition, Geisel published several other books under the pseudonym "Theo LeSieg" ("LeSieg" is "Geisel" spelled backward).

Young fans were frequent, albeit uninvited, visitors at the Seuss home in La Jolla, California, and letters of admiration poured in by the thousands (Clifford, 1991). One 9-year-old once wrote Seuss that "This was the funniest book I ever read in nine years," while another declared, "Dr. Seuss, you have an imagination with a long tail!" (Freeman, 1969, p. 12).

The secret to the enduring popularity of Seuss books lies in the fact that Seuss wrote with a "sense of anarchy," claims Peter Neumeyer, children's literature professor at San Diego State University (Lamb, 1991). But children's literature critic Lorrene Love Ort offered a different explanation in 1955 when she asserted that Seuss provided children with a sense of "secure suspense" in his wild explorations of the imagination (Ort, 1955). Maurice Sendak, author of such children's favorites as *Where the Wild Things Are*, saw Seuss as a "mischief-maker and revolutionary" who was "on the side of the kids" (Emerson, 1991). Sendak called Seuss "the big papa," saying that the inspiration for his own books was drawn from the early work of Dr. Seuss (Lamb, 1991). Charlotte Zolotow, author and publisher of children's books, said of Seuss, "He went straight to the most elemental feeling that people had, and the characteristics of certain personalities, and he caught it with a sense of mischief and fun and compassion and understanding" (Emerson, 1991, p. E8). In his essay "Psychological Aspects of Nonsense Literature for Children," Leo Schneiderman credits Seuss with providing children an opportunity to experiment with independence, imagination, and problem-solving (Schneiderman, 1989).

Such sentiments are heard not only from fellow writers and children's literature critics, but from children, parents, and teachers who have spent time with Dr. Seuss over the last half-century. In fact, we asked several *RT* readers to reminisce about Dr. Seuss so we could share these thoughts. The first respondent, Jackie Conaway, a grandmother who often buys Dr. Seuss books to augment her grandchildren's collections, related this anecdote:

> When my children were young, we spent several vacations at cabins in Wisconsin fishing with my in-laws. We, of course, always took along a large bag of books for the trip and for any rainy days we might encounter. My father-in-law was a very loving, caring man who would do anything for his grandchildren. He was not a skilled "read-aloud" reader, but he always obliged the children when they requested a story. They usually chose a book by Dr. Seuss. They would race for a spot right next to Grandpa, and once they were settled, he would read along gamely in his monotone, "Fox, Socks, Box, Knox, Knox in box.... Sue sews socks of fox in socks now." He hesitated at times, grinning at the potpourri of language. The children's eyes were glued to the pages—they knew every word—it did not matter that Grandpa was reading in a monotone. What mattered to them was that Grandpa was sharing himself with them. What a winning combination—Grandpa and Dr. Seuss!

"He Never Even Really Grew-Up"

Theodor Seuss Geisel worked diligently at his craft of entertaining children and adults with fun stories that often carried important messages, intended or not. Writing was a struggle for him because he had such a high regard for children. "Children have as much right to quality as their elders," Seuss stated in one interview (Bunzel, 1959, p. 113). Perhaps Seuss realized the importance of amusing, exciting, exuberant literature for children because he was still a child at heart. According to Judith Morgan, friend and biographer of the late author, "Ted never grew old. He never even really grew up. Each of our visits ... was a joyful, mischievous revelation with his wonderfully skewed view of the world which was also his defense against its pomposity and foolishness" (Lamb, 1991, p. A8). Morgan's statement leaves us with an optimistic feeling. Although Dr. Seuss is gone from our world, he has not, like the fickle cat he created, simply disappeared with a tip of his hat. Dr. Seuss has left us a treasury of literature by which we can visit and journey with him for generations to come.

Oh, the places you've taken us! Thanks, Dr. Seuss.

References

Brezzo, S.L. (1986). *Dr. Seuss from THEN to NOW.* New York: Random House.

Bunzel, P. (1959). Wacky world of Dr. Seuss. *Life*, 46, pp. 107–108, 110, 113.

Clifford, J. (1991, September 25). A farewell to Dr. Seuss, *San Diego Tribune*, pp. C1–2.

Commire, A. (Ed.). (1982). *Something about the author.* Detroit, MI: Gale Research Company, pp. 107–116.

Emerson, B. (1991, September 25). So long, Dr. Seuss, *Atlanta Journal*, pp. E1, 8–12.

Freeman, D. (1969). Who thunk you up, Dr. Seuss? *San Jose Mercury News*, pp. 12–13.

Hopkins, L.B. (1969). *Books are by people.* Citation Press.

Kanfer, S. (1991, October 7). The doctor beloved by all. *Time*, p. 71.

Lamb, J.R. (1991, September 25). Dr. Seuss dies. *San Diego Tribune*, pp. A1, 8.

Lingemann, R.R. (1976, November). Dr. Seuss, Theo LeSieg…. *The New York Times Book Review*, pp. 24, 48.

Orr, L.L. (1955). Theodor Seuss Geisel—The children's Dr. Seuss. *Elementary English*, 32, 135–142.

Schneiderman, L. (1989). Psychological aspects of nonsense literature for children. In C.C. Anderson & M.F. Apseloff (Eds.), *Nonsense literature for children: Aesop to Seuss* (pp. 94–109). Hamden, CT: Library Professional Publications.

Many magazines have recognizable personalities. Over the years, Time *has been cynical, skeptical and prickly. Yet after Ted Geisel's death,* Time's *Stefan Kanfer warmly and generously called Dr. Seuss "one of the last doctors to make house calls."*

Time *was not the first (and won't be the last) to write about Seuss in rhyme.*

25

The Doctor Beloved by All

STEFAN KANFER

Time, **October 7, 1991**

He was one of the last doctors to make house calls—some 200 million of them in 20 languages. By the time of his death last week at 87, Dr. Seuss had journeyed on beyond Dr. Spock to a unique and hallowed place in the nurseries of the world.

Actually, the title was as imaginary as the name. The first doctorate Theodor Seuss Geisel ever earned was an honorary one, given by his alma mater, Dartmouth. Young Theodor began his education in the public schools of Springfield, Mass., where his father was a part-time zookeeper. The avid student decided to become a professor. After college he went to Oxford, where his attention was diverted by Helen Palmer, a fellow American student who would remain his wife until her death 40 years later. The couple returned to the States just in time for the Depression: Theodor fed his soul by trying to write serious novels and filled the refrigerator by concocting an ad campaign for a spray insecticide: "Quick, Henry, the Flit!"

"I was successful but frustrated," he recalled. To amuse himself he wrote a volume for the very young: *And to Think That I Saw It on Mulberry Street.* In the Dick-and-Jane atmosphere of '30s children's books, it became an instant hit. The Seuss style was born fully developed: looping free-style drawings; clanging, infectious rhymes; and a relentless logic. "If I start with a two-headed animal," he maintained, "I must never waver from that concept. There must be two hats in the closet, two toothbrushes in the bathroom and two sets of spectacles on the night table." Each succeeding book was a refraction of some life experience. *If I Ran the Zoo* acted out a childhood fantasy: the postwar *Horton Hears a Who!* ("A person's a person no matter how small") poignantly echoed the emotions he felt after visiting Hiroshima.

In the 1950s, Seuss began a one–Dr. battle against illiteracy. For beginning readers he created an overnight success, *The Cat in the Hat*, with a vocabulary of 220 words. Best seller followed best seller: prize followed award. He was given an Oscar for the animated cartoon *Gerald McBoing-Boing*, Emmys for Grinch TV specials, a Pulitzer citation. Generations devoured *Green Eggs and Ham* ("Sam! If you will let me be, I will try them. You will see"), *The 500 Hats of Bartholomew Cubbins* and *Yertle the Turtle*. As Geisel remembered it, "I used the word burp, and nobody had ever burped before on the pages of a children's book. It took a decision from the president of the publishing house before my vulgar turtle was permitted to do so." The childless author eventually lost interest in writing for grownups. He believed that "adults are obsolete children, and the hell with them."

For the past several decades, the white-bearded, bow-tied figure was a fixture in La Jolla, Calif., along with his second wife Audrey. He tooled around in a car with the license plate GRINCH and continued to work despite four cataract operations and a heart attack. His later volumes revealed the teacher hidden beneath the torrent of mirth. *The Butter Battle Book* spoke of the dangers of the nuclear-arms race; his final work, *Oh, the Places You'll Go!*, took on the meaning of life.

For Geisel, that meaning was never in doubt: "It's wrong to talk about what's wrong with children today," he insisted. "They are living in an environment that we made. When enough people are worrying enough—about war, the environment, illiteracy—we'll begin to get those problems solved." Reason enough to believe:

> It was T.S. Geisel who provoked all the chortles.
> But it's old Dr. Seuss who has joined the immortals.

We end with a very personal tribute from Peter Bernstein, son of Robert Bernstein, Geisel's publisher for so many years. As a child, Peter Bernstein was introduced to Dr. Seuss ... the real Dr. Seuss, in person, in La Jolla. Needless to say, when Peter Bernstein grew up, his own children were introduced to the Dr. Seuss books.

26

Epitaph: Green Eggs and Me

Peter W. Bernstein

U.S. News and World Report, **October 7, 1991**

Dr. Seuss didn't like children. At least that's what my parents told my brothers and me as we drove to see him at his hilltop home in La Jolla, Calif., in the mid-'60s. I was 13 and anxious not to embarrass my father, Dr. Seuss' publisher. That Dr. Seuss didn't have any children of his own made my parents' assertion all too believable.

The house loomed behind a gate high above the Pacific Ocean. Only a tower had stood there when Dr. Seuss bought the land. By the time of our visit, however, a spacious house surrounded the tower, which was topped by an office lined with sketches. I remember his eyes were always dancing. He showed us around, taking delight in pointing out the heads of Seussian creatures with long, crinkly horns that were mounted on the walls. Our fears faded away.

Though he labored over his books, he seemed to me a quick sketch artist. On one visit to New York, he drew us a picture of a Wild Idlewild on hotel stationery as we drove him to the airport that then bore that name. As a small child, I once asked my mother as she worked in the garden what manure was. Her explanation prompted another question: How did they get the cow to do it in a bag? Hearing that story on a trip to Paris, Dr. Seuss drew a quizzical bovine clutching a burlap sack asking "Dans un bag?"

Any Seuss fan knows he loved to make up silly names and use them to good effect. When he needed a plumber, he would call and say, with a touch of hysteria, that the dipilator was broken. The plumber, embarrassed to admit his ignorance of dipilators, would show up promptly. Last summer, in his last

Ted Geisel at his desk. (Photo courtesy of Dr. Seuss Enterprises, L.P.)

letter to my father, shortly after Clarence Thomas was nominated to the Supreme Court, he wrote, "Dear Robert, I would not wish to be quoted on this and I have absolutely nothing whatever against Grimalken, Drouber-hannus, Knalbner and Fepp, but as the Supreme Court moves farther and farther to the right, I am placing more and more of my litigation into the hands of Abernathy, Arbuthnot, Proudfoot and Cadwallader."

Yankee that he was, he liked to keep his comments brief. When Lake Forest College, outside Chicago, asked him to give its commencement address, he decided to make it the world's shortest and got it down to 1 minute, 14 seconds. His title was "My Uncle Terwilliger on the Art of Eating Popovers," which went like this:

> My uncle ordered popovers
>   from the restaurant's bill of fare.
> And, when they were served,
>   he regarded them with a penetrating stare...
> Then he spoke great Words of Wisdom
>   as he sat there on that chair:
> "To eat these things," said my uncle:
> "You must exercise great care.
> You may swallow down what's solid...
>   BUT ... you must spit out the air!"

And ... as you partake of the world's bill of fare,
   that's darn good advice to follow.
Do a lot of spitting out the hot air
   And be careful what you swallow.

When I told my youngest son, Nicky, age 5, that Dr. Seuss, age 87, had died last week, he put his head down on the dinner table and cried. It turned out, of course, that Theodor Seuss Geisel loved children of all ages: we felt the same way about him.

Appendix: All-Time Bestselling Hardcover Children's Books

Twenty titles by Dr. Seuss (and one by Theo. LeSieg) made it onto this list from *Publishers Weekly* (Feb. 5, 1996), which is based on publishers' sales figures through 1995. The list reflects domestic sales only and does not include book club sales.

The sales for the Dr. Seuss and Theo. LeSieg titles on this list amount to 50,579,846 copies. These 21 top sellers make up less than half of Theodor Geisel's published work.

Bold italics indicating Dr. Seuss titles have been added by the editor.

1. *The Poky Little Puppy* by Janette Sebring Lowrey (Golden, 1942) *14,000,000*

2. *The Tale of Peter Rabbit* by Beatrix Potter (Frederick Warne, 1902) *9,331,266*

3. *Tootle* by Gertrude Crampton (Golden, 1945) *8,055,500*

4. *Saggy Baggy Elephant* by Kathryn and Byron Jackson (Golden, 1947) *7,098,000*

5. *Scuffy the Tugboat* by Gertrude Crampton (Golden, 1955) *7,065,000*

6. *Pat the Bunny* by Dorothy Kunhardt (Golden, 1940) *6,146,543*

7. ***Green Eggs and Ham*** by Dr. Seuss (Random House, 1960) *6,065,197*

8. ***The Cat in the Hat*** by Dr. Seuss (Random House, 1957) *5,643,731*

9. *The Littlest Angel* by Charles Tazewell (Children's Press/Ideals, 1946) *5,424,709*

10. ***One Fish, Two Fish, Red Fish, Blue Fish*** by Dr. Seuss (Random House, 1960) *4,822,331*

11. *Where the Sidewalk Ends* by Shel Silverstein (HarperCollins, 1974) *4,623,762*

12. ***Hop on Pop*** by Dr. Seuss (Random House, 1963) *4,398,271*

13. ***Dr. Seuss's ABC*** by Dr. Seuss (Random House, 1960) *4,266,910*

14. *The Tale of Benjamin Bunny* by Beatrix Potter (Frederick Warne, 1904) *4,105,757*

15. *The Giving Tree* by Shel Silverstein (HarperCollins, 1964) *4,075,925*

16. *The Children's Bible* (Golden, 1965) *4,025,749*

17. *Disney's the Lion King* adapted by Justine Korman (Golden, 1994) *3,900,150*

18. *The Tale of Jemima Puddle-Duck* by Beatrix Potter (Frederick Warne, 1908) *3,825,819*

19. *Richard Scarry's Best Word Book*

OP: Out of print.

Ever by Richard Scarry (Golden, 1963) *3,798,953*

20. *The Real Mother Goose* illus. by Blanche F. Wright (Rand McNally, 1916 OP*) *3,600,000 (as of 1989)*

21. *The Cat in the Hat Comes Back* by Dr. Seuss (Random House, 1958) *3,445,303*

22. *A Light in the Attic* by Shel Silverstein (Collins, 1981) *3,302,278*

23. *Are You My Mother?* by P. D. Eastman (Random House, 1960) *3,277,939*

24. *The Tale of Squirrel Nutkin* by Beatrix Potter (Frederick Warne, 1903) *3,079,317*

25. *The Tale of Tom Kitten* by Beatrix Potter (Frederick Warne, 1907) *2,986,005*

26. *Fox in Socks* by Dr. Seuss (Random House, 1965) *2,949,628*

27. *Where's Waldo?* by Martin Handford (Little, Brown, 1987) *2,911,190*

28. *The Great Waldo Search* by Martin Handford (Little, Brown, 1989) *2,819,504*

29. *The Polar Express* by Chris Van Allsburg (Houghton Mifflin, 1985) *2,734,670*

30. *Winnie-the-Pooh* by A. A. Milne, illus. by Ernest Shepard (Dutton, 1926) *2,730,398*

31. *Find Waldo Now* by Martin Handford (Little, Brown, 1989) *2,730,306*

32. *Go, Dog. Go!* by P. D. Eastman (Random House, 1961) *2,715,788*

33. *Oh, the Places You'll Go!* by Dr. Seuss (Random House, 1990) *2,658,935*

34. *Macmillan Dictionary for Children* edited by Judith Levey (Simon & Schuster, 1975) *2,560,281*

35. *My Book About Me (by Me, Myself)* by Dr. Seuss, illus. by Roy McKie (Random House, 1969) *2,491,445*

36. *Walt Disney's Storyland* by Walt Disney (Golden, 1962) *2,400,904*

37. *The Cat in the Hat Beginner Book Dictionary* by P. D. Eastman (Random House, 1964) *2,382,269*

38. *The Rainbow Fish* by Marcus Pfister (North-South, 1992) *2,357,700*

39. *How the Grinch Stole Christmas* by Dr. Seuss (Random House, 1957) *2,251,625*

40. *Richard Scarry's Best Mother Goose Ever* by Richard Scarry (Golden, 1961) *2,040,125*

41. *The Touch Me Book* by Pat and Eve Witte (Golden, 1961) *2,040,125*

42. *Goodnight Moon* by Margaret Wise Brown, illus. by Clement Hurd (Harper-Collins, 1947) *2,039,916*

43. *I Am a Bunny* by Ole Risom, illus. by Richard Scarry (Golden, 1963) *2,003,832*

44. *The Little Engine That Could* by Watty Piper (Platt & Munk, 1930) *1,993,043*

45. *Charlotte's Web* by E. B. White, illus. by Garth Williams (Harper Collins, 1952) *1,933,710*

46. *Never Talk to Strangers* by Irma Joyce (Golden, 1967 OP) *1,916,040*

47. *When We Were Very Young* by A. A. Milne, illus. by Ernest Shepard (Dutton, 1924) *1,800,687*

48. *Richard Scarry's Best Storybook Ever* by Richard Scarry (Golden, 1968) *1,764,176*

49. *Barney's Magical Picnic* by Stephen White (Golden, 1993) *1,743,700*

50. *I Can Read with My Eyes Shut* by Dr. Seuss (Random House, 1978) *1,739,355*

51. *The Secret of the Old Clock (Nancy Drew #1)* by Carolyn Keene (Grosset & Dunlap, 1930) *1,700,979*

52. *The Tower Treasure (Hardy Boys #1)* by Franklin Dixon (Grosset & Dunlap, 1927) *1,694,286*

53. *Just Imagine* (Lyons/Barney, 1992 OP) *1,588,233*

54. *Put Me in the Zoo* by Robert Lopshire (Random House, 1960) *1,584,471*

55. *Disney's 101 Dalmatians* adapted by Ronald Kidd (Golden, 1991) *1,520,900*

56. *The Very Hungry Caterpillar* by Eric Carle (Philomel, 1969) *1,519,677*

57. *Barney's Farm Animals* (Lyons/Barney, 1993) *1,498,274*

58. *Where the Wild Things Are* by Maurice Sendak (Harper Collins, 1964) *1,486,903*

59. *Richard Scarry's Cars and Trucks and Things That Go* by Richard Scarry (Golden, 1968) *1,483,285*

60. *Disney's Beauty and the Beast* adapted by Ronald Kidd (Golden, 1992) *1,479,350*

61. *The Little Prince* by Antoine de Saint-Exupéry (Harcourt Brace, 1943) *1,478,530*

62. *Eloise Wilkin's Mother Goose* by Eloise Wilkin (Golden, 1961) *1,471,000*

63. *Disney's The Little Mermaid* adapted by Ronald Kidd (Golden, 1991) *1,467,300*

64. *Oh, The Thinks You Can Think!* by Dr. Seuss (Random House, 1975) *1,448,144*

65. *Love Is a Special Way of Feeling* by Joan Walsh Anglund (Harcourt Brace, 1960) *1,384,375*

66. *Big Bird's Color Game* by Children's Television Workshop (Golden, 1980) *1,354,626*

67. *Disney's Aladdin* adapted by Ronald Kidd (Golden, 1992) *1,354,500*

68. *The Hidden Staircase (Nancy Drew #2)* by Carolyn Keene (Grosset & Dunlap, 1930) *1,323,265*

69. *The House on the Cliff (Hardy Boys #2)* by Franklin Dixon (Grosset & Dunlap, 1927) *1,282,153*

70. *Meet Samantha* by Susan Adler (Pleasant Co., 1986) *1,266,746*

71. *Animalia* by Graeme Base (Abrams, 1987) *1,258,000*

72. *Barney's Favorite Mother Goose Rhymes Vol. 1* (Lyons/Barney, 1993 OP) *1,237,897*

73. *Disney's The Lion King* adapted by Ronald Kidd (Golden, 1994) *1,212,200*

74. *Meet Addy* by Connie Porter (Pleasant Co., 1993) *1,204,528*

75. *Oh Say Can You Say?* by Dr. Seuss (Random House, 1979) *1,198,643*

76. *Barney's Color Surprise* (Lyons/Barney, 1993) *1,159,190*

77. *The Way Things Work* by David Macaulay (Houghton Mifflin, 1988) *1,148,818*

78. *Tawny Scrawny Lion* by Kathryn Jackson (Golden, 1952) *1,126,000*

79. *Make Way for Ducklings* by Robert McCloskey (Viking, 1941) *1,122,213*

80. *Meet Kirsten* by Janet Shaw (Pleasant Co., 1986) *1,108,740*

81. *There's a Wocket in My Pocket!* by Dr. Seuss (Random House, 1974) *1,107,265*

82. *Millions of Cats* by Wanda Gág (Coward, 1928) *1,106,586*

83. *ET—The Extra-Terrestrial Storybook* by William Kotzwinkle (Grosset & Dunlap, 1983) *1,096,338*

84. *A Fly Went By* by Mike McClintock, illus. by Fritz Siebel (Random House, 1958) *1,092,967*

85. *The Bungalow Mystery (Nancy Drew #3)* by Carolyn Keene (Grosset & Dunlap, 1930) *1,091,897*

86. *Santa Mouse* by Elfrieda Dewitt (Grosset & Dunlap, 1966 OP) *1,078,215*

87. *The Magic Locket* by Elizabeth Koda-Callan (Workman, 1988) *1,062,000*

88. *The Secret of the Old Mill (Hardy Boys #3)* by Franklin Dixon (Grosset & Dunlap, 1930) *1,056,053*

89. *Mr. Brown Can Moo! Can You?* by Dr. Seuss (Random House, 1970) *1,052,582*

90. *If You Give a Mouse a Cookie* by Laura Numeroff, illus. by Felicia Bond (Harper Collins, 1985) *1,025,422*

91. *Richard Scarry's What Do People Do All Day?* by Richard Scarry (Random House, 1968) *1,007,177*

92. *Where's Spot?* by Eric Hill (Putnam, 1980) *992,956*

93. *House at Pooh Corner* by A. A. Milne, illus. by Ernest Shepard (Dutton, 1928) *992,911*

94. *The Tall Book of Nursery Tales* illus. by Feodor Rojankovsky (Harper-Collins, 1944 OP) *968,218*

95. Yertle the Turtle and Other Stories by Dr. Seuss (Random House, 1958) *915,313*

96. *Richard Scarry's Early Woods* by Richard Scarry (Random House, 1976 OP) *914,174*

97. *The Jolly Postman* by Janet and Allan Ahlberg (Little, Brown, 1986) *890,808*

98. *The Mystery of Lilac Inn (Nancy Drew #4)* by Carolyn Keene (Grosset & Dunlap, 1930) *887,870*

99. Dr. Seuss's Sleep Book by Dr. Seuss (Random House, 1962) *881,029*

100. *Baby Bop's Counting Book* (Lyons/Barney, 1993) *881,019*

101. *The Eleventh Hour* by Graeme Base (Abrams, 1989) *878,000*

102. *Babies So Tall Board Book* by Gyo Fujikawa (Grosset & Dunlap, 1963) *872,068*

103. *The Silver Slippers* by Elizabeth Koda-Callan (Workman, 1989) *867,000*

104. *The Mitten* by Jan Brett (Puttnam, 1989) *861,819*

105. *Baby Bop's Toys* (Lyons/Barney, 1993 OP) *861,020*

106. *The Secret of Shadow Ranch (Nancy Drew #5)* by Carolyn Keene (Grosset & Dunlap, 1931) *853,043*

107. Horton Hatches the Egg by Dr. Seuss (Random House, 1940) *834,803*

108. *Soft as a Kitten* by Audean Johnson (Random House, 1982) *823,234*

109. The Sneetches and Other Stories by Dr. Seuss (Random House, 1961) *819,085*

110. *The Missing Chums (Hardy Boys #4)* by Franklin Dixon (Grosset & Dunlap, 1930) *815,073*

111. *The True Story of the Three Little Pigs* by Jon Sciszka, illus. by Lane Smith (Viking, 1989) *802,530*

112. *Hunting for Hidden Gold (Hardy Boys #5)* by Franklin Dixon (Grosset & Dunlap, 1928) *800,248*

113. *Now We Are Six* by A. A. Milne, illus. by Ernest Shepard (Dutton, 1927) *799,762*

114. Happy Birthday to You! by Dr. Seuss (Random House, 1959) *799,091*

115. Ten Apples Up on Top! by Theo. LeSieg, illus. by Roy McKie (Random House, 1961) *791,178*

116. *The Story of Babar* by Jean de Brunhoff (Random House, 1937) *788,971*

117. *The Star Wars Storybook* adapted by Geraldine Richelson (Random House, 1978 OP) *779,259*

118. *Super Songs with Silly Sounds* (Golden, 1992) *778,300*

119. *Baby Animals So Tall Board Book* by Gyo Fujikawa (Grosset & Dunlap, 1963) *774,050*

120. *Kids Songs with Crazy Sounds* (Golden, 1992) *758,700*

121. *Charlie and the Chocolate Factory* by Ronald Dahl (Knopf, 1964) *758,624*

122. *Bennett Cerf's Book of Riddles* by Bennett Cerf (Random House, 1960) *755,075*

123. *It's Not Easy Being a Bunny* by Marilyn Sadler, illus. by Roger Bollen (Random House, 1983) *751,010*

Annotated Bibliography

Additional Articles About Theodor "Dr. Seuss" Geisel:

Bandler, Michael J. "Dr. Seuss: Still a Drawing Card." *American Way*, Dec. 1977, 23–27.

Cahn, Robert. "The Wonderful World of Dr. Seuss." *The Saturday Evening Post*, July 6, 1957, 17–19, 42–46.

Corwin, Miles. "Author Isn't Just a Cat in the Hat." *The Los Angeles Times*, Nov. 27, 1983, 1, 3.

Crichton, Jennifer. "Dr. Seuss Turns Eighty." *Publishers Weekly*, Feb. 10, 1984, 22–23.

Curley, Suzanne. "The Nuclear Dr. Seuss." *Newsday*, March 5, 1984, 3.

Dow, Maureen. "Novel 'Ironweed' and Mamet Play Are Awarded Pulitzer Prizes." *The New York Times*, April 17, 1984, A1, B4. Geisel is mentioned among other Pulitzer Prize winners of 1984.

Hacker, Kathy. "Happy Eightieth Birthday, Dr. Seuss." *The Philadelphia Inquirer*, March 7, 1984, E1, E8.

Katz, Lee Michael. "Most Kids Say Yooks Should Talk to Zooks." *USA Today*, June 29, 1984, A11.

Kupferberg, Herbert. "A Seussian Celebration." *Parade*, Feb. 26, 1984, 4–6.

Lamb, J.R. "Dr. Seuss Dies." *San Diego Tribune*, Sept. 25, 1991, p. A18.

Lyon, Jeff. "Writing for Adults, It Seems, Is One of Dr. Seuss' Dreams." *Chicago Tribune*, April 15, 1982, 3:1, 10.

Ort, Lorrene Love. "Theodor Seuss Geisel: The Children's Dr. Seuss" *Elementary English*, vol. 32, (1955), 135–142.

Smith, Dinita. "Seuss Creatures Go Commercial." *Houston Chronicle*, Feb. 17, 1997, 4c. Describes how Dr. Seuss characters are now appearing on neckties, sweatshirts, t-shirts and the like.

Sullivan, Emilie. "Brightening Our Years: A Half-Century of Laughter and Learning with Dr. Seuss." *The Delta Kappa Gamma Bulletin*, vol. 59, (Fall 1992), 47–51.

Sullivan, John. "Growing Up with Dr. Seuss." *American Way*, Aug. 1984, 46, 52.

Sullivan, Robert. "The Boy Who Drew Wynnmphs." *Yankee* magazine, Dec. 1995, 54–59, 120–121. Feature obituary, from the perspective of Geisel's home of New England. Below the title, a headline reads, "Four years ago, the world mourned the death of Dr. Seuss, the man who created the Grinch and the Cat in the Hat. But in Springfield, Massachusetts, they mourned for Teddy Geisel."

Thistlewaite, Susan B. "Dr. Seuss: Getting Christmas Back." *Christianity and Crisis*, vol. 51, no. 18 (Dec. 16, 1991), 370. How the Grinch offers a vision of Christmas to children.

Wilder, Rob. "Catching Up with Dr. Seuss." *Parents Magazine*, June 1979, 60–64.

Wolf, Tim. "Imagination, Rejection and Rescue: Recurrent Themes in Dr. Seuss." *Children's Literature*, vol. 23 (1995), 137–164. Long scholarly analysis of recurring themes in Seuss books.

By Theodor Geisel:

"If at First You Don't Succeed—Quit!" *The Saturday Evening Post*, Nov. 28, 1964, 8–9.

Books about Theodor "Dr. Seuss" Geisel:

Dr. Seuss from Then to Now. New York: Random House, 1986. A book version of a retrospective exhibition of his works organized by the San Diego Museum of Art, 1986. Contains much interesting material about his early days in advertising. (Some of his advertising sketches later appeared, virtually unchanged, in the Dr. Seuss books.) Also contains rough drawings from *You're Only Old Once!*, then in progress. Worth finding through a rare book dealer.

Greene, Carol. *Dr. Seuss: Writer and Artist for Children*. Chicago: Children's Press, 1993. A juvenile biography.

MacDonald, Ruth K. *Dr. Seuss*. Boston: Twayne. 1988. An analysis of his books through 1987.

Marschall, Richard, ed. *The Tough Coughs as He Ploughs the Dough: Early Writing and Cartoons by Dr. Seuss*. New York: William Morrow, 1987.

Morgan, Judith, and Morgan, Neil. *Dr. Seuss and Mr. Geisel*. New York: Random House, 1995. Reprint ed.: New York: DaCapo, 1996. The authorized biography of Theodor Geisel, written by Geisel family friends in LaJolla.

Wheeler, Jill C. *Dr. Seuss*. Minneapolis: Abdo & Daughters, 1992. A juvenile biography.

Weidt, Maryann. *Oh, the Places He Went: A Story about Dr. Seuss—Theodor Seuss Geisel*. Minneapolis: Carolrhoda, 1994. A juvenile biography.

Books by Dr. Seuss:

1931: *Boners*. (Illustrated by Dr. Seuss) New York: Viking.
1931: *More Boners*. (Illustrated by Dr. Seuss.) New York: Viking.
1937: *And to Think That I Saw It on Mulberry Street*. New York: Vanguard.
1938: *The 500 Hats of Bartholomew Cubbins*. New York; Vanguard.
1939: *The King's Stilts*. New York: Random House.
1939: *The Seven Lady Godivas*. New York: Random House.
1940: *Horton Hatches the Egg*. New York: Random House.
1947: *McElligot's Pool*. New York: Random House.
1948: *Thidwick the Big-Hearted Moose*. New York: Random House.
1949: *Bartholomew and the Oobleck*. New York: Random House.
1950: *If I Ran the Zoo*. New York: Random House.
1953: *Scrambled Eggs Super!* New York: Random House.
1954: *Horton Hears a Who!* New York: Random House.
1955: *On Beyond Zebra!* New York: Random House.
1956: *If I Ran the Circus*. New York: Random House.
1957: *How the Grinch Stole Christmas*. New York: Random House.
1957: *The Cat in the Hat*. New York: Random House (Beginner Books).
1958: *The Cat in the Hat Comes Back*. New York: Random House (Beginner Books).
1958: *Yertle the Turtle and Other Stories*. New York: Random House.
1959: *Happy Birthday to You!* New York: Random House.
1960: *Green Eggs and Ham*. New York: Random House (Beginner Books).

1960: *One Fish Two Fish Red Fish Blue Fish.* New York: Random House (Beginner Books).

1961: *The Sneetches and Other Stories.* New York: Random House.

1961: *Ten Apples Up on Top!* (Theo. LeSieg, pseudonym). New York: Random House (Beginner Books).

1962: *Dr. Seuss's Sleep Book.* New York: Random House.

1963: *Dr. Seuss's ABC.* New York: Random House (Beginner Books).

1963: *Hop on Pop.* New York: Random House (Beginner Books).

1965: *Fox in Socks.* New York: Random House (Beginner Books).

1965: *I Had Trouble in Getting to Solla Sollew.* New York: Random House.

1965: *I Wish That I Had Duck Feet.* (Theo. LeSieg, pseudonym). New York: Random House (Beginner Books).

1966: *Come Over to My House.* (Theo LeSieg, pseudonym). New York: Random House.

1967: *Dr. Seuss's Lost World Revisited: A Forward-Looking Backward Glance.* New York: Universal Publishing Co. A curious book—a combination of early Seuss with a touch of Rube Goldberg. A rare paperback. This consists of material by Seuss published in *Liberty,* a highly popular weekly magazine published 1924–1951. It appears that this Seuss material was published in *Liberty* throughout 1932; publication rights were resold to Universal Publishing for this 1967 edition. Surely not part of the Seuss canon. Not mentioned in most Seuss bibliographies.

1967: *The Cat in the Hat Song Book.* New York: Random House (Beginner Books).

1968: *The Eye Book.* (Theo. LeSieg, pseudonym). New York: Random House (Bright and Early Books).

1968: *The Foot Book.* New York: Random House (Bright and Early Books).

1969: *I Can Lick 30 Tigers Today! And Other Stories.* New York: Random House.

1969: *My Book About Me—By Me, Myself, I Wrote It! I Drew It!* New York: Random House (Beginner Books).

1970: *I Can Draw It Myself.* New York: Random House (Beginner Books).

1970: *Mr. Brown Can Moo! Can You?* New York: Random House (Bright and Early Books).

1971: *I Can Write—by Me, Myself.* (Theo. LeSieg, pseudonym) New York: Random House (Bright and Early Books).

1971: *The Lorax.* New York: Random House.

1972: *In a People House.* (Theo. LeSieg, pseudonym). New York: Random House (Bright and Early Books).

1972: *Marvin K. Mooney Will You Please Go Now!* New York: Random House (Bright and Early Books).

1973: *The Many Mice of Mr. Brice.* (Theo. LeSieg, pseudonym). New York: Random House (Bright and Early Books).

1973: *The Shape of Me and Other Stuff.* New York: Random House (Bright and Early Books).

1974: *Great Day for Up!* New York: Random House (Bright and Early Books).

1974: *There's a Wocket in My Pocket!* New York: Random House (Bright and Early Books).

1974: *Wacky Wednesday.* (Theo. LeSieg, pseudonym). New York: Random House (Beginner Books).

1975: *Because a Little Bug Went Ka-Choo!* (Rosetta Stone, pseudonym). New York: Random House (Beginner Books).

1975: *O, the Thinks You Can Think!* New York: Random House (Beginner Books).

1975: *Would You Rather Be a Bullfrog?* (Theo. LeSieg, pseudonym). New York: Random House (Bright and Early Books).

1976: *Hooper Humperdink ... ? Not Him!* (Theo. LeSieg, pseudonym). New York: Random House (Beginner Books).

1976: *The Cat's Quizzer.* New York: Random House (Beginner Books).

1977: *Please Try to Remember the First of Octember.* (Theo. LeSieg, pseudonym). New York: Random House (Beginner Books).

1978: *I Can Read with My Eyes Shut!* New York: Random House (Beginner Books).

1979: *Oh Say Can You Say?* New York: Random House (Beginner Books).

1980: *Maybe You Should Fly a Jet! Maybe You Should be a Vet!* (Theo. LeSieg, pseudonym). New York: Random House (Beginner Books).

1981: *The Tooth Book.* (Theo. LeSieg, pseudonym) New York: Random House (Bright and Early Books).

1982: *Hunches in Bunches.* New York: Random House.

1984: *The Butter Battle Book.* New York: Random House.

1986: *You're Only Old Once!* New York: Random House.

1987: *I Am Not Going to Get Up Today!* New York: Random House (Beginner Books).

1990: *Oh, the Places You'll Go!* New York: Random House.

1991: *Six by Seuss.* New York: Random House.

Includes *And to Think That I Saw It on Mulberry Street; The 500 Hats of Bartholomew Cubbins; Horton Hatches the Egg; Yertle the Turtle; How the Grinch Stole Christmas* and *The Lorax.*

Published Posthumously:

1995: *Daisy-Head Mayzie.* New York: Random House. The only Dr. Seuss title with a girl as the lead character.

1995: *The Secret Art of Dr. Seuss.* New York: Random House. This book reprints abstract art which Geisel completed but did not use in the Dr. Seuss books. Some of the titles are fanciful, to say the least, such as "The Rather Odd Myopic Woman Riding Piggyback on One of Helen's Many Cats."

1996: *My Many Colored Days.* Illustrated by Steve Johnson and Lou Fancher. New York: Alfred A. Knopf. Before his death, Theodor Geisel gave instructions that this manuscript be illustrated by someone else, for he didn't want it to be a typical Seuss book. The someone else turned out to be two illustrators, Johnson and Fancher, and indeed the book has a look very different from Dr. Seuss.

1996: *A Hatful of Seuss.* New York: Random House. Includes *If I Ran the Zoo; The Sneetches and Other Stories; Horton Hears a Who!; Dr. Seuss's Sleep Book* and *Bartholomew and the Oobleck.*

1997: *Seuss-isms: Wise and Witty Prescriptions for Living from the Good Doctor.* New York: Random House. A slim volume, 4¼ x 5¾, 25 pp. A collection of epigrams from assorted Seuss books.

Index